WAR AND THE CHRISTIAN CONSCIENCE / *How Shall Modern War Be Conducted Justly?*

Paul Ramsey

Princeton University

PUBLISHED FOR THE LILLY ENDOWMENT RESEARCH PROGRAM IN CHRISTIANITY AND POLITICS BY THE DUKE UNIVERSITY PRESS, DURHAM, N. C.   1961

L.C.C. card no. 61-10666
Paperback edition I.S.B.N. 0-8223-0361-2

Printed in the United States of America

Dedicated

to

Effie Register Ramsey

Foreword

The mushroom-like clouds that rose from the ruins of Hiroshima and Nagasaki a short sixteen years ago ushered in a new age in the life of mankind. Not only must we come to terms with the fact that all civilized life upon this planet may come to an end but that this is possible through human decision and action. So frightful is the prospect that many have been led to declare that there is no evil greater than the risk of nuclear warfare. Thus Mr. Philip Toynbee has declared that "surely anything is better," including the domination of the world by Russian tyranny, "than a policy which allows for the possibility of nuclear war." On the other hand there are those who speak recklessly of "preventive war" and of "massive retaliation." Both positions spring from fear, and we are told that we must choose between unlimited warfare by any means or the total abolition of force. The first alternative is wholly immoral and purposeless while the second is utopian and unattainable. Such are the counsels that spring from fear.

If we are to find some way out of the dilemma which confronts us we must listen once again to the counsel of reason and to the voice of conscience. This is not to say that the "answer" is obvious but it is to say that we have an obligation to seek the best possible answer which reason and faith can help us find. Professor Ramsey's analysis is an important contribution to that search. His book is concerned primarily with only one facet of the problem, namely, the nature and meaning of rational armament. The earliest Christians were pacifists but during the early centuries A.D. there was developed a doctrine of the just war which has continued in its development down to the present day. Its proponents did not conceive of it as a rejection of the commandment that we should love one another but as a fulfillment of that commandment in socially responsible service. The doctrine not only justified the use of force in defense of the moral order but limited, in the name of the same moral order, the kind of warfare that could justifiably be fought. It is Professor Ramsey's contention that the doctrine of the just war is not only applicable today but that to depart from it is to surrender to irrationality and gross immorality. Not only does he examine the origins and development of the just war doctrine but he subjects much of the current literature on the problem of armaments to a searching analysis from the perspective of a Christian humanist. Although a Protestant, he is critical of many current trends in Protestant ethical thought and he is especially critical of those who regard policy decisions as wholly relative or "contextual." He prefers to think of the Christian statesman as operating of necessity within a realm which he suggestively calls the realm of "deferred repentance."

As the author of *Basic Christian Ethics* (1950) and of numerous articles in the same field, Professor Ramsey is well qualified to undertake the present inquiry. A native of Mississippi, he graduated from Millsaps College in 1935. He holds the B.D. degree from Yale as well as a Ph.D. which he received in 1943. He began teaching at Princeton University in 1944 and since 1957 has been the Harrington Spear Paine Professor of Religion and since 1959 Chairman of the Department at that university. He is a member of the National Council on Religion in Higher Education.

The present volume represents an extension and an elaboration of a series of three lectures which Professor Ramsey delivered at Duke University in May, 1960 under the auspices of the Lilly Endowment Research Program in Christianity and Politics. It should be understood, of course, that although the publication of this book was made possible by funds provided by Lilly Endowment, Inc., the Endowment is not the author or publisher and is not to be understood as approving, by virtue of its grant, any of the statements or views expressed in the pages that follow.

John H. Hallowell, *Director*
Lilly Endowment Research Program in Christianity and Politics

Acknowledgments

I am grateful to the Lilly Endowment Research Program in Christianity and Politics at Duke University, and particularly to its Director, Professor John Hallowell of the Department of Political Science, and to the other distinguished members of the Advisory Committee of the Program, for inviting me to deliver a series of lectures at Duke in May, 1960, on the theme of this volume. This was not only an enjoyable week spent among hospitable friends, but also an intellectually stimulating one to me, in which I was forced to correct and restate at least some of my thoughts on this most crucial subject of morality and war. It ought also to be acknowledged that I have benefited by the discussions in Duodecim Theological Society and the American Theological Society of the matter of this volume; and from the discussion and criticism that followed the presentation of a version of Chapter XI, at the invitation of the Church Peace Union, as a paper entitled "National Security: Its Moral Aspects" before the Union's annual interfaith, interdisciplinary Seminar on Ethics and Foreign Policy in November, 1960. Finally, portions of two of the following chapters have previously been published as articles in the journal of The Church Peace Union, which has generously granted me permission to revise and reprint: "Right and Wrong Calculation," *Worldview*, December, 1959, and "The Politics of Fear," *Worldview*, March, 1960. My daughter, Marcia, typed the Index.

Paul Ramsey

Department of Religion
Princeton University
Princeton, New Jersey

Table of Contents

Author's Introduction

For almost two centuries of the history of the early church, Christians were universally pacifists. Christ, in disarming Peter, they said, had unbelted every soldier; or if not every soldier, this at least meant that the disciples of Jesus Christ were not to engage in armed violence for any cause. Such pacifism was a withdrawal from political and military affairs to which the early Christians were driven, no doubt, from a mixture of motives. As a sect of Judaism, they at first shared in the exemption of all the Jews from military service—which exemption had been granted by the Romans not because the Jews had conscientious objection to fighting but against fighting on the Sabbath Day. The early Christians avoided the life of a soldier also in order to avoid the requirement of emperor-worship, since everyone whose office was that of a soldier or commander, judge or magistrate, was forced on numerous occasions to throw incense on the altar. Thus, a religious refusal to commit idolatry may have been the main motive, and not always a refusal, on ethical grounds, to engage in war. Many apparent pacifists, in North Africa and elsewhere, were simply anti-imperialists. Moreover, the dualism and otherwordly spirituality widespread in a decadent Hellenism had its effect. Just as in sexual morality there was among the Christians a strong tendency to reject the body and its passions altogether, so also to engage in physical struggle seemed to many of them a contamination of the soul with the impurities of matter.

To engage in conflict meant not only a violation of love. It meant also a devotion of the human spirit to physical and this-wordly goods. Early Christian pacifism resulted also from specialization in "love for the brethren" so long as the Christians were a small mutual-aid society with little or no responsibility for the political community as a whole. It resulted from apocalyptic expectation severing them from political responsibility, or from the inability of individuals or small groups even to dream of affecting the course of events in the wide reaches of the Roman Empire, and doubt-less also from those leaner motives that soon were to drive thousands of men from the normal life of family, city, or state to people monasteries on islands in the Mediterranean far removed from the time of troubles and famine in which the father of a family had to endure, as one of them said, seeing his children's tongues cleave to the roofs of their mouths.

Yet there can be no doubt that early Christian pacifism was in the main a consistent deduction from the new foun-dation laid by Christ in the lives of men for a new kind of exercise, in intention and in practice, of love for every man for whom Christ died. How could anyone, who knew him-self to be classed with transgressors and the enemies of God whom Christ came to die to save, love his own life and seek to save it more than that of his own enemy or murderer?

How this early Christian pacifism came to be replaced by the justification of Christian participation in warfare in the church during the era of the Emperor Constantine is a story that need not be told in detail. It seems fairly well estab-lished that the first Christians known to have been soldiers were recruits under the Stoic Marcus Aurelius fighting in the provinces on the Danube in A.D. 177; and that engage-ment in political and military action only gradually came to be accepted practice for Christians, until in A.D. 403 there is evidence that *only* Christians were allowed to enter the military profession. The important thing is how we are to explain or interpret this seeming reversal of Christian practice. A pacifist today viewing this period writes a book with the title "The Fall of Christianity." A responsibilist, using the same data, entitles his book, "The Social Triumph of Christianity." The question this poses about the consistency or the continuity and discontinuity in the Christian ethical tradition can be answered only by probing deeply into the motives of men, available to us only in the literature in defense of Christian participation in war; and by exposing to view the basic anatomy of the doctrine of justifiable war, first formulated by St. Ambrose and St. Augustine and continued in its development throughout the Middle Ages and by Thomas Aquinas, and into the present day.

Our examination of the theory of the just war has in view the demonstration of the following propositions—each of which is of more than historical significance, each of which is of the highest importance for constructive ethical analysis today:

1. The change-over to just-war doctrine and practice was not a "fall" from the original purity of Christian ethics; but, however striking a turning-full-circle, this was a change of tactics only. The basic strategy remained the same: responsible love and service of one's neighbors in the texture of the common life. The primary motive and foundation for now approving Christian participation in warfare was the same as that which before, in a different social context, led Christians out of Christlike love for neighbor wholly to disapprove of the use of armed force. Christians simply came to see that the service of the real needs of all the men for whom Christ died required more than personal, witnessing action. It also required them to be involved in maintaining the organized social and political life in which all men live.

Non-resisting love had sometimes to resist evil. Just-war theorists did not first adopt an ethic that intrinsically justifies self-defense in general, and then simply apply this general principle to the just defense of the nation. Instead, the very men who first justified participation in warfare for the protection of justice and the public order continue to prohibit the Christian from under any circumstances killing another man, or even resisting him, in the private defense of his own life or property when that alone was at stake. If in the private realm defensiveness was not regarded as ever justified, then, the root reason for engaging in public defense most likely was not self-preservation.

2. Of course, it is possible that the foundation of just-war theory and practice was a new kind of exercise that was laid in the principles of natural justice or natural law, and that on this a Christian's participation in political and military action depended, *alongside* the foundation that was laid by Jesus Christ in the private lives of men and in their personal relations for a new kind of exercise of love for every man, even the enemy or the onrushing assailant, for whom Christ died. Thus, natural justice may have governed in requiring responsible political participation, while love still prevailed in the private realm only. My second proposition is therefore of the utmost importance, namely, that the limits placed upon the just conduct of war at the same time that this was said to be permitted to the Christian bear significant traces of the fact that the norm of Christian love, and not natural justice only, was still the main source both of what the Christian could and should do and of what he could and should never do in military action. It was to be expected that political vocation and participation in war, if these were justified and motivated by what love required the Christian to do, would at the same time be surrounded by very severe limits upon what love permitted him ever to

do if he was under the necessity of killing another man. It was to be expected that natural justice would not be the only or even the main source of the Christian's conduct, and that, in the special case of war, certain clearly limiting definitions had to be given of the military conduct permitted or prohibited to the Christian in justifiable warfare.

The question to be raised is *whence* came the prohibition of indiscriminate killing in warfare or the direct killing of the innocent in combat between nations? These applications of the rule of "double effect" in traditional Christian morality, like the rule itself, can be shown to be a deposit or creation of the Christian love ethic itself, and not merely the result of an independent natural-law reason. Thus, the conscience schooled by Christ which first compelled Christians to justify warfare at the same time proscribed for them its moral limits. What they still declared always to be illicit was internally related to what they declared to be licit on some occasions in the taking of human life.

The constructive question that arises from an historical account of just-war theory and practice (in the opening chapters of this book) is this: Can the Christian ever discover sufficient grounds for setting aside the judgment that any act of war is intrinsically immoral which directly and intentionally attacks persons other than those directly or closely co-operating in the force that should be repelled? Can obliteration bombing, much less the all-out use of thermonuclear weapons, ever be justified? The answer must be that Christian love in action should, at the least, renew and re-create its own ancient principle which for a thousand years governed the conscience of all the Christians who ever justified participation in war. If today the Christian affirms that the right conduct of war can never include the strategic bombing of whole civilian populations and that it is never right to intend to kill directly millions of babies and school children in order to get at their fathers, the reason is not that he adopts (and "seasons" with love) a rigorous alien natural-law principle drawn from some source outside of Christian morals, but that he finds himself still required to do only what love requires and permitted to do only what love allows to be right. An ethic of Christian love has no alternative but to renew and re-create its own articulation in the rule or principle which surrounds non-combatants with moral immunity from direct attack.

It is true that Christian love continues to exert a free and sovereign pressure toward fresh determination of what should be done in situations not covered by the law, natural justice, or its own former articulation in principle. But it is also the case that love often acts within the law and it is always at work laying down rules or principles for the guidance of action. In determining justifiable and unjustifiable warfare, the work of love will be to return ever again to the prohibition of the direct killing of any person not directly or closely co-operating in the force which should be resisted. This it must say, if ever it justifies resisting by violence anyone for whom Christ died. That product of *agape* in Western thought, the doctrine of the just or limited war, must happen again as an event in the minds of men and in Christian ethical analysis in every age. He who has gone so far as to justify, for the sake of justice and the public order, wounding anyone whom by his wounds Christ died to save, will find no way of escape from the moral limitation upon the conduct of war which requires that military force be mounted against the attacking force and not directly against whole populations. Christian love should again, as in the past, surround the little ones with moral immunity from direct killing. It should discern the difference between just war and murder.

3. A third thesis is this: It has often been pointed out that the main contribution of Christianity to Western political life is that, by its doctrine of the "two cities" and by relating men to an eternal end and not only to the earthly end of the common good, Christianity broke open the one-world view of classical politics with its incipient totalitarianism that viewed individual men as belonging to only one city and that embraced their whole lives in one commonwealth. That meant incipiently that the individual might properly be reduced to a mere means ordered to the achievement of the good of the classical commonwealth; and it does not much matter that classical conceptions of the common good included many excellent values. It is only the Christian view that man belongs to a city above all earthly commonwealths that in principle prevents reducing him, to the whole extent of his being, to his contribution to the common good. In Christian political theory, the mere fact that a man is a citizen elsewhere keeps him from being only a citizen here. By distinguishing two cities, Christianity corrected the implicit absolutism of loyalty to earthly kingdoms.

It has less frequently been pointed out, however, that, since the nature of that City in which men together attain their final end is divine charity, as a consequence even earthly cities began to be elevated and their justice was infused and transformed by new perspectives, limits, and principles. Proof of this is to be found in the fact that the Christians who justified participation in warfare also sought to limit morally the conduct of the warfare that was regarded as permissible; and that the limit they formulated had especially to do with exempting as many persons as possible from becoming objects of direct killing, and surrounding with immunity everyone not directly involved in the cause of war—especially the weak and the helpless.

The reverse has been happening in the modern period as the just-war theory has eroded from the minds of men. Pragmatic politics, a complete distinction between personal and political morality, and the analysis of political and military decision wholly in situational terms (not only by secular political realists but also by all too many Protestant statements and all too many writers on Christian ethics and poltics) have only exhibited or accomplished the return of mankind to significant citizenship in only one city; and that city has now lost most traces of its original moralization by a love-transformed-justice and the morally limiting rules of justified warfare. We live now in one unelevated commonwealth, where the end pursued in common (ends themselves not so intrinsically excellent as in classical political theory) is sufficient justification of any means; and this unfortunately means nothing at all abstract, but that there is no limit to the direct, mass killing of people which political or military ends seem to require, and that murder becomes just whenever it is done, not for some private good, but for the public good and when planned on a grand scale. If there are any lessons from the past, surely it is this: that we should not go about revising our moral tradition by pragmatically justifying what we are now preparing to do, but that we should frankly state—if this is the case—that wholly unjustifiable, immoral warfare has now become a necessity.

4. Finally, an assumption made in this volume is that the chief problem facing us in not *what* are the moral limits upon the just conduct of war, but *where* are these principles,[1] i.e., *where* are the men in whose minds and *where* is

---

[1] Cf. Julian N. Hartt, "Religion and the Bomb," *Worldview*, April, 1959, p. 7: "*Where*, not *what:* can we make out the lineaments of the community which is the living repository (as it were) of the ethical principles relevant and efficacious to the moral determination of the limits of warfare?" And John Courtney Murray, S. J.: "Morality and Foreign Policy: II," *America*, CII, XXV (March 26, 1960), 766; or in *Worldview*, May, 1960 p. 8.

the community of men in whose very *ethos* the propelling reason for ever engaging in war also itself lays down intrinsic moral limits upon how the defense of civilized life should proceed? If we live in a post-Christian age, it is not surprising that we also live in a post-just-war age. Instead of tinkering with this age by making scientific studies of how policy decisions are in fact made in it, it may be necessary for us to awaken to the fact that we have to go forward with the patient work of entering a new age. To this end, perhaps it may be helpful to take a look backward into that period of Christian history in which, whatever the brutalities of actual war, war was in theory never to be engaged in unless it was just to do so, and then only in a just manner, and when war was at least attempted to be kept just in practice— precisely because generations of men had their consciences formed by love-directed conceptions of justice and of right conduct. It may be helpful for us to consult the wisdom contained in that most uninterrupted, longest-continuing study of *moral decision-making* known in the Western World, the just-war theory.

The subtitle of this volume asks the question, "How Shall Modern War Be Conducted Justly?" The words "How *Shall* . . . ?" are intended to ask both "How *Should* . . . ?" and "How *Can* . . . ?" Our undertaking will be to examine policy decisions that *can* possibly be made only in the context of the moral principles that *ought* to govern the practice of governments with regard to modern weapons and warfare. He may be well advised to leave off reading at this point who believes that there is only one important question, namely the technical question, "How *Will* Modern War Be Conducted?" or who seeks to derive what "ought" to be done from what "is" now being done in the world, and who determines the practice that "should" be adopted by simple reference to what amorally must and, at the maximum, can be done in the face of an immoral, tyrannical enemy. Nevertheless, I do propose to proceed from the "should" to the "can" be done, in attempting a complete answer to the question "How *Shall* Modern War Be Conducted Justly?"

WAR AND THE CHRISTIAN CONSCIENCE

Chapter One

THE PROBLEM OF PROTESTANT
ETHICS TODAY

Protestant ethics today comes from a long line of prudent people. The pacifism which between the world wars
spread widely in the non-peace churches, the non-pacifism
which gradually overcame this as World War II approached
and which continues today, the increasing pragmatism of
the Niebuhrians, the current increase of "no greater evil"
nuclear pacifism, and in general the rejection of natural law
and "middle axioms" in favor of contextualism and the
study of "decision making"—all this has been largely a matter of determining the "lesser evil" or perchance the "greater
good" among the supposed *consequences* of actions. By
calculating the facts and speculating about the expected results, we have sought to find the path along which action
should be directed in order to defend or secure some sort
of values at the end of the road toward which action reaches,
yet never reaches. We have had an ethics derived from
some future good (or evil), not in any significant degree an
ethics of *right*, right action or proper conduct. We have
understood morality to be a matter of prudential calculation. This is the case even if Christian *agape* directs the
estimate made of the utility of an action to be done. Such
an ethic is well calculated to reduce every present reality—
people and principles no less than facts—to what may be
done to bring in the future.

Against this, it should be affirmed, first of all, that "prudence" has rightly to be understood to be in the service of some prior principle, whether in application of natural-law principles or (if, as I believe, these alone are inadequate) in application of divine charity. Against this, secondly, it should be affirmed that *agape* does not first and always face toward the future alone. Rather does *agape* face in the present also toward a man's existing neighbors and companions in God, seeking to determine what love permits and requires to be now done or not done toward them. Thus, love posits or takes form in principles of right conduct which express the difference it discerns between permitted and prohibited action, and these are not wholly derived from reflection upon the consequences.

In what way, then, should moral decision be based on anticipation of greater good or lesser evil among the consequences of action? Not every action that is licit is therefore to be done; what love permits, it does not without more ado require. For sound judgment to be made that a certain conduct is commanded, the Christian must, of course, also consult the consequences to see as best he can that the good outweighs the evil, or that evil is minimized by his proposed action. Yet, in order to make a decision about what should *be done,* a Christian would attempt to trammel up the consequences only among alternative courses of action which do not directly violate the love-commandment, or fall outside of the work of love in depositing, in-forming or taking the form of certain principles of right conduct. The good or the best or the lesser evil among the goals of action is to be chosen, yet by action that is not intrinsically and from the beginning wrong in itself.

We must affirm that a wholly teleological ethic—even a *wholly future-facing agape*-ethic—amounts to the suspension of a great part of morality. If no more can be said about the morality of *action* than can be derived backward from the future goal (thus unrolling toward the present the path that we shall have to tread by deeds determined by calculating their utility) ethics has already more than half-way vanished, i.e., it has become mere calculation of the means to projected ends. Of course, the ends and values toward which ethico-political calculation or prudence is directed may in themselves be of great importance; and we cannot deny that it makes a great deal of difference what the objectives a society seeks are, especially when, so far as Christian action is concerned, *agape* is in any measure the director of action toward the greater good or lesser evil (which, of course, means the same as the greatest possible good). Still, to say only this about morality is to say that there is nothing that should not be done which a future-facing calculation seems to require; and no action which can be prudently calculated to produce the described result which should not *therefore* be defined as a right action. Such a view has to be rejected as the suspension of a great part of ethics, without in any sense minimizing the significance of calculation, in its proper place, both for morality and for political decision.

When, for example, Reinhold Niebuhr writes "To serve peace, we must threaten war without blinking the fact that the threat may be a factor in precipitating war,"[1] It should not first be asked whether the suggested political calculation is right or wrong but whether this is right or wrong calculation. And the answer to the latter question depends in large measure upon the sort of military action, or the conduct of war, that was threatened and the threat in turn foreknown perhaps to precipitate. That peace was thought to be served (however good that end may be), and a precarious

[1] "From Progress to Perplexity," in *The Search for America*, ed. Huston Smith (Englewood Cliffs, N. J.: Prentice-Hall, 1959), p. 144.

calculation of the mixed tendency our actions may have to produce peace, do not provide an entirely adequate determination of right action. There is little to be gained from questioning the accuracy of such realistic, prudential political judgments, when the real issue to be raised concerns the establishment of moral and political judgment also upon some other, and logically prior, ground. In undertaking to state the moral grounds for political action, this book will attempt, at one and the same time, to distinguish between right and wrong calculation and to locate the proper place for prudential consideration of consequences. This must be done before asking the question whether a given calculation of the expected results of an action is correct or not. In the past an ethics that attempted to determine right action and the proper conduct of affairs may have been too rigid, too certain in its statements about legitimate means; and "moralism" may often have prevented good people from being sufficiently wise or free or flexible in their deeds or in the choice of political programs. However, this should not blind us to the fact that rigid moralism has long since been overcorrected; and that today Protestant ethics points every which way in search of the useful and prudent thing to do. We call by the name of "social ethics" our wanderings over the wasteland of utility since the day we completely surrendered to technical political reason the choice of the way to the goals we seek.

Morality, including political morality, has to do with the definition of right *conduct*, and this not simply by way of the ends of action. *How* we do *what* we do is as important as our goals. An "idealist" in politics is one who goes on his way and finds his way under the lure of such goals as the greatest happiness of the greatest number, etc. A "realist" is one who knows that there are many ways that may reasonably be supposed to lead there, ranging all the way from the noblest to the most wicked political decisions and actions; and he reminds the calculative idealist that in politics he had better know more than this about right and wrong conduct. No properly ethical statement has yet been made so long as our moral imperatives are tied to unlimitedly variable ends. Nor has a properly ethical statement yet been made so long as the means are unlimitedly variable that are supposed to lead to fixed, universal ends, even the ends determined by *agape*.

Of course, ends and means mutually interpenetrate each other. But surely the means-end relationship should always be read both ways. Surely war will never be kept a just endurable human enterprise if it is sought to be kept limited only by political *objectives* and *therefore* limited in terms of the weapons employed. Limited ends do tend to moderate the means ventured and the cost paid and exacted in warfare. But not only does the military force made possible by modern technology work against our being able to achieve the control of warfare by aiming at modest ends, but also the endless restless aspiration of the human spirit, which displays its want of heaven even in man's towering attempts at grandeur and wickedness with which history is replete. The interpenetration of means and ends should also be stated: limited (or unlimited) means or weapons are available and resolved to be used, and *therefore* limited (or unlimited) political objectives may be thought to be proper goals in war. Calculative morality and politics cannot dispense with exhortations to whole peoples to adopt only limited goals. It must therefore rely upon a revival of this aspect of the moral tradition of civilized warfare.[2] At the

[2] Consider, for example, the national self-control on the part of combatants assumed by the following paragraph: "The limited objectives must be adhered to by the winning party. In other words, if the fortunes of war go to one side they must be exploited in a limited sense only. The winner must not allow himself to be carried away by success, raising the demands he has made initially regarding the conditions for which he would settle.

same time (if means and ends interpenetrate), there is need for a re-creation, in both thought and feeling, of the moral tradition of civilized warfare in the right *conduct* of war and the moral limitation to be placed upon means. Surely, the immunity of non-combatants from indiscriminate, direct attack may come again to govern the consciences of men as readily or with as great improbability as they will set limits to the political objectives they pursue.

The morality of means referred to in the "justified" war theory meant more than the inert weapon as such; it meant the *conduct* of war as such, the action as a whole and its nature, which had a morality or an immorality not wholly swallowed up in consequences or in motive to ends believed to justify any action that might be thought to have military decisiveness. This was an application of the Christian love-ethic in principles of *right,* and not only, as today, an application of Christian love through prudence teleologically oriented toward ends only.

A wholly future-facing love-ethic necessarily produces some version of the opinion that the end justifies the means, and a reading of the means-end situation only from the end backward. Nevertheless, an emphasis upon the significance of means, and upon principles of justice and right conduct, need not neglect concern with the good and evil consequences. For while the end may never justify the means, one effect often justifies another effect that is linked with it. Thus, moral theology has long taught that an unavoidable evil effect may be produced if that is the only way, by an action not wrong in itself, to secure some very good re-

The loser must admit defeat and not go on fighting beyond the point at which he would initially have conceded loss. In other words, the limited response to a limited challenge must never be lost sight of. Even the preservation of the *status quo ante* must be considered as a solution." Oskar Morgenstern: *The Question of National Defense* (*New York*: *Random House*, 1959), pp. 140-141 (italics omitted).

sult. Now only at this point do we come to the proper work of calculation, in the comparison of the mixed effects of right or neutral actions, weighing their gravity, estimating the sufficiency of the reasons for them, and balancing greater against lesser goods or lesser evils.

It was a *late* Spanish schoolman, Francesco Vittoria, who first made explicit the teleologically prudential criterion in the just-war theory. To be finally justified there should be some reasonable expectation that a war can produce more good than evil, or at least achieve a lesser evil than not resorting to arms would lead to. To be justified, Luther said, a war must not, like fishing with a golden net, involve more risk of loss than realistic hope of gain. This, of course, requires calculation to determine whether warfare, already and on other grounds believed to be licit, should in fact be undertaken. It seems to me of the highest significance that discussion of the problem of war in Protestant circles today consists so largely of the principle of expediency alone out of the ancient theory. Thus prudential pacifism, prudential non-pacifism, and now prudential nuclear pacifism emphasize in the main our responsibility for judging concerning greater good or lesser evil among the consequences of political decision. Their conclusions disagree, of course, but the ethical orientation is the same.

If pacifism as an analysis of the right Christian conduct is wrong, it is wrong not first of all because it is imprudent, but because it has mistaken the principles of right political conduct and of justifiable war in which Christian love should take form, today as in the past. If non-pacifism is correct, it is correct not first of all because we can foreknow that there can be no greater evil than the consequences supposed to follow from non-resistance to tyranny and aggression, but because there is a perennial truth in the just-war doctrine which in every epoch of our human history Christian love, of its own inner logic, will be impelled to affirm and renew as proper Christian action, even in face of a great deal of ignorance of what the actual consequences will be. Of course, a balance of greater evil over the good expected to result would render unchoiceworthy an action otherwise right in itself. Calculation of the consquences may in any given instance be sufficient to prove that an act of justified warfare cannot effectively, and therefore should not, be undertaken; but this alone would never establish the right-fulness of such action as legitimate or permitted by love in the first place. By the same token, moral limits upon mili-tary action that is licit spring from the same source that al-lows it to the Christian. If today nuclear pacifism is cor-rect in any of its conclusions, the reason is not first of all that there can be "no greater evil" than the *event* of nuclear destruction but that there can be no greater evil than an *act* of all-out nuclear warfare. This is not only or first be-cause of the destructiveness of it but because of the intrinsic immorality of indiscriminate, direct killing; and that was all along the teaching of that product of *agape* in Western thought, the doctrine of the just war.

It is striking that Christian theories of justified war in the past have directed attention at least as much to the con-duct as to the ultimate and large-scale consequences of mili-tary action. In Chapter III we shall attempt to answer the historical question: Whence came the prohibition of indis-criminate killing in warfare? It is also significant that, at least at the outset, the just-war theory did not suppose that men possess the ability to discriminate between social orders at large by means of *clear and certain* principles of justice so as to declare one side or social system to be just and the other unjust in universal terms, in a case of conflict. Augus-tine does not seem to have needed to believe this as premise for a confident enough judgment as to a Christian's responsibility for action in justifiable (if not unambiguously just) war. To demonstrate this conclusion will be our concern in the next chapter. Perhaps the lesson to be drawn from this is that Christian ethics has reason to know more clearly and certainly the moral limits pertaining to the armed action of a man or nation than we can claim to know about the over-all justice of regimes and nations; and still more reason for knowing something significant about proper conduct than we have the competence to count up all its remote effects, subject as these are to the erosions, reversals, and glacial changes of history yet to come.

Before we attempt to recount the historical development of the just-war theory, however, and the moral and political wisdom to be drawn from it, two conclusions may be drawn from the foregoing analysis—one for the Christian public official and another for the shape (or lack of shape) of Protestant Christian ethical theory today. The Christian statesman who is responsible for policy decisions lives in a realm where "the science of the possible" is definitive for all his actions so long as he remains convinced that politics is his vocation. Politics is also, for the Christian, a realm of "deferred repentance." This means that there is not an essential difference between private morality and public morality. Murder, or the intentional, direct killing of persons not immediately involved in force that should justly be repelled, means the same whether this is done by individuals or by states. Moreover, readiness and preparation to kill the "innocent" partake of the crime of actually doing so. Therefore, the Christian statesman has no escape from his evil necessities in the assertion that his nation's power to retaliate against whole peoples is for the purpose of deterrence. No ethics—least of all Christian ethics—gives us leave to kill another man's children directly as a means of weakening *his* murderous intent. Preparation to do so—if that is the real and the only object of our weapons—is intrinsically a grave moral evil.

But politics and military planning may be a realm of deferred repentance. Whatever is immoral an individual, in his private capacity, should cease doing at once. But there should be statesmen who themselves are quite clear as to the immorality of obliteration warfare (and as well the wrong of deterring evil by readiness to do the same thing) who are still willing to engage in negotiation directed to the end of limiting war to justifiable means and ends through a period of time in which they may have to defer their nation's repentance. This may be better than keeping personal conscience clean by getting out of office. Thus, it may be that a "just war" Christian may sometimes find himself supporting a nation's preparations for unjust warfare—as there have been pacifist Christians in public office who have been willing to vote for a military appropriation. The important thing is to make clear and keep clear in the public conscience the moral *context* of political action that should surround every specific policy decision and should be the aim of political practice and of negotiation between nations. Just war must be made possible, and only just war should be allowed as a possibility. Meantime, repentance may have to be deferred. This is the main difference between public and private morality; and no case can be made for the view that what is wrong for a man may be right for a government. Only the statesman who knows this may be trusted not to defer his nation's repentance forever; and he will have the most powerful incentive to guide the thrust of political action into ways that are right, and toward international agreements and institutions that prevent wrong-doing on a national scale.

Finally, we must conclude that today Protestant theories of politics have a very odd shape indeed. Those theologians who most stress the fact that Christian ethics is wholly predicated upon redemption or upon the Divine indicative, and who say that decisive action is made possible by virtue of *justification* in Christ and by God's *forgiveness*, are often precisely the thinkers who strip politics of norms and principles distinguishing between right and wrong action. For them policy decisions are always wholly relative or "contextual," pragmatically relating available means to ends. On their view, a policy may be inept or erroneous, but it is difficult to see how decision could be *wrong*. This makes it difficult to see what there is in need of forgiveness, except inner motives. Even the politics of deferred repentance is made quite impossible, where there is nothing in violation of fundamental principle to repent of, and to negotiate out of the realm of possibility. It would seem that an ethics grounded in justification in Christ has no such urgent need to avoid making judgments of right and wrong in politics. The statesman who lives out of faith and love is under no necessity of theorizing contextually to the effect that there is no right he did not do and no wrong he was under continuing complicity in doing. This is not to say that sin must abound in order that faith may the more abound. But where there is faith there is surely no need for the removal of the principles of civil righteousness by which wrong gains some meaning; and where there is justification it is sinners and wrong-doers who may be sustained in office, and not merely prudent politicians. It is only an *agape*-ethic facing exclusively toward the future consequences that today allows outstanding theologians to reduce the morality of means to prudential calculation of results. Certainly, the moral problem of war will never be correctly analyzed unless there is a return to a morality of means as well as ends in warfare that can at all be justified for the Christian. This requires also an *agape*-ethic precipitating some principled judgment about means that are permitted or prohibited. Such an understanding of Christian morality may be described as "faith effective through in-principled love." The task of Christian ethical analysis is to articulate what this should mean in political action, and for the vocation of citizen or statesman.

Chapter Two

THE JUST WAR ACCORDING TO
ST. AUGUSTINE

Whoever wishes to understand the theory of the *justum bellum* (which should perhaps be translated the "justified war" rather than the "just war") must understand, in the writings of St. Augustine, the similarity between his critique of the pagan personal virtues and his critique of the social justice of any of the nations or empires of this world, in defense of which participation in warfare still could, he believed, be justified in Christian conscience. Augustine is not more severe in his criticism and rejection of the natural personal virtues as only "splendid vices" than he is in his analysis of the actual nature of that justice which prevails in the common life of a nation. Yet he was the first great formulator of the theory that war might be "just," which thereafter has mainly directed the course of Western Christian thinking about the problem of war. A brief inspection of Augustine's views will show that most later formulations of the theory of the *justum bellum* and, as a consquence, the verdict that no actual war can meet the conditions of the just-war theory, are radically un-Augustinian. It will show that the political experience and ethical analysis summarized in the so-called just-war theory cannot be dealt with all in one lump, as if it were a simple system of moral rules for the classification of cases, subject to no significant historical development, freighted with few ambiguities, there to be accepted or rejected as a single, if ancient or "classical," formulation of one possible position in Christian ethics, with no significant decisions to be taken *within* this tradition itself.

It is well known that, according to Augustine, the "fourfold division" of personal virtue (i.e., the cardinal virtues of prudence, justice, courage, and temperance) is "taken from four *forms* of love";[1] and that these dependable structures in human behavior or character "arise from" a man's loves,[2] as their habitual actualization, in order that the desired end (be it health, wealth, pleasure, or honor) may better be served and more steadily attained. These *ends* Augustine criticized, because, as temporal, they perish and can be lost against the will; and this judgment, in turn, was based on his analysis that all men in their desiring desire not only some good, not even a good higher than all others, but also the permanent enjoyment of it. A man necessarily wills and loves more than he gets in this world. Thou hast made us *toward* Thyself, and our hearts are restless until they rest in Thee. Until it rests in God, something was sought in the desire of the soul, no matter to what it was directed, that was not obtained.

These earthly *loves* Augustine criticized as not only vain but also selfish; and he was equally severe in his criticism of the love wherewith men love whatever they love, no matter how high it may be on some scale or in the order of natures Augustine derived from Neo-Platonism. The height of the value makes no essential difference; and, for all his respect for the typical Roman or Stoic virtues, arising from love of honor and informed by this love, in comparison with the Epicurean "virtues," Augustine wrote that "he has the

---

[1] *On the Morals of the Catholic Church,* xv (italics added). Except where otherwise indicated, citations to the works of St. Augustine are from *Basic Writings of Saint Augustine,* ed. Whitney J. Oates. (Two vols.; New York: Random House, 1948).

[2] *Ibid.,* xxv.

soundest perception who recognizes that even the love of praise is a vice,"[3] and that "though that glory be not a luxurious woman [i.e., pleasure], it is nevertheless puffed up, and has much vanity in it."[4] Even when men pursue virtue for its own sake, and, as they say, for no other reward or benefit than virtue itself, still virtue is the form to which their secret love gives the substance: "For although some suppose that virtues which have a reference only to themselves, and are desired only on their own account, are yet true and genuine virtues, the fact is that even then they are inflated with pride, and are therefore to be reckoned vices rather than virtues." If Augustine believed that Roman morality was "less base" than some of the types of character he knew to be cultivated under the sun, this can only mean that he paid it paradoxical tribute as more splendidly vicious than others. "Where there is no true religion"—bringing the soul to rest in the one good End that eternally endures, and converting, transforming, and redirecting the love wherewith a man loves every good—"there can be no true virtue."[5] Upright pagans have the form but not the substance of true virtue. As to this, there can be no distinction among men.

The word "form" is Augustine's own, but not the word "substance," in the foregoing statement of his theory of moral virtue. The latter term, and the distinction to follow between the mere form and the real substance of justice, is used, not in the somewhat different sense in which later scholasticism may have used "form-substance," but to direct attention to that charity which makes virtue virtuous. The heart of the matter of virtue or of justice consists in a matter of the heart. The right inner intention or direction of the will alone "rightwises" every virtue, regardless of the "for-

[3] *The City of God,* V, 13.
[4] *Ibid.,* V, 20.
[5] *Ibid.,* XIX, 25.

mal" identity there may be between one "justice" and another "justice," warranting the use of the same word to point to patterns of behavior, character, or relationships which arise from and are in-formed by quite different sorts of love.

What Augustine says about social justice and the nature of the state in Book XIX of *The City of God* can best be comprehended by means of this distinction between form and substance. Moreover, his radical critique of such justice as characterizes, has characterized, or ever will characterize, the kingdoms of this world should be held firmly in mind whenever the question arises concerning the theory of a *justum bellum,* of which he was the primary architect. Properly grasped, even more than when improperly grasped, Augustine's views on political justice are apt today to occasion considerable puzzlement in a person who holds idealistic and universalistic conceptions of justice, and consternation in the Christian who may want *real* justice on the side he supports in war and who may have been informed that the theory of a just war is supposed to tell him clearly when this is the case and when not.

Here it is necessary to oppose and reject Ernest Barker's interpretation of St. Augustine's political theory, and especially of Book XIX, set forth in his Introduction to the Temple Classics edition of *The City of God*.[6]   Barker's key distinction is only a relative one, between "absolute" and "relative righteousness."   By the latter he means "a system of right relations mainly in the legal sphere" or "a system of right relations reckoning with, and adjusted to, the sinfulness of human nature."[7]   The State has relative justice (rel-

---

[6] Trans. John Healey. (One volume ed.; London: Dent; New York; E. P. Dutton, 1931, 1934, 1940).

[7] *Ibid.*, p. xxvi. The objection to this definition of the justice of nations is that it states only that the sinfulness of human nature is reckoned with and adjusted to. There is no suggestion that this "system of right relations" itself gives form to unrectified love and participates in the sin it represses.

ative natural law?); the City of God, absolute justice (absolute natural law?); and the terrene city, absolute unrighteousness.[8] Absolute righteousness goes further than the relative justice of states, but it does not fundamentally challenge this justice. Any flaw there may be in worldly justice is not intrinsically a flaw in the *morality* of it; and, on Barker's showing, love of God would, theoretically, only add to earthly justice a religious dimension. Such an interpretation does not take seriously into account Augustine's belief that there can be no justice, or rendering man his due, unless God is given His due.

In passing, it should be pointed out that Barker makes a similar *donum superadditum* analysis of Augustine's treatment of the personal moral virtues. "One by one," he writes, "St Augustine examines the four cardinal virtues of ancient theory . . . and of each in turn he proves that so long as it is a merely moral virtue, without the comfort of faith in God and the corroboration of the hope of eternal life, it must necessarily absent itself from felicity."[9] Love of God adds "comfort," "corroboration," and saving "felicity" to virtues that are already intrinsically, even if "merely," moral. Surely Augustine meant and said more than this. Moral virtue without charity not only "must necessarily absent itself from felicity"; it also, and primarily, necessarily absents itself from virtuousness and lacks the very essence of virtue.

Barker's eloquent words of tribute to the significance of St. Augustine fail, therefore, to communicate the full measure of the tumult and dialectical encounter that was going

[8] "The earthly city, like the heavenly city, is an ideal conception; or rather, and to speak more exactly, it may be called the ideal negation, or antithesis, of the ideal. . . . The actual State, as it really exists, is something different. It is not absolutely unrighteous. On the contrary, it has a sort of *Justitia* of its own. . . ." *Ibid.*, p. xxv. This is not to be denied. But the question is whether this sort of justice ought properly to be called "relative," or merely formal.

[9] *Ibid.*, pp. xxv-xxvi.

on in his mind. "It it the great fascination of *The City of God* (and particularly perhaps of the nineteenth book) that we see the two men ["the antique man of the old classical culture, and the Christian man of the New Gospel"] at grips with one another. This is what makes the work one of the greatest turning points in the history of human destiny: it stands on the confines of two worlds, the classical and the Christian, and it points the way into the Christian."[10] Or again: "The nineteenth book particularly illustrates this sentinel attitude."[11] Augustine is not only a sentinel on the ramparts. He not only points the way into the Christian world. He also attacks, in order to capture and, afterward, to conserve. His critique and rejection of the humanistic autonomy of classical moral achievement—the substance of its virtue—was most thoroughgoing and severe (as Cochrane has shown), in order that that world might be torn from its foundations, and turn if possible and be converted. The new direction of morality required more of a transformation than an addition, and Augustine's new direction in moral and political analysis proceeds not by distinctions in degree. Given man's citizenship in the City of God, his citizenship elsewhere is not merely relatively inferior; it must be seen as radically deprived of the ethical substance formerly attributed to it before that which is new had come. We may now turn to see confirmation of this in Book XIX, *contra* Barker.

Notice first that Barker insists on translating *Justitia* always as "righteousness" (even though, in the reverse, he notes the fact that the term for righteousness in Plato and in the New Testament was "received in the Latin" as *Justitia,* with large and sometimes disastrous consequences in the field of theology and of moral philosophy).[12] The idea of

[10] *Ibid.,* p. iv.
[11] *Ibid.,* p. xxxiii.
[12] *Ibid.,* p. xx-xxi.

"righteousness" was, for Plato, St. Paul, and St. Augustine, without much distinction, according to Barker, "a moral idea (which at its highest seemed to pass into a religious idea) rather than an idea of law."[13] This means that in the thought of Augustine, Platonic "righteousness is lifted to a higher plane" rather easily and smoothly. Righteousness simply "ceases to be a system of right relations between men, based on the idea of social stations, and it becomes a system of right relations between man and God (but also, and consequently, between man and man)."[14] If righteousness already seemed about to pass over into a religious idea, this higher plane has already been envisioned and in some degree attained. On this interpretation, there would be no mounting of an attack upon the will (or love) that governs, directs, and determines the innermost nature of the systems of justice and relationships within and among the nations.

Consequently, Barker affirms that the State "has its own 'order': it has its own relative 'righteousness.' It is not a *magnum latrocinium;* for you *cannot* remove righteousness from it and St. Augustine only said that kingdoms were great bands of brigands if you remove righteousness."[15] However, it befalls this interpretation that Augustine also said that you cannot remove justice from a band of brigands! You would have left neither band nor brigands, for there is nothing so clearly contrary to nature as to display no order and no remnant of interrelationships that may be termed "due," by common consent or habitual acceptance.[16]

---

[13] *Ibid.,* p. xxi.
[14] *Ibid.,* p. xxiii.
[15] *Ibid.,* p. xxxviii.
[16] The same point may be stated in terms of "peace." When discussing peace as the *end* of "just" wars, Augustine clinches his point by saying, "Even robbers take care to maintain peace with their comrades." An earthly kingdom, while it abhors "the just peace of God and loves its own unjust peace," "cannot help loving peace of one kind or other. For there is no vice so clean contrary to nature that it obliterates the faintest traces of nature" (XIX, 12). "There may be peace without war, but there cannot be war without some kind peace, *because war supposes the existence of*

Barker affirms not only that states have "a sort of *Justitia*" of their own, but also that "the citizens of the heavenly city avail themselves of this *Justitia* in the course of their pilgrimage, so that the State is thus, in its way, a coadjutor of the City of God."[17]   Now, it is significant that this is precisely what Augustine avoids saying, even when he might have done so, in the formal sense of the existing legal system or system of social relationships, not in the sense of substantive justice.   One passage that Barker cites says not this, but that the children of God make use of earthly *peace;*[18] and Augustine ordinarily describes this as an "*unjust* peace."[19] The Heavenly City also uses the "order" of the world in the course of its pilgrimage. Augustine explicity says *pax-ordo,* not *justitia,* in this connection.   Barker places the term in the text, because what he wants to be able to take out of it is his own scheme of continuous religio-political concepts, e.g.: "*Ordo* is a great word in St. Augustine; and *ordo* is closely allied to what I have called a 'system of right relations,' and that in turn is closely allied to, and indeed identical with, the idea of Righteousness."[20] Augustine would not have said the relations were "right."   Instead, he might have said that it is an "unjust order" as well as an "unjust peace" that the Heavenly City uses in its pilgrimage.   That City does not rescind or destroy, rather it preserves and pursues those orders, *different though they be in different na-*

---

some natures to wage it, and these natures cannot exist without peace of one kind or other" (XIX, 13, italics added).

[17] *Op. cit.,* p. xxv.

[18] "Therefore the heavenly city rescinds and destroys none of those things by which earthly peace is attained or maintained: rather it preserves and pursues that which, different though it be in different nations, is yet directed to the one and selfsame end of earthly peace.... Therefore, again, the heavenly city uses earthly peace in its pilgrimage: it preserves and seeks the agreement of human wills in matters pertaining to the mortal nature of man...." *The City of God,* XIX, 17; quoted by Barker, p. xxvii. See also XIX, 26.

[19] *Ibid.,* XIX, 12.

[20] *Op. cit.,* p. xxiii.

tions, by which earthly peace, doubtless an unjust peace and a just endurable order, is maintained. It seeks every "agreement of human wills in matters pertaining to the mortal nature of man." The Heavenly City, therefore, preserves, pursues, and uses the forms of justice, different though they may be in different nations, for that is but a necessary part of their *pax-ordo,* and the agreement of human wills about goods that are mortal, in the midst of which it continues on its journey. There is continuity among *pax, ordo,* and *justitia* in this sense; but a great gulf is fixed between these and either ultimate Righteousness or justice that is the substance of right human relations. Human wills are in themselves divided and sinful wills, and of course the same is the case also in their agreements of will, no matter how inclusive these may be.

In summary, Barker elevates *Justitia* by translating it as "righteousness"; yet at the same time he continues to regard it as closely associated with the concrete order or system of relations that necessarily exists in any State. This brings about a seemingly smooth Christianization of classical politics. Such an interpretation is incapable of appreciating the passages in which Augustine evacuates the ethical idealism from Graeco-Roman definitions of the commonwealth before and in the course of pointing the way to the Christian world. To Barker, this—the most startling thesis of Book XIX—seems to be only a matter of language, a *tour de force,* or an unwarranted quarrel resulting from purely religious (i.e., non-political, non-moral) preconceptions on Augustine's part. The point here has to do with Cicero's definition of *res publica* as "as assemblage associated by a common acknowledgment of right *(jus)* and by a community of interests."[21] Barker comments:

[21] *The City of God,* XIX, 21.

It is the word Right, or *Jus,* which offends St. Augustine. In the Latin usage *Jus* is a legal term; and it signifies simply the body of legal rules which is recognized, and can be enforced, by a human authority. On the basis of this significance of *Jus* there is little in Cicero's definition with which we need quarrel. It might, perhaps, go farther; but it is correct enough so far as it goes. But St. Augustine has his own preconceptions; and they made him resolve to quarrel with Cicero's definition. With his mind full of the idea of Righteousness (the Greek *dikaiosune,* as it appears in Plato and in St. Paul), he twists the sense of *jus.* He identifies *jus* with *justitia;* he identifies *Justitia* with *vera justitia;* and he argues accordingly that "where there is no true righteousness, there cannot be a union of men associated by a common acknowledgement of Right."[22]

On the surface, of course, Barker is correct. In Cicero, and elsewhere in Latin political writings, *jus* signifies simply the body of legal rules recognized and enforced by the State. But when Augustine moves quickly on to the assertion that where there is no true justice (*justitia*) there can be no right (*jus*), more is involved than the mistaken replacement of one word for another. Augustine goes behind the words, behind the system of legal rules, to the common assumption of Graeco-Roman political theory that justice is the ethical substance of a commonwealth. This he gets a grip on; and, therefore, it is a theoretical *argument,* not mere logomachy, when he contends that "where there is no true justice there can be no assemblage of men associated by a common acknowledgment of right, and therefore there can be no people . . . ; and if no people, then no weal of the people"—and therefore "there never was a Roman republic." Whether contained in the term *jus,* or not, there is a real difference between Augustine's and the classical conception of the State; and this difference is at the level of the analysis of the actual justice present in the commonwealth. When Augustine writes that the virtues which a soul or a State seems to

[22] *Op. cit.,* p. xlvii

possess "are rather vices than virtues, so long as there is no reference to God in the matter,"[23] he is not calling for a mere religious addendum, or for a State that goes further than its existant, intrinsic justice to become a denominationally Christian State. Rather he is making a judgment in political analysis itself, a judgment upon such seeming justice. When, therefore, Barker rejoins that "this has only been proved on the basis of assumptions about the significance of *Jus* which Cicero would never have admitted,"[24] he may be correct so far as this word alone is concerned; but the challenge to Cicero's assumptions, not about religion, or *jus*, but about secular *justitia*, remains. Incidentally, if Augustine's meaning in himself using *Justitia* (despite its translation as Righteousness) was to signify a system of right legal relations; if, as Barker contends, the word *ordo* is closely allied with such a system of relationships or functions in society, and this in turn is "closely allied to, and indeed identical with the idea of Righteousness," then one wonders what led him to make the mistake, even verbally, of objecting at all to Cicero's definition. He did this because behind *jus* he seemed to discern pretentions to a quality of justice he could not allow to be the case in any earthly kingdom.

By discarding the definition of a commonwealth which was so idealistic as to be a logical class without any members, and adopting another, Augustine reaches the conclusion that Rome, after all, was a "people." If only there is an assemblage of reasonable beings, and not of beasts, and they are bound together by an agreement as to the objects of love, it can reasonably be called a people. Thus Augustine demoralizes *res publica*. For the word "love" as used here has no specially laudable denotation or connotation. It simply means the activity of "will." "An assemblage of reasonable beings bound together by a common agreement as to the

---

[23] *The City of God*, XIX, 25.
[24] *Op. cit.*, p. xlviii.

objects of their love, ... whatever it loves";[25] or, as Barker translates, "a reasoning multitude associated by an agreement to pursue in common the objects which it desires."[26] Neither a common language nor a common ethnic origin nor common and universal conceptions of the norms of justice nor the substance of justice in the common life constitute a people, but a common will or love. "This is practically Cicero's definition," the Carlysles comment, "but with the elements of law and justice left out. No more fundamental difference could well be imagined, although St. Augustine seems to take the matter lightly; for Cicero's whole conception of the State turns upon the principle that it is a means of attaining and preserving justice.... It would appear, then, that the political theory of St. Augustine is materially different in several respects from that of St. Ambrose and other Fathers, who represent the ancient tradition that justice is the essential quality, as it is also the end, of the State."[27]

As with justice as a personal virtue, so with social justice. "When a man does not serve God what justice can we ascribe to him...? And if there is no justice in such an individual, certainly there can be none in a community of such persons."[28] Indeed, what justice can be ascribed to such communities? The forms of justice, lacking the inner rectitude that makes justice just or relationships right among men.

[25] *The City of God,* XIX, 24.

[26] *Op. cit.,* p. xlix. Yet it was Augustine who first fully formulated the "justice" of Christian participation in war to preserve earthly *pax-ordo!* One may compare this with the way C. C. Morrison, in a remarkable series of editorials in the *Christian Century,* removed clear judgments of greater justice from among the grounds for a Christian's positive involvement in his nation's cause in World War II (*The Christian and the War,* Willett, Clark & Co., 1942); and with Reinhold Niebuhr's wonderfully ironic and self-analytic remark about the occasion he has to thank God for placing him on the just side in three wars in one lifetime.

[27] R. W. Carlyle and A. J. Carlyle: *A History of Medieval Political Theory in the West* (Edinburgh and London: W. Blackwood and Sons, 1903-1936), I, 166, 170.

[28] *The City of God,* XIX, 21.

Then should be kept clearly in mind the justice of which Augustine was speaking when he wrote of wars in which Christian engagement was justified.

How many great wars, how much slaughter and bloodshed, have provided this unity [of the imperial city]! And though those are past, the end of these miseries has not yet come. For though there have never been wanting, nor are yet wanting, hostile nations beyond the empire, against whom wars have been and are waged, yet, supposing there were no such nations, the very extent of the empire itself has produced wars of a more obnoxious description—social and civil wars—and with these the whole race has been agitated, either by the actual conflict or fear of a renewed outbreak. If I attempted to give an adequate description of these manifold disasters, these stern and lasting necessities, though I am quite unequal to the task, what limit could I set? But, say they, the wise man will wage just wars. As if he would not all the rather lament the necessity of just wars, if he remembers that he is a man; for if they were not just he would not wage them, and would therefore be delivered from all wars. For it is the wrongdoing of the opposing party which compels the wise man to wage just wars; and this wrongdoing, even though it give rise to no war, would still be matter of grief to man because it is man's wrong-doing. Let every one, then, who thinks with pain on all these great evils, so horrible, so ruthless, acknowledge that this is misery. And if any one either endures or thinks of them without mental pain, this is a more miserable plight still, for he thinks himself happy because he has lost human feeling.[29]

Notice that Augustine writes of "the wrong-doing of the opposing party which compels the wise man to wage just wars," as incidental to his stress upon the mental pain this misery should cause every man to feel. It is not made incidental to justifying the right side specifically in terms of universal standards of justice. The same is true of his statement that "even when we wage just war, our adversaries must be sinning:" this is prefatory to pointing to the fact

[29] *Ibid.*, XIX, 7.

that "every victory, even though gained by wicked men, is a result of the first judgment of God, who humbles the vanquished either for the sake of removing or punishing their sins."[30] It is a lively sense of man's common plight in wrong-doing and of the judgment of God that overarches the justified war, and not—except perhaps as an incidental implication of what Augustine says—a sense of or clarity about the universal ethical standards that are to be applied. On the face of it, therefore, the statement of the Calhoun Commission (in the course of outlining "three main attitudes toward participation in war which developed in the life of the Christian Church:" pacifism, the just war, and the holy war) that "the just war was carefully defined, in such terms that only one side could be regarded as fighting justly,"[31] cannot certainly be read back as far in this tradition as Augustine's first statement of it.

If Augustine believed that there is always only one side that can be regarded as fighting justly in the wars in which a Christian will find himself responsibly engaged, he should not have believed this. For his own analysis of the *pax-ordo*-formal *justitia* or *jus* of nations gives no ground for any such conclusion in every case, perhaps not in most cases. Justice is the form of men's loves; in the State it is the form of that love or agreement to pursue in common the objects which a "people" desire. Moreover, social justice "arises from" a common agreement as to the objects of their love (will); and, since the agreement would break down and the people become a mere multitude without minimum or greater degrees of participation in the life of a nation, accepted schemes of justice serve to strengthen that common will or love which constitutes *res publica*. The Christian has reason to endeavor to strengthen "the combination of

[30] *Ibid.*, XIX, 15.
[31] "The Relation of the Church to the War in the Light of the Christian Faith," *Social Action*, Dec. 1944, p. 61.

men's wills to attain the things which are helpful to this life." The "heavenly city, while it sojourns on earth . . . , not scrupling about diversities in the manners, laws, and institutions whereby earthly peace is secured and maintained, but recognizing that, however various these are, they all tend to one and the same end of earthly peace . . . [is] so far from rescinding and abolishing these diversities, that it even preserves and adopts them. . . . Even the heavenly city, therefore, while in its state of pilgrimage, avails itself of the peace of earth, and . . . desires and maintains a common agreement among men regarding the acquisition of the necessities of life. . . ."[32] Thus, a Christian in this life finds his own life and will bound up inextricably with such a common agreement among men as to the objects of their political purposes, and he is bound to foster the combination of men's wills to attain the things which are helpful to this life. Doubtless he seeks not only to preserve but also to enlarge such agreements of will and the scope of peaceful orders on this earth. But is it not likely that there will be occasions on which the love or will in-forming secular justice cannot be extended into greater combinations, that appeal must then be made the *ultima ratio* of war, and that the existing justice Augustine has in mind when speaking of the "just" war may tragically be on both sides? In any case, all Augustine's language about the purpose that lies at the root of the State, and his severe castigation of the resulting justice which still must be what justifies warfare, brings us remarkably close to that remarkable statement in the best book about "limited warfare" that has appeared in recent years, to the effect that "nations might better renounce the use of war as an instrument of *anything but* national policy."[33]

[32] *The City of God*, XIX, 17.
[33] Robert Osgood: *Limited War: The Challenge to American Strategy* (Chicago: The University of Chicago Press, 1957), p. 21.

In elevating a better peace as one criterion of the just war (we may also say the limited war), Augustine was not unaware that there slips into the national policy which constitutes the multitude a people, an attitude according to which "even those whom they make war against they wish to make their own, and impose on them the laws of their peace."[34]   And so the "just" war which seeks peace, in the sense of a larger and better and more stable agreement of wills, has its own intrinsic limits which it may overstep. Nations may seek to extend *pax-ordo* by mere compulsion, and not by agreement of wills. Yet Augustine could not have supposed that warfare is justified only on the part of the side which is driven by none of the desire to impose the laws of its own peace.   Such a supposition would be contrary to his basic analysis of the reality of States, and of the love basic to their nature.   Whether of individuals or of communities of individuals who are agreed to be a people, the love for temporal goods and for those material things necessary for individual or collective life must of necessity be a love in which *men must fear to have colleagues*.   All men's loves, for any other good than the *bonum summum et commune,* is of its nature fratricidal.   That is why Cain, who killed his brother, is the founder of the earthly city.   If it be said, quite correctly, that the earthly city is an "ideal negation" and that actual societies are not necessarily like that, then we must remember Remus and point to Romulus, who was the founder of Rome.   The truth is that, according to Augustine, fratricidal love and brotherly love based on love of God are always commingled in human history.   There is no heart, no people, and no public policy so redeemed or so clearly contrary to nature as to be without both.   Communities are built over fratricidal love by men with divided hearts.   We must not only say that, according to the doc-

[34] *The City of God*, XIX, 12.

trine of the divided will, Augustine was unable to will entirely, and with a whole heart, to love God, because at the
same moment he nilled this for the will (or love) of his
"ancient mistresses" (the adjective I understand to indicate
the span of time that had elapsed, not to characterize his
mistresses when he had them).[35] We must also say that he
was equally unable to will entirely to love his mistresses
with a whole heart, because of the foundation of the love of
God that was laid in him. Them he also nilled for the love
of God, for God had made him for himself.[36] The same complex analysis must be given of the love or will in common
which makes a people. It, too, cannot will any finite thing
entirely. Something is sought in every human desire, no
matter to what it is directed, that is not obtained. That is
the created good, and at the same time the misdirected evil
of it; for men and States necessarily will and love more than
they get in this world. They desire not only some good, or
even a good higher than all others, but also the permanent
enjoyment of it. An unrectified *nisus* toward the eternal
disturbs every people's purpose: that is why they see in their
good *the* Good, in the laws of their peace the conditions of
universal peace, and are resolved that this too shall not pass
away. Yet Augustine, who saw all this so clearly, not as
an aloof spectator of the human scene or of the rise and fall
of empires but as one who was content to dwell in the midst
of this since God had placed him there, was almost the first
thinker known in our literature to justify Christian participation in wars. The just-war theory cannot have meant
for him the presence of justice (i.e., the temporary order and
form of these divided loves) on one side, its absence on the
other.

　These conclusions, then, have been demonstrated from a
review of St. Augustine's views of political justice and the

[35] *The Confessions*, VIII, 26.
[36] *Ibid*, VIII, 20-22.

justum bellum. At least at the outset, the just-war theory did not rest upon the supposition that men possess a general competence to discriminate with certainty between social orders at large by means of clear, universal principles of justice, so as to be able to declare (without sin's affecting one's judgment of his own nation's cause) one side or social system to be just and the others unjust. This was not the premise by which Augustine came to a confident enough judgment as to a Christian's responsibility in justifiable (if not unambiguously just) war. My contention is that Christian ethics may attribute to ordinary men, and to their political leaders, a capacity to know more clearly and certainly the moral limits pertaining to the armed action a man or a nation is about to engage in, than they are likely to know enough to compare unerringly the over-all justice of regimes and nations. There is still more reason to believe that men know something of moral significance about proper conduct than to believe that they are able to count up all the remote effects of their actions, so as to measure their actions by the standards of any consequentialist system of ethics.

Two main alterations of the just-war doctrine took place between Augustine and Aquinas. First, a shift from voluntarism to rationalism in understanding the nature of political community, and therefore an increasing emphasis upon the natural-law concept of justice in analysis of the cause that justifies participation in war. This is what is usually meant by the doctrine of the just war. I shall reject this, in the belief that Augustine was more correct and realistic in believing people to be bound together more by agreement of will and purpose than by agreement in their general conceptions of justice. Secondly, rules for the right *conduct* of war were drawn up, particularly for the protection of noncombatants. This is usually dismissed as the weakest part of the traditional theory of the just war. I propose, however, that we seriously reconsider this question of the just conduct of war. For, it may well be the case that natural reason falters in attempting to make large comparison of the justice inherent in great regimes in conflict but is quite competent to deliver verdict upon a specific action that is proposed in warfare. It is striking that Christian theories of justified war in the past have directed attention at least as much to the conduct as to the ultimate and large-scale consequences of military action.

In any case, the work of love (or of "faith effective through in-principled love") in limiting the conduct of war, or acts of war that are ever justified, can be clearly demonstrated. This will be our task in the following chapter. At the same time, a study of the genesis of the so-called rule of double effect, prohibiting the direct and intentional killing of anyone besides "combatants" in warfare, will show that, in very large measure, "natural law" judgments do not proceed from autonomous reason alone, but are derivative principles in which *agape* shapes itself for action.

Chapter Three

THE GENESIS OF NONCOMBATANT IMMUNITY

A great deal of the history and later meaning of the just-war theory may best be comprehended from two passages— one from St. Augustine and the other from St. Thomas Aquinas—and by a careful study of the movement of thought from one of these positions to the other and thence into contemporary treatments of the just or limited war. In this survey the issues which will be raised are these: In participating in warfare, is it his sense of justice and injustice or of what love requires that motivates the Christian? When did the requirements of natural justice become so complete and clear that Christian ethics claimed to be able to define exhaustively and with considerable certainty those inherently wrong means that may never be used to accomplish directly any good, however great, even the ends of charity? When and in what way may it be said that to bring about the death of an unjust aggressor is *intrinsically* justifiable? What is the meaning of the natural law immunity and rights of the innocent (the noncombatant)?

The striking thing about the views of Augustine is that, while he was quite realistic, as we have seen, about the necessity and justifiability of public defense and the Christian's responsibility for it, nevertheless he saw no cause for private self-defense. And the striking thing about the views of Thomas Aquinas is that, despite the development of the theory of the just war by the Canonists over the intervening centuries and despite his own theory of natural law, he was almost equally reluctant to justify the direct killing even of the enemy, or of an unjust aggressor, as in itself intrinsically right. The thought of these two men on this subject is worth profound consideration, if only in order to understand the background and shape of the ethical judgments that are made in the natural-law tradition which followed from the development we will trace, and which persists to the present day.

The passage from Augustine is to be found in a chapter on the question "whether *Libido* dominates also in those things which we see too often done."[1]

For me the point to be considered first is whether an onrushing enemy, or an assassin lying in wait may be killed with no wrong-headed desire [for the saving] of one's life, or for liberty or for purity.... How can I think that they act with no inordinate desire who fight for that [i.e., some creaturely good], which they can lose without desiring to lose it?... Therefore the law is not just which grants the power to a wayfarer to kill a highway robber, so that he may not be killed [by the robber]; or which grants to any one, man or woman, to slay an assailant attacking, if he can, before he or she is harmed. The soldier also is commanded by law to slay the enemy, for which slaying, if he objects, he will pay the penalty by imperial order. Shall we then dare to say that these laws are unjust, or more, that they are not laws? For to me a law that is not just appears to be no law.... For that he be slain who lays plans to take the life of another is less hard [to bear] than the death of him who is defending his own life [against the plotter]. And acting against the chaste life of a man in opposition to his own will is much more evidently wrong than the taking of the life of him who so does violence by that one against whom the violence is done. Then again the soldier in slaying the enemy is the agent of the law [in war], wherefore he does his duty easily with no wrong aim or purpose.... That law therefore, which for the

[1] *De Libero Arbitrio*, Bk. I, chap. v (trans. F. E. Tourscher; Peter Reilly Co., 1937), pp. 25-29. Cf. Ep. XLVII, 6.

protection of citizens orders foreign force to be repulsed by the same force, can be obeyed without a wrong desire: and this same can be said of all officials who by right and by order are subject to any powers. But I see not how these men [who defend themselves privately], while not held guilty by law, can be without fault: for the law does not force them to kill, but leaves it in their power. It is free therefore for them to kill no one for those things [life or possessions] which they can lose against their own will, which things therefore they ought not to love.... Wherefore again I do not blame the law which permits such aggressors to be slain: but by what reason I can defend those who slay them I do not find.... How indeed are they free of sin before Providence, who for those things which ought to be held of less worth are defiled by the killing of a man?

In this passage Augustine acknowledges that there is a difference between killing an unjust aggressor and killing the innocent. The latter act, he says, is "more evidently wrong than the taking of the life of him who so does violence by the one against whom the violence is done." But this difference in the natural justice of the two cases is quite insufficient to be made the basis for Christian action. Near the beginning of this quotation Augustine leans toward the opinion that the law is not just which grants a wayfarer the right to kill an attacking assailant, and he says that to his way of thinking such an unjust law is no law at all. Here the "just" standard he has in mind can only be a justice radically transformed by supernatural charity; and he seems for a moment to hold open the possibility that the laws of society might be brought to accord with such a principle. At the end, however, Augustine refrains from blaming the law which permits the slaying of unjust aggressors, and reserves his condemnation for anyone, especially any Christian, who avails himself of this right which the law only allows. No disciple of Christ should love life or property, both of which are creaturely goods that may be lost against his will, more than he loves God, and his neighbor in God, who may not be so lost. No Christian should be thus "defiled by the killing of a man."

What in him, we may ask, would be defiled by the inordinate self-love or "wrong-headed desire" necessarily involved even in killing an unjust man? The answer is stated by Ambrose, with whom Augustine agrees in this as surely as he agreed with him in justifying public defense, that the wise man "when he meets an armed robber ... cannot return his blows, *lest in defending his life he should stain his love toward his neighbor.* The verdict on this is plain and clear in the books of the Gospel. . . . What robber is more hateful than the persecutor who came to kill Christ? But Christ would not be defended by the wounds of the persecutor, *for He willed to heal all by his wounds.*"[2] It is clear that supernatural charity is the basis of Augustine's judgment in the matter of private defense, that he would see this extended quite far into the actual affairs of men, and that his analysis of how hostility is to be met has not shifted over to be based on natural, intrinsic justice alone.

This confirms the conclusion (already reached in our analysis of Augustine's treatment of justice in the State) that he does not justify Christian participation in warfare on the grounds of intrinsic justice alone. For surely whatever is intrinsically and substantially just the Christian may perform, whether in the matter of public or private defense. If it is not from justice in any adequate ethical sense, the question remains whether instead it is from love that the Christian engages in public defense, just as it is from love that he renounces the same in the private realm. We may not be quite able to attribute to Augustine in describing the relation of the Heavenly City to earthly kingdoms the words of Luther in relating the Two Realms: "In what concerns

[2] *The Duties of the Clergy*, III, iv, 27 (*Nicene and Post-Nicene Fathers of the Christian Church*, ed. by Philip Schaff; New York: Chas. Scribner's Sons, 1887, vol. X; italics added).

you and yours, you govern yourself by the Gospel and suffer injustice for yourself as a true Christian; in what concerns others, you [still] *govern yourself according to love,* and suffer no injustice for your neighbor's sake."[3] Augustine's political realism probably prevented his elaborating any such explicit, individualistic (and doubtless somewhat abstract) conception of the relation of a Christian as such to his political duties in wartime. Augustine says simply that "that law therefore, which for the protection of citizens orders foreign force to be repulsed by the same force, can be obeyed without wrong desire: and this same can be said of all officials who by right and by order are subject to any powers." This means, at least, that the Christian citizen who obeys an order to fight may do so without, on his own part, an inordinate desire for worldly goods; and so far Augustine is in agreement with Luther. Inordinate self-love may be *absent* when the public good is in question; but whether it is love that is *present,* governing the Christian in what concerns the public good, and leading him to suffer no injustice to be done, may be questioned.

I once expressed the opinion that the reason Augustine justified the Christian citizen in obeying the orders of his prince (while at the same time he denied him the exercise of any right of private self-defense) was that he supposed the prince, like a judge on the bench, to be in a position to render more impartial judgment as to the justice of the cause than a private individual when his own life or property is in peril.[4] The possibility of more impartial judgment concerning the true justice of the matter now seems to me

---

[3] *Secular Authority: To What Extent It Should Be Obeyed, Works* (Philadelphia: Muhlenberg Press, 1943), III, 242 (italics added). Bearing the sword is an alien work yet still the proper work of love. This is the very essence of Luther's political ethics, and not "a somewhat labored argument" (as Preserved Smith believed. *The Life and Letters of Martin Luther,* Boston and New York: Houghton Mifflin Co., 1911, p. 216).

[4] *Basic Christian Ethics.* (New York: Chas. Scribner's Sons, 1950), p. 175.

to have played a much larger part in later formulations of the just-war theory (in support of the criterion that a war, to be justified, has to be publicly declared by the highest official) than it does in Augustine. While not excluding this basis in some degree, it seems much more likely that the reason Augustine required declaration of war on the part of the highest official authority was because the existing political authority has the responsibility for that combination of wills or agreement as to goods necessary to the earthly life of a multitude if it is a people. The king, more than any individual or party, could be expected to be the voice of this alignment of wills, and he is therefore charged with the responsibility of preserving it. When this condition is fulfilled, when the highest official authority has initiated a war and made a judgment as to its necessity for the preservation of the laws of its peace, the Christian citizen finds himself called into responsible action because of the alliance of his will with the will (and love) that constitutes him with the rest of the multitude a people. It is not that he, not at least explicitly, makes the ethical judgment that Christian love requires just this participating action, for it is a very earthly love that requires it; nor does he—he is even less in the position to do this than the ruler—make the ethical judgment that intrinsic justice requires it.

The passage from Aquinas is his reply to the question, whether it is lawful to kill a man in self-defense.[5]

I answer that, Nothing hinders one act from having two effects, only one of which is intended, while the other is beside the intention. Now moral acts take their species according to what is intended, and not according to what is beside the intention, since this is accidental as explained above. . . . Accordingly the act of self-defense may have two effects, one is the saving of one's life, the other is the slaying of the aggressor. Therefore this act, since one's intention is to save one's own life,

[5] *S-T.*, II-II, Q. 64, art. 7.

is not unlawful, seeing that it is natural to everything to keep itself in being, as far as possible. And yet, though proceeding from a good intention, an act may be rendered unlawful, if it be out of proportion to the end. Wherefore if a man, in self-defense, uses more than necessary violence, it will be unlawful: whereas if he repel force with moderation his defense will be lawful, because according to the jurists, *it is lawful to repel force by force, provided one does not exceed the limits of a blameless defense.* Nor is it necessary for salvation that a man omit the act of self-defense in order to avoid killing the other man, since one is bound to take more care of one's own life than of another's. But as it is unlawful to take a man's life, except for the public authority acting for the common good, as stated above, it is not lawful for a man to intend killing a man in self-defense, except for such as have public authority, who while intending to kill a man in self-defense refer this to the public good, as in the case of a soldier fighting against the foe, and in the minister or the judge struggling with robbers, although even these sin if they be moved by private animosity.

This is a remarkable passage, deserving close scrutiny. In it Aquinas does *not* say that, because of the principles of natural justice, an unjust assailant may be killed without more ado or more to think about. The only case in which it is right to intend to kill even an unjust assailant would seem to be when, in acting for the public defense, one refers this intentional killing as a means to the public good. Aquinas does not require, as Augustine does, the individual who is unjustly attacked to omit the *act* of private self-defense; but he does require him to omit directing his *intention* against even an unjust man. This "doubling" of the will's intention for love's sake produces, as we shall see, the first formulation of the rule of "double effect." No more than Augustine does Aquinas first justify direct killing in self-defense. He does not say that it is intrinsically right to intend to kill an onrushing, unjust assailant, and then apply this general rule to the case of action in defense of the common good. Intending to kill a man as a means to the public good is clearly an exception to the basic rule (which still remains in force) that no Christian shall intend to kill any man.

Instead, in terms of the ethical standard he has in mind, the only case of direct, intentional killing Aquinas, no less than Augustine, finds warranted he regards as an exception to the rule. "It is not lawful for a man to intend killing a man in self-defense," he says without any qualification, "except for such as have public authority," or who are acting for the public authority charged with preserving the common good. These "while intending to kill a man in self-defense refer this to the public good." Such would still be a direct intention to kill, even though as a means referred to the public good as an end. Shall we say that in this instance, it is right to do evil that good may come of it? Or that, in this instance alone as an exception, the means used—the direct killing of the unjust aggressor—should be judged to be right in itself?

Be that as it may, it is significant that Aquinas has much the same trouble in his Christian conscience as Augustine did when dealing with the case of private self-defense. He does not subsume the just war and domestic police action, along with action to be approved when an individual's life or property are attacked, all under the same rubric of the intrinsic justifiability of killing an unjust aggressor, nor even under the principle that "one is bound to take more care of one's own life than of another's," which has in Aquinas' thought a controlling position it did not have for Augustine. For only in taking responsibility for the public good to which one has allegiance more than for the public good of another, is the direct killing of an unjust aggressor justified; while this is not the case in taking more care of one's own life than of another's. No matter how many Canonists may have declared it always to be right, as a general principle, to defend, with every proportionate and necessary means, justice against injustice, it is clear that Aquinas still thinks about these questions from the point of view of love, or of love-transformed-justice, even if not to the measure this was operative in Augustine's thought. In order to wrest from his ancient moral heritage practical, down-to-earth conclusions, while as a Christian unable to depart wholly from it, this great Doctor of the Church was driven to formulate, for the first time clearly, the principle of the double effect.

This principle has two aspects, one subjective and primary, the other objective and secondary. As to the first, Aquinas observes that one and the same action may have two effects, only one of which is intended, the other unintended or beside the intention of the other (the good) effect. In the case of private self-defense, the intention is ordered directly to the good of saving one's own life, while the other effect, unavoidably associated with the first, the slaying of the aggressor, is beside the intention. No more in Aquinas (who allows killing the onrushing assailant) than in Augustine (who does not) is the direct intention to kill justified on the part of a Christian or a truly "just" and "wise" man. This is, indeed, a justice and a wisdom schooled by Jesus Christ; and, indeed, the "law" has been transformed by love in reaching the conclusion that, under these conditions, self-defense is not "unlawful." This first aspect of Aquinas' view may be illustrated by the modern criminal law of "excusable homicide," enforced daily in our courts, which requires a man in a "sudden affray" and "chance-medley," or in mutual combat where the other person suddenly becomes angry, to give evidence that he does not share with this other man a mutual murderous intent, that in short he does not mean to kill him, by retreating as far as he safely can, to the wall, ditch, or other impediment, before, if he must, killing him in self-defense. Subjectively, the Christian must never intend to kill a man, since love refuses to allow that motive, and countenances only the intention of saving life, even one's own.

Then, in addition to this definition of the right intention, there are more objective aspects of the action to be taken into account, for "though proceeding from a good intention, an act may be rendered unlawful, if it be out of proportion to the end." To kill even an unjust man, as an indirect effect beside the intention to save one's life, would be unjustified if by any means it may be avoided. There must be due moderation in the action put forth out of good intention. The evil, secondary effect only allowed must not be out of proportion to the good effect one intends to obtain. This second aspect of Aquinas' view may be illustrated by a few cases (not, it is significant, today the prevailing rule of law) where the courts in interpreting the criminal law have required that a man retreat as far as he safely may even when he is *felonously* assaulted, where killing the assailant would be "justifiable" (as distinct from the above cases of "excusable") homicide, in order that possibly even a felon's life may be saved by means of only a moderate defense on the part of a man who has (because of the assailant's injustice) every "right" to kill him.

Let us not be deceived by the apparent proportion in weighing the good and evil effects, at which we have now arrived, nor even by the judgment that a man should take more care of his own life than of another's. It is not reciprocity or the standards of an equal justice alone that are here being applied in analysis of the action. If this were so, then without doubt Aquinas would simply have said that, since it is intrinsically right to kill an unjust assailant, no guilt is to be imputed to the direct intention to do so. Profoundly at work in his line of reasoning is what justice transformed by love requires to be extended even to him

who wrongfully attacks. This is what produced the original
statement of the so-called rule of double effect. This principle was born precisely out of an attempt to put into practice a not so equal, Christian regard for the unjust man.
Anything less flows from "private animosity" which should
be declared to be unrighteous and unbecoming to wise action.

In the matter of action on behalf of the public good,
there is in Aquinas nothing comparable to Luther's statement that the Christian still does what love requires and
suffers no injustice to be done. There is only mention of
the public authority and what this requires to be done, with,
of course, the assumption that this forecloses private animosity, or, if it does not, that an unlawful act has been done.
In the matter of private defense, however, there still sounds
a nobler music, if from a greater distance than in St. Augustine. We may *not* say that, in the primary intention of the
action Aquinas describes, a man does what love requires;
rather, he does overtly *what* natural justice requires. The
objective good intended is seen in that "it is natural to
everything to keep itself in being, as far as possible;" and
while this natural right may not be exercised always, or
necessarily, in the face of innocent aggression, it surely *may*
be used in an external act of self-defense in the face of
wrongful aggression. Herein what is of itself just is to be
the rule, as can be clearly seen in comparison with Augustine's judgment that, while he cannot condemn the law
which allows this, he cannot see how those are blameless
who avail themselves of the law's permission. But what love
requires manifests itself in Aquinas' analysis in the *non-in-
tention* of even this overt act of self-defense—in what is permitted though not willed for itself, not even as a means but
only as one of twin, unavoidably connected effects, namely,
the death of even an unjust man, which was not intended,

but only beside that other and just intention, when anyone wills and wills with a right mind to resist the one who is evil. Herein is prohibited, at the least, what love *prohibits,* namely, the direct killing of any man, as an end in itself or as a means of preserving the life that a Christian should love far less than he loves God and his neighbor in God who stands before him in the guise of a robber or a murderer.

If at this point the natural man in us exclaims, or the man insufficiently schooled by Christ, that it is humanly impossible to let go the blow and withhold the animosity, or to let go the bullet and withhold the intention in the manner Aquinas describes, and moreover that it is bad casuistry to suppose there is much difference anyway between an act which is good and right in its "species" according to what is intended and one that is not, since both bring about the death of the attacker with equal certainty, if any Christian should say this, and should he also propose as an alternative that the matter be settled more simply on grounds of the plain right of self-defense, then it might be replied that this means to let go justice at an attacker and withhold love, and that this shows the complex intentionality of any Christian action in such critical situations—except, of course, an act of non-resistance, to either innocent or unjust aggressors alike. Neither the theory of the natural law nor its less rigorous "kissin' cousin," the ethics of mutuality, or the latter in the form of contextualist ethics (whose advent much-heralded by now aging evangelists keeps on being delayed) have yet faced up to the problem of love and justice in the full magnitude it must have in any Christian ethics; and they all might learn a great deal about in-principled love by a return to the sources we have traced.

The foregoing interpretation is strikingly borne out by the moral theology of later centuries, which (1) achieved a fuller and clearer (or at least a different) distinction between

means that are intrinsically right and means that are intrinsically wrong in natural law; and therefore concluded both
that wrong means may never be used for however good an
end and that, of course, means that of themselves are right
may be directly intended, thus abolishing or bypassing the
Christian ethical problem Aquinas still had on his hands;
(2) gave more careful and exact formulation to the rule of
double effect, safeguarding from abuse particularly the subjective or intentional aspect of it, by not leaving the determination of the direct and indirect effects altogether to the
self-direction of the will; (3) concluded from both these
points, taken together, that the rule of double effect can
correctly be applied only to the indirect killing of the innocent, not to the indirect killing of the unjust assailant, who,
of course, may be killed directly however regrettably; and
finally (4), looking back upon this passage in Aquinas from
the later point of view, contended, at least in the person of
certain moralists, that it does not contain double effect
at all, that Aquinas did not know this principle "as we know
it today," or at least that he applied it very badly, and in
a case to which, rightly understood, it does not apply.   So
do men cease to praise their fathers who were before them;
or rather, so did natural justice triumph over love in Christian ethical theory.

The subsequent history of the rule of double effect may
be sketched as follows.[6]   In the early sixteenth century,
Cardinal Cajetan, in his commentary upon St. Thomas, interpreted the passage with which we have been dealing as
expressing this rule and himself accepted it as valid, and he
also continued, with St. Thomas, to justify self-defense at the
expense of killing even an unjust aggressor only in terms of
this principle.   Cajetan also seems to have been the first to

[6] See Joseph T. Mangan, S. J.: "An Historical Analysis of the Principle of
Double Effect," *Theological Studies*, X, 1 (March, 1949), pp. 41-61.

use this rule extensively in attempting to solve cases involving necessarily the death of innocent persons. Thereafter, from the early seventeenth century to the present day, the generality of moral theologians *ceased* to use this rule to solve the problem of the unjust aggressor. Killing such a man they regarded as inherently justifiable, and precisely *not* a use of wrong means to attain some good. There was then no need not to intend such killing. Instead, the rule of double effect came to be applied mainly to the problem of killing the innocent. The death of an innocent man might be brought about, without guilt to the agent, as the unavoidable yet indirect effect of an action whose primary intention and whose primary and physically independent effect was to secure some good. Thus, Samson killed himself in bringing down the house of the Philistines upon himself and them; he did not intend to kill an innocent man (himself) as a means of bringing just punishment upon them.[7] The same thing applies to the case of Eleazer, who fought his way to the center of the fray where sat the commanding enemy prince upon an elephant and thrust his spear into that ponderous animal by whose fall he was killed along with its rider.[8] Then, finally, in the nineteenth century, this principle came to be not only used and explained where it seemed needed to deal with specific cases but set in the forefront of Roman Catholic moral theology, among its basic principles applicable to the whole field, usually in the section dealing with imputability: *viz.* No one is to be held accountable, or said to be guilty, for the evil consequence of his action, provided the following four conditions are verified at one and the same time: (1) the action itself must be good in its nature and object, or at least indifferent,

---

[7] Not having in mind the distinctions made in this rule, Augustine says Samson did wrong, unless the Holy Ghost secretly commanded him to do this. *The City of God,* I, 21.

[8] II Macc. 6.

(2) a good effect and not the evil effect must be intended, (3) the good effect must not be produced by means of the evil effect, but both effects must arise simultaneously from the (at least) morally indifferent action as cause, and (4) there must be in the good effect a proportionately grave reason for permitting the evil effect. Then the proposed action is lawful (which does not mean that it is always to be recommended or to be done).

The modern elaboration of this rule in terms of these four (sometimes summarized as three) main points goes beyond Aquinas in exactitude, perhaps in substance. It has now become clear that the agent must not only be certain that, in the self-direction of his will in putting forth the action, his subjective intention is right. It has also to be objectively determined that, whatever his intention may be, the action is good or indifferent in itself and that the evil effect is not (in *fact*, again, not simply in intention) the means to the good effect, but that both are associated effects of the action as prior cause. (Here the word "prior," and the proviso that the two effects should be "simultaneous," need not be taken only in a temporal sense.) So stated, it may indeed be difficult to bring the case of killing an unjust aggressor *and* saving one's life under this principle. There may have been an inner logic by which moral theology during the modern period, as it came to greater clarity about its meaning in this principle, also gave up applying it to the killing of the unjust aggressor (which thereupon was declared to be inherently just, and no wrong means to use when necessary); and by which at the same time certain moral theologians found themselves unable to discover this rule in Thomas Aquinas at all.

In any case, looking back from the vantage point of the developed theory, whether to find it in Aquinas or to find it absent, recent interpreters show a not unnatural tendency to press him into their mould. Those who deny it to him say, for example, among other things, that the rule as we understand it today could not have been in his mind because it was not needed, since in itself it is right to protect one's life by killing an unjust aggressor; while those who recognize Aquinas as the first progenitor of this rule often do not deny this but say only that, in Aquinas' view, a man defending himself should merely indirectly intend what is just anyway. For this reason, the extent to which, still even in Thomas Aquinas, love transforms justice, or even displaces it, in the foundation of Christian ethical analysis has not heretofore been given sufficient prominence. For this reason, also, it is difficult to weave one's way through contemporary moral theology, especially where it addresses itself to this crucial passage in Thomas Aquinas. Nevertheless, there may be some advantage to be gained from attempting briefly to do this, before drawing this chapter to a close.

In an excellent article that deserves to be better known in Protestant circles on "The Morality of Obliteration Bombing,"[9] Fr. John C. Ford vigorously opposes that barbaric departure from the tradition of civilized warfare which bears the name of "strategic" or "area" bombing. In order to do this effectively he found it necessary to reject any such interpretation of the rule of double effect, when applied to the killing of innocent people, as would "find a simple solution to the moral problem merely by advising the air strategist to let go his bombs, but withold his intention."[10] Since this opens the whole question of the meaning of the principle of the double effect, and depends on a correct understanding of it, Fr. Ford in the course of his argument also contends that the rule of double effect, when

[9] *Theological Studies*, V, 3 (Sept., 1944), pp. 261-309.
[10] *Ibid.*, p. 289.

applied, as is supposed, by Thomas Aquinas to the killing of
unjust aggressors, could not have had a meaning analogous
to the one Ford decisively rejects in the present case; and
therefore that "St. Thomas did not know the principle of the
double effect as we formulate it."[11] He argues, I believe correctly, that reasoning about moral issues after the fashion
of double effect, however "basic in scientific Catholic morality," is not simply to apply a rigid mathematical formula or
an analytical principle from which certain conclusions may
be deduced with absolute certainty. Rather is it "a practical formula which synthesizes an immense amount of moral
experience," which, by clarifying this experience, can then
serve "as an efficient guide in countless perplexing cases."[12]
Even Protestants use it every day in making decisions, although a bourgeois mentality which never faces crucial
choices between actions with mixed consequences may seem
to avoid doing so.[13] On the other hand, the rule of double
effect is not so flexible as to state conditions that may be
satisfied merely in the inwardness of intention. Intentions
alone are always open to suspicion, unless they are also con-

[11] *Ibid.*, p. 290, n. 57.
[12] *Ibid.*, p. 289.
[13] A not so everyday example, drawn from *The Cruel Sea*, is that of the
destroyer commander who located a submarine just below the spot where
some hundreds of men, previously torpedoed, were swimming in the water,
and who nevertheless let go the depth bomb knowing that no choice available could be anything but death-dealing to these men he did not want to
hit. "One must do what one must do," he said, "and say one's prayers."
Joseph Sittler calls this "an eloquent condensation of the ethical situation"
(*The Structure of Christian Ethics,* Baton Rouge: The Louisiana State University Press, 1958, p. 83); and so it is. But it is not very good as an *analysis*
of the ethical situation. The post-bourgeois generation of men who have
regained a moral sensitivity their fathers did not possess should not think
it possible to restore their connection with their grandfathers in the faith
(the Reformers) merely by condensed expression of ethical dilemmas, or by
burying analysis of principles of action underneath contextualism. Thereby
they succeed only in preventing themselves from coming to clarity about
exactly what was contained in this commander's "must" and the warrant for
it. Nor is it to be feared that careful ethical analysis in and of itself con-
tests the ground with "justification" or with the self-understanding that "no
decision fulfills the will of God or releases man from that relation to God
which dares to live only by the daily forgiveness of sins" *(ibid.).*

trolled by some more objective determination of right *action*. Double effect cannot mean merely letting the bullet go and withholding the intention (in the case of unjust attack by an aggressor) or letting go the bomb and withholding the intention (in the case of the killing of non-combatants in wartime). Such interpretations of the rule Fr. Ford has in mind when he writes that "some applications of it can only be called casuistical in the bad sense of that word."[14] To avoid accusing St. Thomas of bad casuistry, a note appended to this last statement asserts, that "even St. Thomas has been accused repeatedly of defending the subtle proposition: When you kill an unjust aggressor you merely permit his death while intending to save your own.... St. Thomas held that the killing of an unjust aggressor must be willed only as a means, not as an end in itself. St. Thomas did not know the principle of the double effect as we formulate it."[15] Now, it seems obvious to me that Fr. Ford would not affirm so boldly that Aquinas meant that the killing of an unjust aggressor might be willed as a means unless, from the perspective of the later theory, no doubt is allowed to arise concerning the fact that St. Thomas and every other right thinking man believes that such killing in itself is right; else the position attributed to him would imply that St. Thomas did not know an even more basic principle in Christian morality, namely, that no one should do wrong that good may come of it. It also seems obvious that we must search in later centuries for the unquestionable ethical assumptions upon which ground this interpretation strives to maintain itself against St. Thomas' plain words that "it is, therefore, wrong for a man to intend to kill another as a means to defend himself."

[14] *Op. cit.*, pp. 289-290.
[15] *Ibid.*, p. 290 n. 57, citing Vincent Alonso, *El principio del doble efecto en los comentadores de Santo Tomas* (Rome: Gregorian University dissertation, 1937).

Side by side with the foregoing viewpoint we may place the one to be found in T. Lincoln Bouscaren's exhaustive study of the *Ethics of Ectopic Operations*.[16]   The author of this book propounds the thesis, now widely accepted, that in cases of tubal pregnancy certainly endangering the life of both mother and child an operation may be performed to save the mother which *in fact and in intention* unavoidably kills the fetus *indirectly*. As background to his argument and in order to reject more decisively the solutions of some few moral theologians of the past who seem to have permitted a direct attack upon the fetus in cases of this sort, Bouscaren seeks first to establish the proposition that according to the principles of Christian morality, *any* lawful killing must be indirect, or in accord with the rule of double effect. Since killing even an unjust aggressor is permissible only beside the intention, *how much more* certainly must this be the rule in the case of a fetus who is innocent of any injustice. This is the form of the argument; and how may its major premise be better established than by an appeal to the authority and reasoning of Thomas Aquinas?

Indeed, Bouscaren is of the opinion that one reason false solutions of the problem of tubal pregnancy, permitting direct killing of the child, have arisen in the past is precisely "the fact that according to a fairly common opinion—which we, for intrinsic reasons, decline to admit—it is allowed to kill [directly] even an unjust aggressor upon one's life; and it makes no difference whether the aggressor be formally unjust or only materially so, as in the case of a drunken or insane person whose attack is a serious menace to one's life."[17]   Of course, the child is not "formally" an unjust aggressor, since he does not have rational control of his action.

---

[16] Gregorian University dissertation, 1928, supervised and approved by Arthur Veermeersh, S. J. (Milwaukee, Wisconsin: the Bruce Publishing Co., 2nd ed., 1943, 1944).
[17] *Ibid.*, p. 49.

The question is whether he is a "material" aggressor, and "materially" an *unjust* aggressor. If the latter, he may be intentionally killed to save the mother's life, according to the before-mentioned "fairly common opinion" which this author rejects. Now, there may be good reason to suppose that the child is at least a material aggressor, even though the way in which his deadly action takes place in the tube is itself an astonishing example of the rule of double effect: merely by doing what comes naturally and struggling to be born, the fetus causes the death of the mother without intending to do so. Yet it is not utterly impossible for a strong argument to be advanced in behalf of the proposition that the child is materially an unjust aggressor, as is shown by examples from moral theology in the past. Therefore Bouscaren concludes that, omitting for the moment the decrees of the Holy Office which have settled this issue, and "considering the merely intrinsic reason pro and con, one must admit that, *as long as that principle is granted which allows the direct killing of a materially unjust aggressor* on private authority, *it will be very difficult to take the ectopic fetus outside the operation of that principle.* It is far from easy to indicate the difference between a morally irresponsible aggressor and the child who is unwittingly causing a deadly peril to its mother."[18]

Or, to express the author's thesis positively: ". . . direct killing, even in self-defense, is unlawful. If that view be admitted, it is evident that direct destruction of the fetus is always wrong, quite regardless of the question whether the fetus is or is not an aggressor."[19] Now, is not this an astonishing end result of the history of the idea we have been tracing? The gulf that separates Roman Catholic and Protestant teaching on this matter, and indeed their divergence in *feel-*

[18] *Ibid.,* p. 50 (italics added).
[19] *Ibid.,* p. 52.

ings upon the subject, does not arise first of all—as appears upon the surface—from an excessively rigid application by the Roman moralists of the principles of equal justice or of such rules as "the fetus has a right to life equal to that of the mother," or "it is never right to do something that is intrinsically wrong in order that good may come of it." No matter to what extent one may still disagree with specific judgments made in practice, it must be admitted that the force profoundly at work here is not the natural-law immunity of every life from direct attack, unless this right to life has first been sacrificed by some injustice done, but instead the immunity with which love surrounds the weak, the helpless, even the unjust, and those who are in fact or intention our enemies, for while we were all ungodly Christ died for us. This is the clear inference to be drawn from Bouscaren's reliance upon the rule of double effect in the shape in which it was first fashioned when Aquinas modified Augustine's complete rejection of the right of private self-defense. The construction Bouscaren places upon the passage from Aquinas must be accepted, or else Aquinas has not really answered the objection he himself takes from Augustine, and to which he replies by saying, "The words quoted from Augustine refer to the case when one man intends to kill another to save himself from death."[20] This intention to kill another to save oneself is ruled out by Aquinas as well as by Augustine. "Nature teaches" that "it is natural to every being to preserve its life as far as possible," as Aquinas says; but a decisive limit is placed upon the natural right of self-preservation it is *ethically* permissible for me to *exercise,* not by the aggressor's attitude toward me or by his injustice but by my only right attitude toward him, in that I should never will his non-existence either as an end or as a means but should accept him with

[20] *S-T,* II-II, Q. 64, a 7, ad. 1; cf. Bouscaren, *op. cit.,* p. 32.

the intentionality of my every act and should conserve his being if possible.[21]

I have said that the modern refinements of the rule of the double effect have cast doubt upon whether *this* in substance was Aquinas' teaching. The modern improvements of the rule make it clear that the good effect must not only be the formal object of the intention but also the immediate material object of the physical act. More simply, the good must be not only willed directly but also done directly, if the agent is not to be held directly accountable also for the foreknown evil consequence of his action. It would seem that, in the case of self-defense, killing the assailant is what is done directly. If this is the immediate material object of the physical act as such, it then seems that what is here done directly would have to be defensible as an inherently right means (because of the injustice of the aggression) if it is to make any difference that what the agent directly wills, or the formal object of his intention, is a good thing. This I understand to be the thesis of Vincent Alónso, which Fr. Ford accepts as the construction to be placed upon Aquinas.

He summarily concludes that the principle according to which St. Thomas considers that one act can have two effects, one of

[21] One of Bouscaren's footnotes seems too much affected by the modern formulations of natural-law theory, in that he simply adds together the natural-law right of self-defense *and* St. Thomas on indirect intention: "We do not, of course, deny the right of self-defense; but we hold, with St. Thomas, that even in the case of real aggression, the death of the assailant cannot be directly intended even as a means, but only permitted as a consequence of the act of defense, in accordance with the principle of the double effect" (*op. cit.*, p. 52 n. 8). To this the retort is correct which says that, if the right of self-defense remains in full force, one need not take the precaution of exercising it only unintentionally in accord with double effect. Another footnote reproduces Aquinas' position more faithfully: "... since he does not admit that the death of even an unjust aggressor may be directly intended, but only permitted as a consequence of an otherwise lawful act, it is evident that the Angelic Doctor in this connection *treats the aggressor just as if he were innocent*" (p. 37 n. 22, italics added). In other words, the rule seems to be that a Christian should let his care and will (love) rain upon the just and unjust alike. Only the intervention of the public authority, and not natural right, ever makes it just to intend to kill, even to save one's life.

which is *ex intentione,* and the other *praeter intentionem,* has nothing at all to do with the principle of the double effect as it is understood today. For, inasmuch as these effects are considered materially (in the physical order), the death of the aggressor is a means or a *conditio sine qua non* for the preservation of one's life. By no means is the death considered as an effect that comes equally immediately from the cause as the defense of one's life. And in the intentional order, the term *praeter intentionem* by no means prohibits the effect, death, from being deliberate and from being chosen directly by the will as a lawful means toward an equally lawful end.[22]

It seems clear to me that the significant issues in the interpretation of Aquinas do not depend decisively upon searching his texts to determine the meaning of his terms *intendere, non intendere, ex intention,* and *praeter intentionem,* or upon whether the term "to intend" refers only to the ultimate end of an action or may also embrace the means.[23] The difference in interpretations of this passage in Aquinas depends on whether one stands with Aquinas close to Augustine's rejection of private self-defense lest a man inordinately love his life and property more than God and his neighbor in God or whether one stands closer to the fully developed modern theories of natural justice. The latter position renders superfluous any use of double effect in or in interpreting this passage, and makes the means-end meaning plausible, while the former requires some form of the principle of double effect in order at all to take care of a problem which was then still a problem for Christian conscience. However, any suggestion of mere subjective prejudgment on the part of his interpreters should be avoided. The objective situation seems to be that Aquinas devised an early formulation of the principle of double effect, and *we have*

---

[22] Joseph T. Mangam, *op. cit.,* p. 46. This article, which gives a rather full treatment and, in its author's opinion, refutation, is as close as I can come to Alonso's thesis.

[23] See *ibid.,* p. 44-45.

seen why he did so. Yet at the same time it is certainly true that he did not have in mind later augmentations of the rule which stipulate that in addition to the good as the only proper object of one's formal intention it must also be capable of being done directly, and with at least as much immediacy to the act as the evil effect.

Perhaps for good reason, then, this tradition in moral theology ceased to employ the rule of double effect in attempting to solve the problem of self-defense against an unjust aggressor, and to confine its use, after Aquinas and Cajetan, to the problem of the killing of an innocent person.   Largely unnoticed was the fact that, if the principle cannot be applied to the killing of an unjust aggressor (or is not needed), neither can it be applied, and for about the same reasons, to the act of killing oneself.   Toward that one "innocent" man, whose death may be willed only "indirectly," I stand in about the same situation, so far as concerns the practice of this principle, as I stand toward an unjust assailant whose death was once said to be only "indirectly" an effect beside the will of any man who intends to do right. Can I, any more in one case than in the other, let go the bullet and withhold the intention?   Granting that a general captured in wartime may swallow a suicide pill with the primary *intention* of saving the military secrets in his head or his comrades in arms from being betrayed by him under torture, can he *do* this directly?   How can a suicidal act for some good cause be *not* done directly, as the immediate material object of the physical act, therefore as inherently wrong means to some remote good? Supposing the formal object of my intention is that good effect, supposing the good is willed directly, this would still not be enough to qualify the action as without guilt, if it is not that good rather than this evil which is done directly.   The fact that, in the intentional order, killing myself may be beside my intention would seem not to prevent this from being gravely sinful if, when considered materially, in the physical order, my death is the means by which the attainment of an ulterior good actually takes place. Perhaps Samson intended only to save his people from the unjust Philistines, perhaps it was beside his intention to kill himself, even though this was unavoidable. On the other hand, perhaps he only "enlarged the target," intending his own death, for itself or as a means, no less than theirs. Such questions are bound to arise where the intentions and the action with both its consequences adhere so closely together. These are the same doubts which arise about Aquinas' application of the rule of double effect to the single individual over against me in private self-defense. Here, too, the intentions and the twin effects cohere so closely together as to raise doubt about the rectitude of the will in doing any such thing. This forced the tradition to seek to clear the matter up by adding the more objective stipulation that the good effect must be done directly. When this became the understanding of the rule, the application of it to the case of self-defense against unjust attack appears like a "casuistical device in the bad sense of that word," and so it became difficult to believe that St. Thomas meant any such thing. The intention to sacrifice one's life by primarily putting forth one's will toward some good goal may be as suspect as the intention to "sacrifice" the life of another (just or unjust) man as one effect beside another, good effect (saving one's life). In both cases, the rectitude of the will seems not to be sufficiently determined by a merely inward, conscious turning of the intention away from the secondary evil known to come to pass because of a deed done primarily for another purpose. There is need for a decisive objective reference to what is *done* directly, or *in fact* only indirectly permitted. When this was added, and as finally formulated, the principle of double effect could have a significant future mainly as applied to cases of the unavoidable killing of *innocent* persons and of innocent persons *other than oneself*. So the rule of double effect came to focus upon the moral immunity of noncombatants from direct attack.

This, however, is a topic for the next chapter. Then, in Chapter VIII and elsewhere, we will ask whether today, under the changed conditions brought about by modern technology and because of the nature of warfare in an industrial society, there is any escape in morality from this judgment that would surround noncombatants with immunity from directly being killed in any war that is conducted justly, or in which either Christian or just men should engage. In the course of this argument yet to come, the reader should have in mind the ground we have traversed in telling the genesis of noncombatant immunity. The historical account given in this chapter should not be forgotten when today, and later on in this book, we face the question whether Christian action can discover sufficient grounds for setting this principle aside in order to justify military action that makes all-out use of nuclear weapons. The point that needs stressing is that the limitation placed upon conduct in the just-war theory arose not from autonomous natural reason asserting its sovereignty over determinations of right and wrong (and threatening to lead Christian faith and love, which are and should be free, into bondage to alien principles), but from a quite humble moral reason subjecting itself to the sovereignty of God and the lordship of Christ, as Christian men felt themselves impelled out of love to justify war and by love severely to limit war.[24]

[24] See especially, pp. 177-9, 182, 185-6, 190-91 below.

Chapter Four

THE JUST WAR IN CONTEMPORARY
ROMAN CATHOLIC THOUGHT

The main features of the Roman Catholic doctrine of just warfare today may be exhibited by a consideration of the previously mentioned article, which should be basic to all discussion of this subject, on "The Morality of Obliteration Bombing," written by Fr. John C. Ford during World War II,[1] and articles of his that have continued to appear as weapons of obliteration have increased in power. He rejects the opinion that the air strategist may enlarge his target to include objectively whole areas of the civilian population as such, provided only that he does not subjectively intend to kill non-combatants. In bombing whole areas as such, it is impossible to let go the bombs along with the intention to kill directly the combatants, while simply inwardly withholding the intrinsically murderous direct intention to kill the innocent. Death to the innocent is done directly in strategic bombing. Morally, this is the same act as it would have been had their death been willed directly. Only in tactical bombing, where a military target is attacked directly both by the deed and by the intention of the will, can it be said that the unavoidable and foreknown death of the innocent was not the direct object of the action, or was beside the intention to kill them as a means to victory, or a regretably necessary secondary effect of action justifiable in itself.

[1] *Theological Studies,* V, 3 (Sept., 1944), 261-309.

In order to pursue the meaning of noncombatant immunity
to complete understanding, I propose in this chapter that
we examine at some length the views of Fr. Ford, especially
in this article. This will be followed by an equally thorough,
if briefer, consideration of the writings of other outstanding
Roman Catholic authors on the subject of morality and warfare, including Francis J. Connell, John Courtney Murray,
and recent Papal pronouncements. Throughout, we will
bring into view the proper location of calculating the consequences by a comparison of good and evil effects.

The vast immorality of strategic or area bombing, Fr.
Ford writes, "would not be subject to dispute, at least
amongst Catholics, were it not for the appeal to the principle of the double effect" that sometimes has been made.
The misapplication of this rule which Ford rejects says simply that the air strategist may enlarge the target to include
objectively whole areas of the civilian population as such of
an enemy nation, provided only that he does not directly intend to kill them. What is done directly may be not directly willed; and so, it is believed, a simple solution may
be found for the avoidance of murder "merely by advising
the air strategist to let go his bombs, but withhold his intention,"[2] so far as the innocent are concerned.[3] This meth-
od of warfare cannot honestly be brought under the rule
that innocent people may be killed if this takes place beside

[2] *Ibid.*, p. 289.
[3] *Ibid.*, p. 293. It is at this point that Fr. Ford gives us his interpretation of Thomas Aquinas. His argument is, therefore, curiously the reverse
of Bouscaren's. The latter, as we have seen, attributed to or found in
Aquinas a complete rejection of any and all direct killing, whether of the
unjust or the just, in order to reach the conclusion, in face of the uncertainty whether a fetus may be classed as an aggressor or not, that he can
in no case be killed directly. Fr. Ford, on the other hand, attributes to or
finds in Aquinas no use of the rule of double effect with regard to the
unjust aggressor, and no judgment that such a man may not be killed
directly as a means, in order the more decisively to rule out what he can
only regard as a comparable, badly casuistical, device for justifying the
slaying of the innocent in obliteration bombing.

the intention, even if perhaps this may be the case in tactical bombing. Area bombing, unlike the destruction of a specific target, cannot be regarded as "twofold in its immediate efficiency," either in fact or (by a subterfuge) in intention. It *de facto* contributes as a means to the victory (the good) desired, even if by a great deal of peculiar psychological effort it may not be explicitly willed as a means. A man could not, even if he wanted to, avoid the direct willing of an evil effect so immediately consequent upon his action as this is;[4] moreover, he would not if he could, and there is plenty of evidence that he does not endeavor to do so. Thus Fr. Ford states together the first two points in the logic of his argument, which is more succinctly expressed elsewhere: "It is my contention that the civil and military leaders who would plan and execute the dropping of a series of high megaton H-Bombs on an area like Moscow or New York: (1) *would not* in practice avoid the direct intention of violence to the innocent; (2) *could not* if they would; and (3) even if they would and could avoid it, would have no proportionate justifying reason for permitting the evils which this type of all-out nuclear warfare would let loose."[5]

Even to devise a policy of area bombing contains the implicit distinction between this and the aim of only allowing the death of many innocent people while destroying specific military targets, and only by explicitly rejecting the latter as not enough does a policy of obliteration come to

[4] *Ibid.*, p. 290.
[5] John C. Ford: "The Hydrogen Bombing of Cities," *Theology Digest,* Winter, 1957, p. 7. This article (now reprinted as chap. vii in the symposium *Morality and Modern Warfare,* ed. Wm. J. Nagle, Baltimore: Helicon Press, 1960, pp. 98-103) contains the substance of Fr. Ford's address to the conference on ethics and nuclear weapons sponsored by the Church Peace Union in 1957. Criticisms of his remarks on that occasion were written by John Cogley, *The Commonweal,* Dec. 13, 1957 ("the problem he spoke about is not the moral problem that actually faces our political and military leaders") and by William Lee Miller, in the first issue of *Worldview,* Jan., 1958 (who unfortunately opens by saying, "he granted that it is often necessary to do evil in order to do good").

be adopted by our military leaders. The objective immorality of such a policy seems evident, and the measure of this is taken from the fact that the rule of the double effect cannot rightly be applied to the killing of the innocent in this manner. Indeed, the reverse relation between the two effects or two intentions is more likely the case. "When an entire city is destroyed by such means," Fr. Ford quotes John K. Ryan with approval,

the military objectives are destroyed indirectly and incidentally as parts of a great civil center, rather than vice versa. It is the case of the good effect coming along with, or better, after and on account of the evil, instead of a case where the evil is incidental to the attainment of a good.... It is hardly correct to think and speak of the damage done to life and property in such situations as being 'incidental destruction.' Rather it is the realistic interpretation of this situation to hold that any good gained is incidental to the evil.... The evil effect is first, immediate and direct, while any military advantage comes through and after it in a secondary, derivative, and dependent way.[6]

Concerning the evident solicitude and care the Allies used in bombing the city of Rome, Fr. Ford doubts whether this was based on any moral principle worthy of respect.

I do not think it is cynical to believe that they were more interested in religious *feelings* and world reaction than they were in the morality of killing the innocent whether directly or indirectly, and of destroying non-military property.... From the moral point of view, the lives of the innocent inhabitants of Germany or any other country are far more precious than the religious monuments of Rome, or the real estate of the Holy Father. But we hear nothing of a week's preliminary briefing to insure the safety of non-military targets in Berlin. We hear just the opposite. We hear the word obliterate.[7]

---

[6] John K. Ryan, *Modern War and Basic Ethics* (Milwaukee: The Bruce Publishing Co., 1944), pp. 105 f., quoted by J. C. Ford, "The Morality of Obliteration Bombing," *loc. cit.*, pp. 291-292.
[7] "The Morality of Obliteration Bombing," pp. 295-296.

We hear, instead, of "terror and devastation carried to the core of a warring nation."[8]   We hear that "our planes are to bomb, burn, and ruthlessly destroy in every way available to us the people responsible for creating the war."[9]   We hear advice to these people to escape these severities by taking to the hills and fields, there to "watch the home fires burning from a distance" and to "find time for meditation and repentance."[10]   We hear the roar of unlimited war.

It is the virtue, and perhaps the irrelevance, of modern formulations of the rule of double effect in the theory of the just war that, by requiring more than subjective intention, by requiring that objectively also the intrinsically evil effect of the slaying of innocent people be not a means to whatsoever military advantage, we are brought close to the rejection of all modern warfare.   Fr. Ford recognizes this,[11] and does not hesitate to say that "If anyone were to declare that modern war is necessarily total, and necessarily involves the direct attack on the life of innocent civilians, and, therefore, that obliteration bombing is justified, my reply would be: So much the worse for modern war. If it necessarily includes such means, it is necessarily immoral in itself."[12]

It is worth pointing out that, by basing the morality of a military action upon something more than subjective intention alone, Fr. Ford does not mean to require that the destruction of innocent people, to be justified as a second effect, must always come later in time than the military effect sought.   It is a question of which effect is, in the objective

---

[8] *Target: Germany*, p. 19 (quoted, *ibid.*, p. 294), the U. S. Army Air Force's account of its first year's work over Germany, in co-ordination with the RAF.   "The purpose of this book," it is declared, "has been factually to record *the testing of a new concept of vertical warfare*" (p. 115, quoted in "The Morality of Obliteration Bombing," p. 299 n. 82, italics added).

[9] British Minister of Information, August, 1943 (quoted, *ibid.*, p. 262).

[10] Winston Churchill, Broadcast of May 10, 1942 (quoted, *ibid.*, p. 273).

[11] *Ibid.*, p. 267.

[12] *Ibid.*, p. 268.

order, incidental to which, even when both effects are produced at the same time from a single action.

There comes a point where the immediate evil effect of a given
action is so overwhelmingly large in its physical extent, in its
mere bulk, by comparison with the immediate good effect, that
it no longer makes sense to say that it is merely incidental. . . .
[This is] not a question of the physical inevitability of the evil
effect. It is a question of its incidentality. I can see how a
bombardier could drop a hydrogen bomb on an enemy fleet at
sea, intending directly only the destruction of the fleet, while
permitting reluctantly the inevitable deaths of some innocent
women and children by chance aboard. But I doubt that the
man with the sledgehammer can intend to kill the poisonous
spider [on his neighbor's bald pate] and call the death of his
neighbor merely incidental. And I doubt that the air strategist
can drop his H-bombs on New York-Newark and call the resultant death of millions of innocent people merely incidental.[13]

Here the destruction of the target (say, the Port of New
York) is incidental to the destruction of the area; but, in
tactical bombing, the destruction of a considerable part of
the area might be incidental to the destruction of the target,
even though both these effects also take place at the same
time. And we may add, there would be the same crucial
difference in the morality of these actions if we suppose that,
as it turned out, the same number of civilians were killed.
In the cases supposed, their death would be indirect in one
case, direct in the other.

Even if Fr. Ford did not believe as he does about the
abstract possibility of holding back the intention to murder
innocent people, he would still have no doubt about the immorality of area bombing, by reason of the final stipulation
of the rule of double effect, which requires a proper proportion between the evil effect permitted and the good effect
intended. In making a practical estimate whether a grave

---

[13] "The Hydrogen Bombing of Cities," *loc. cit.*, pp. 7-8.

enough reason exists for producing so much devastation, one should begin, he writes, with the asssumption that "an evil which is certain and extensive and immediate will rarely be compensated for by a problematical, speculative, future good." So, even if he were not convinced that obliteration bombing is in itself an immoral attack on the rights of the innocent, and a determination to do them injury, "it would still be immoral, because no proportionate cause could justify the evil done; and to make it legitimate would soon lead the world to the immoral barbarity of total war."[14] Here, calculation of consequences, or the weighing of anticipated greater goods or lesser evils, plays its proper role. We have always to ask whether one effect justifies another—in the final place.

Such is Fr. Ford's finding as to the moral law. What, then, is his finding as to fact? This further question has to be raised, because it is possible, and too frequently contended, that the term "noncombatant" used in the traditional theory of the just war, given the complex interdependency of social relations in an industrial society, has now become obsolete and a mere word for a logical class without any members. Is war now total, i.e., is everyone a fighter? Therefore the question has to be answered, in fact as well as in law, "Do the majority of civilians in a modern nation at war enjoy a natural-law right of immunity from violent repression?"[15]

In taking up the question of fact, two of Fr. Ford's assumptions should be held in mind. One is that it is not necessary to draw an accurate line between combatants and noncombatants, or to tell who and where they are, in order to solve the moral problem of obliteration bombing. "It is enough to show that there are large numbers of people

---

[14] "The Morality of Obliteration Bombing," *loc cit.,* pp. 298, 299, 308.
[15] *Ibid.,* pp. 271, 286.

even in the conditions of modern warfare who are clearly to be classed as innocent noncombatants, and then that, wherever the line is drawn, obliteration goes beyond it and violates the rights of these people."[16] Given *that* there are large numbers of "noncombatants" in our modern cities, this is sufficient to base the conclusion that area or indiscriminate bombing of them is wrong. The difficulty of telling *who* and *where* they are only qualifies them as possible objects of indirect attack in raids limited to specifically military targets.

This is a point of prime importance, and one that is too often forgotten, as we shall see, in Protestant and in secular writings on the subject of morality and war. There where it is erroneously supposed that *direct* killing is the only kind of killing sought to be justified, where war and murder have been indiscriminately mixed together by a widespread cryptopacifism, it has come to be an unquestioned maxim that, for war to be justly conducted, noncombatants have to be *clearly* distinguishable from combatants, and moreover we would have to be sure that *where* they live is not within any legitimate target area. As a consequence, if this distinction is not simply ignorantly ridiculed, the nullity of it is assumed as a premise rather than as a conclusion proved by disciplined intellectual reflection. Plainly, it is necessary for most people to come to terms again with the terms of the ancient limits of civilized warfare. How can the "facts" prove that there are now no noncombatants when this conclusion depends in every respect upon whether we have in our heads such notions as the moral significance of the degrees of closeness or remoteness of co-operation in aggression? It is the *concept* of noncombatancy that has been jettisoned first from our thought; and this has happened because the *concept* of degrees of co-operation and the *con-*

---

[16] *Ibid.*, pp. 280-281.

cept of an indirect, yet unavoidable and foreknown effect (an evil perhaps tragically necessary to be done, yet quite different from murder) have eroded from the minds of men. *This* then is the reason we are prey to the illusion that modern industrial and metropolitan society has completely changed the nature of warfare, and rendered wholly inapplicable and indeed senseless any attempt to apply the carefully constructed concepts of traditional Christian morality. We only have to know *that* there are noncombatants, not exactly *who* or *where* they are, in order to know that warfare should be forces and counter-forces warfare, and attack be limited to legitimate military targets. This moral limit still holds, even if it must be admitted—nay, even contended—that responsible political and military action has now to assume that civilians with their moral immunity from direct attack are now in far greater danger even in a justly conducted war than ever before in human history, because there are many more legitimate military targets than ever before and because the firepower of even a just war has been vastly increased. This gives greater incentive for the people and nations of the world to settle their disputes and control their resort to arms as an extension of national policy. It may be that under the pressure of the shape that warfare has assumed in our time, a genuine world-wide community, reflected in world law, will come into being over decades to come, and more adequate international instruments will be devised for the proximate resolution of the world's insoluble problems. But until all that is accomplished, or while effort is being exerted in this direction, the justification of war and the moral limits of justifiable warfare remain in force. An understanding of these limits simply has to be recovered, not dismissed out of hand. This, in turn, calls for conceptual clarity in moral and political reasoning.

Our author's second assumption has to do with who has the burden of proof in the determination of this matter of fact. Estimating that three-fourths of the population in a highly industrial area still have noncombatant status and are "certainly innocent," he also says of any single occupation or class of civilians concerning whom there may be doubt, and where the principle of probability may be involved, that these groups still have "a *certain* right not to be deprived of life, family, and property until their combatant or guilty status is proved with certainty."[17]   "The military leader with new and highly destructive weapons in his hands, who claims that he can attack civilians because modern industrial conditions have changed the nature of war radically and made them all aggressors," must bear the burden of proof, and not "the civilian behind the lines, who clings to his traditional immunity."[18]

With this approach, and making use of the government's population figures and its own distinction between "essential," "less essential," and "non-essential" war work, it is not difficult for Ford to show that up to three-fourths of the people in a civilian industrial center such as Boston or New York-Newark should not be classed as "combatants" in the meaning of the traditional theory of just war.   "The word means fighters."[19]   Ford gives an impressive list, running to 20 printed lines, of nearly 120 different occupations in present-day industrial society, constituting a large proportion of the civilian population, and he challenges his readers to answer for themselves whether these people can

[17] *Ibid.*, p. 288 n. 55.
[18] *Ibid.*, pp. 281-282. "If I assert that it is wrong to kill a million school children, I do not have to prove my assertion. It is those who assert the contrary who have the burden of proof." John C. Ford, "The Hydrogen Bombing of Cities," *loc. cit.*, p. 6.
[19] "The Morality of Atomic Bombing," unpublished broadcast talk given over the Vatican Radio in June, 1946.

be regarded as a "nation in arms," "fighters," or closely "co-operating in aggression."[20]

This leads him to warn: "Beware of people who talk of modern war *as total*. It is total not because all the civilians wage it, but because all of them are its targets."[21] The moral decision about what is permissible in the conduct of war has been changed only if modern war is total in the sense that all the people wage it. The fact that as a result of modern technology all of them are potential targets has not changed the morality of the matter. Only the erosion of the tradition of civilized or just warfare could bring it to pass that these people are regarded as the justifiable targets of direct military action. "Everybody in a country at war is a combatant more or less," it is said, "and so everybody in the enemy country is a lawful object of violent attack." This is not a statement of fact about how today a whole people wages war, but of how on their supposed behalf the war may in fact be immorally waged against an enemy, and how the enemy may actually wage it against them. In this regard, the just-war theory has not become inapplicable (or applicable only in such a way as to justify the violent repression of civilian populations who "wage war"); it has simply not been applied. That is a measure of our barbarism, and not a factual report of the changes brought about by modern warfare in placing all the people in the position of making war.[22]

---

[20] "The Morality of Obliteration Bombing," *loc. cit.*, pp. 283-284. There is now greater reason for restoring the distinction between the forces of a nation at war and the population in its industrial centers than may have been apparent during the first and second World Wars: "A future war is going to be fought out of stock and inventory. Thus the things that can hurt the enemy will not be the producing cities but the strategic forces—the bombers, missiles, submarines, and carriers." Herman Kahn, *On Thermonuclear War* (Princeton: Princeton University Press), 1960, Lect. I, chap. iii, p. 104.

[21] "The Morality of Atomic Bombing," broadcast talk.

[22] Cf. E. I. Watkin: "Unjustifiable War," in *Morals and Missiles: Catholic*

The belief that the distinction between combatants and noncombatants has now been erased mistakes the relation of civilians to the conduct of war both in the past and in the present. It is wrongly assumed that, "in the past when the classical formulas were put together, the civilians who were declared untouchable in these formulas had little or nothing to do with the war effort of their countries";[23] and it is wrongly assumed that today the civilians have so much to do with this effort that they are the same as fighters.

But "whole populations" participated to some extent in the war efforts of three or four hundred years ago. They certainly fed and provided the soldiers with supplies, arms, ammunitions, comfort, encouragement, and an occasional love-letter. What has happened in the meantime? To a certain extent civilian participation has increased. But that increase is comparatively insignificant, even if it is double or triple what it used to be. The real, significant difference between war three hundred years ago and war nowadays is that man has increased his destructive attacking power one-thousand-fold or more, and has learned to carry that destructive power hundreds of times faster to the very heart of every civilian population on earth.... The whole civilian population on earth has become liable to total violent attack. It is true to say that modern war is total in the sense that whole populations may have to suffer such an attack and be exterminated by it. But it is not true to say that modern war is total in the sense that the whole population is attacking, is waging war destructively, and is therefore a legitimate target for extermination.[24]

Essays on the Problem of War Today (London: James Clarke and Co. Ltd., 1959), pp. 52-53: "Were this the case such total war, by the mere fact of refusing civilians non-combatant status, offends against the stipulation that a just war must respect the lives of civilians.... In face of this evident relevance, this irrefutable condemnation, to argue that the traditional criteria of just war are no longer relevant is patently false. Never before has their relevance been so clear, their application so easy.... It requires no knowledge inaccessible to the private citizen to be aware of the certain violation on the ... conditions of just war by the nuclear war for which the antagonistic power blocks are arming."

[23] "The Morality of Obliteration Bombing," *loc. cit.*, p. 281.

[24] "The Morality of Atomic Bombing," broadcast talk.

The sea-change that has come about is that today people do not stand even within hailing distance of the meaning that was hammered into the terms of the just- or limited-war theory.   There an "innocent" person did not mean an altogether harmless person, even militarily speaking, but one who did not participate directly, or with immediate co-operation in the violent and destructive action of war itself. And civilian immunity was further bolstered by additional careful distinctions as to co-operation, whether formal or material only, whether immediate or remote only, whether formal and immediate or only remote and material, etc. Today we do not speak in these terms but of "helping the war effort," and therefore we come close to classing as combatants a little boy who "carries his father's dinner pail to the munition factory" or "the little Japanese girl" who "certainly folds up the cardboard boxes in which the ammunition is going to be packed later on. (She does it at home, and meanwhile helps to take care of the baby)."[25] No Catholic theologian should ever assert of a ten-year-old girl who saves bottle caps for the scrap steel drive that "she contributes to the war effort.   In fact, she helps to make munitions;" or that I may "shoot her down on the theory that she is a combatant, an unjust aggressor, and therefore a legitimate target for total violent repression."[26]   And no properly instructed person should ever say that as such the fabric of interdependencies in modern technological society has rendered inapplicable the limits which the just-war theory sought to impose.

But perhaps one aspect of this technology has outdated these limits, namely, the one to which Ford points, the destructive attacking power of our bombs and the capacity of our missiles to carry these warheads with enormous speed

[25] *Ibid.*
[26] "The Hydrogen Bombing of Cities," *loc. cit.,* p. 6.

to the very heart of every civilian population on earth, which presents the stark dilemma of either wiping them out or being wiped out. Of this ultimate issue, Fr. Ford writes, "I do not see how that question has any bearing. If a man attacks me unjustly and tries to kill me, and to make sure of getting at me kills my wife and children first, I do not see that that gives me the right to kill his wife and children on the ground that she cooks his meals and they keep his spirits up when he gets discouraged about his chances of murdering me."[27] He believes that this dilemma may in fact be exaggerated, but states unhesitatingly that "if that were the dilemma, I would consider that we had arrived at the point where absolute moral imperatives were at stake, and that the followers of Christ should abandon themselves to divine Providence rather than forsake these imperatives."[28]

Before attempting to take our bearings toward this theory of limited war, it may be desirable to insert here, in summary fashion, the views of certain other Roman Catholic moral theologians who approach the problem of warfare today from within the same universe of discourse as that of Fr. Ford, even though they may disagree with him in significant detail.

Lawrence L. McReavy[29] apparently agrees with the basic rule of double effect: "The one thing a belligerent state can never lawfully do is this: it may not directly intend to kill the innocent, even only as a reluctantly adopted means to a laudable end, or take measures the only direct effect of which is to bring about their death." But the language of this statement seems to allow them to be among the legitimate objects of direct attack provided there are other objectives as well; and his statement, that "the harmless (if,

[27] "The Morality of Atomic Bombing," broadcast talk.
[28] "The Hydrogen Bombing of Cities," loc. cit., p. 9.
[29] "Reprisals: A Second Opinion," Clergy Review, XX (Feb., 1941) pp. 138 ff.

apart from infants there are any) are of course immune from direct attack on their lives," accepts almost entirely the erosion of the distinction between combatants and non-combatants. The theologian, no less than the airman, does not know where the "guilty" are nor who they are; and so McReavy concludes that "in the modern economy . . . the vast majority of the enemy's non-combatant subjects is co-operating in aggression, and is therefore a legitimate object of violent repression, in the measure warranted by proportionate self-defense." This last provision gives the only remaining limitation in principle upon warfare against civil centers; although from this McReavy himself draws the conclusion that only civilian *property* may be attacked directly, not lives. "For a reason on which we are not entirely in agreement this right violently to repress the cooperation of non-combatants does not extend to their direct slaughter." This seems to mean that a bombardier may let go the bombs at the munition worker's houses, and at the homes of their grocers, cobblers, barbers, etc., *and at their lives,* but withhold the intention so far as their lives are concerned. Presumably, the civil population, whose property is about to be attacked for the purpose of putting an entire city and its productive capacity out of the war, may be invited to take to the fields to watch the home fires burning. In any case, the military end to be gained would not be a proportionate grave reason justifying their direct slaughter. Thus, the civilian does not lose his right to life until he takes up arms or more closely co-operates in violence, because a direct attack on his life would not be a proportionate answer to his present degree of aggressive co-operation. This would exceed the bounds of a moderate self-defense.

Fr. Ford writes that "Dr. McReavy is the only Catholic moralist I know who makes the appalling insinuation that only infants are innocent in modern war. . . . I think it is an appalling insinuation because for all practical purposes it means discarding the distinction between innocent and guilty altogether"; and he also points out that McReavy's substitute for this and his resting the natural-law right to life wholly upon the final provision of the rule of double effect (proportionality) is "no real safeguard against the savagery of total war."[30]   Therefore his own position, as we have seen, rests not only on this one pillar, but on an application of the entire principle of double effect, to prohibit the direct killing of non-combatants.

It ought to be understood that emotional distaste for devastation or even regret over increased violence do not govern in Roman Catholic moral theology.   Let the capacity to make war be whatever it may be, Catholic thought seeks to make its way between the immorality of abandoning the public good to defenselessness and the immorality of an improper defense.   In principle, therefore, the magnitude of the defense permitted increases with the power of attack, so long as this can be brought within the rule we have been examining.   "Neither the intensity of the distress nor the measure of the violence resorted to can be used as independent yardsticks.   The morality of the violence will depend on its proportion to the aggression.   One will not route a burglar with an atomic bomb."[31]   Nor should one give candlesticks to a bombardier, at least not in his official capacity.

Therefore, according to the writer just quoted, "granted a sufficiently important military target which could not be safely eliminated by any less drastic means, nuclear bombing would be morally justified, even if it involved the resultant loss of a large segment of the civilian population."   Provided only that the loss of civilian life be truly an indirect effect,

[30] "The Morality of Obliteration Bombing," *loc. cit.*, p. 276 n. 41.
[31] John R. Conney, S. J.: "Morality of Nuclear Armament," *Theology Digest*, Winter, 1957, p. 9.

the size of it is limited only by a sound estimate that an equivalent loss to the defender is the only alternative.[32] Under certain conditions, on this view, a nuclear attack might even be launched first in a pre-emptive war, provided the enemy also possesses such weapons and is believed about to use them. "His possession of such weapons would never justify a direct attack on his civilian population but it would give me the sufficient reason to knock out his war potential as quickly and effectively as possible, even with a tremendous loss of civilian life. The only alternative to a quick and fatal blow at his war machine would be the destruction of my own population—which is certainly sufficient reason for allowing the incidental, though perhaps staggering, losses to the enemy."[33] On the other hand, this position in general may also yield a sweeping verdict against many of the forms of modern warfare. "No proportionate reason can be assigned," Fr. Ford writes, "for 'permitting' the extinction of the human race."[34] There can be no good, when aimed at, which would warrant this—if certain—effect. That last qualification still allows considerable latitude for judgment; and Catholic thought is not as inclined as are some non-Romans to make the finding in fact that the destruction of the human race is certain if the newer forms of warfare are used, because it is equally concerned about the immorality of any failure to defend the public good and, only in this context, the immorality of improper defense. There can be no greater evil than these types of action, or inaction; no devastation as such is to be compared with them as evils, except, of course, the destruction of mankind as a certain effect.

One Catholic writer, at the time the Cobalt-bomb, or the "open" bomb, one susceptible of limitless extension

[32] *Ibid.*, p. 10.
[33] *Ibid.*, p. 11.
[34] "The Hydrogen Bombing of Cities," *loc. cit.*, p. 8.

of its destructive power, came first under discussion, concluded that such a weapon could not rightfully be used even
in self-defense.   The question this poses is "no longer a
question of justifiable self-defense . . . ; it becomes simply a
matter of full-scale annihilation of all human life.   This is
never permissible." Because of this great immorality which
the use of fractional kiloton weapons may lead to, he judges
it to be impossible to justify an offensive war with lesser
atomic weapons today.   "For the ultimate result of such
warfare may well be the total destruction of mankind.
For such destruction there can never be any appropriate
reason."[35]

What of defense by use of the atom bomb, supposing the
enemy to possess the C-bomb and to be willing to use it?
This writer's answer to this question indicates that by morally discrediting the use of the ultimate military means
available today, this theory may have—retroactively, so to
say—destroyed the moral basis heretofore allowed for making
any defense at all; and thus the possibility of limited war
under the shelter of the threat of unlimited war is called
in question.   "Such resistance [with limited weapons] would
be useless; the desired peace could never be achieved by this
means.   It seems, then, that even limited weapons cannot
be used, because the defender knows that his self-defense
cannot be realized thereby.   But self-defense would be the
only justifying reason.   Yet, if we are going to forbid the
besieged country from using these bombs, we do the equivalent of demanding that this nation put up no resistance."[36]

There is, however, in the case of two belligerents who
both possess A-bombs (but nothing greater) and the aggressor has not used them, an exception to this writer's judgment that offensive use of this bomb may not be initiated:

[35] Pelayo Zamayon, O.F.M., Cap.: "Morality of War Today and in the
Future," *Theology Digest*, Winter, 1957, p. 4.
[36] *Ibid.*

"the justly warring state may use these weapons against the enemy's stockpile of similar weapons when it is clear that he intends to use them; and especially when this aggressor is atheistic and amoral." Again, pre-emptive war seems justified. "In a case, however, where an unjust aggressor has already used A-bombs, the defender may use the same bomb against his enemy. Otherwise there is no way to safeguard the people from the tyranny which defeat would bring."[37] Where, however, the aggressor who first uses the A-bomb also possesses and may use the C-bomb, such defense seems *morally unjustifiable because impracticable,* as we have seen, because such defense will not actually defend the laws of a people's peace.

Our final example of the application of the rule of double effect to the alternatives that may be presented by warfare today is drawn from Francis J. Connell, who, like John C. Ford, is one of the two leading Catholic moralists in the United States today. His article[38] affords us an excellent summary of the theory of the just war. "The Church teaches," he writes, in its theory of the just war, "that the rulers of nations may not declare war against another nation unless they are sure they are in the right, and have first tried all peaceful measures that might contribute toward righting the wrong inflicted by this other nation." Confident that there is an intrinsic, universal justice in terms of which this can be measured, Connell affirms that "it stands to reason that both parties to an armed conflict cannot be objectively right." However, he immediately concedes that "it is possible for the leaders of both countries to be convinced that their cause is just and that they are lawfully defending their rights." This means, it would seem, that for all practical purposes "justice" may be on both sides; and

[37] *Ibid.,* p. 5.
[38] "Is the H-Bomb Right or Wrong," *The Sign,* March, 1950, pp. 11-13, 71.

that—making use of a familiar distinction—it is what subjectively obliges and not what objectively obliges which
determines that appeal to the *ultima ratio* of war is justified.
Against the background of a seemingly greater appeal to the
norms of an objective justice, this means that in actual operation the just war may be but an extension of the public
policy, justice, and laws of their peace informed by that love
and agreement as to the public good which, Augustine believed, constitutes a people. "As far as the ordinary citizen
is concerned, he must obey his country's summons to take
up arms unless he is sure that the war is unjust, and in that
event he must refuse to participate in actual combat, even
though he would be sentenced to death as a consequence."
This seemingly powerful exception, based on clearly know-
able principles of justice, is, however, not greatly different
from the formulations of this theory in the early Christian
centuries when only the topmost public official had responsibility for initiating the use of armed force. What used to
be the august authority of the prince is now replaced by the
difficulty anyone has in determining the justice of the cause
amid the complexities of modern diplomacy. "It is seldom
possible in modern times for an ordinary citizen to acquire
sufficient knowledge of the inner workings of his government to pass a certain judgment on the justice or injustice
of a proposed recourse to arms. Besides, clever propaganda
will convince most civilians their country is fully in the
right." They are then subjectively obliged, and consequently they are justified in fighting. As for distinctions between moral and immoral means that may be employed in
warfare, seemingly open to the competence of the people
to judge, "the fact that some unjust means will be employed
in a war does not render the war itself unjust, as long as lawful means are also used. But a soldier may not participate

in a particular military operation which he is convinced is against the law of God."

Besides decision as to the justice of the cause, the rulers of a nation may not declare war unless they have "good reason to foresee that the benefits that will be effected by their victory will not be outweighed by the evil consequences of the strife." This is the principle of proportionately grave reason with which we have been dealing, or of testing to see whether one effect justifies another by prudent calculation of the consequences. Implicit all along in the tradition of the just war, this condition was made explicit by the Spanish schoolman Francesco Vittoria (1480-1546), and, once lifted up to view, this test of expediency, or of realistically measuring the good to be accomplished against the evil unavoidably done, even after all other criteria of justice were taken into account, became of increasing importance. To be fully just, i.e., to be "justifiable," a war must not be, as Luther remarked, like fishing with a golden net, an enterprise that involves more risk of loss than hope of gain. For Connell writes, "it could happen that a government, though unjustly treated by another government and able to defend its rights through war, would nevertheless not be justified in waging war, because the havoc which is foreseen would outweigh the fruit of victory." This point is especially pertinent to the problem of whether use of the H-bomb would ever be justified.

Fr. Connell then cites the opinion of the Holy Office that, on account of the immense evils which the whole world would suffer inevitably from war in the present day, a nation is never justified in entering upon a war of aggression. A war of defense, however, may be allowed when there are sure indications that the good secured will outweigh the evils that will certainly follow. This proscription of aggression under any circumstances, even to correct some sorely unjust condition, is probably the most significant alteration in the formulation of the just-war theory that has been brought about by the enormous destructivenes of modern warfare. Men of former ages would not have condemned aggression so categorically, or used it as the one main test of an unjustified war. Thus, Aquinas believed that whoever is attacked because of some fault of his own deserves to be attacked, and that it is lawful to attack one's enemies in order to restrain them from sins which are doing hurt to their good and the good of their own neighbor.[39] These former ages believed more that the rule of law or natural justice is indivisible than that peace is indivisible; and, not yet stunned by the enormity of the evil even just war lets loose in the world, for them the prohibition of aggression was not the main rational limit to be imposed upon conflict between peoples.

As for the means that may be employed, Fr. Connell decisively rules out the use of the H-bomb directly against noncombatants, and he points out that "it is certainly the accepted Catholic doctrine that those whose participation is only remote and accidental are not to be reckoned as combatants." Against a military target, however, the verdict must be otherwise, since it is immoral not to make effective defense of the public good. "There is no objection to the use of the H-bomb in a just war, as far as God's law is concerned, if it is launched directly against a military target, such as a fleet at sea, a body of troops, a railroad center, a road used by the enemy's supply trucks, or an ammunition dump." In some if not all of these cases surely we must agree with Fr. Ford that the use of this weapon even against

[39] *S-T*, II-II, Q. 40, Art. 1: Whether It is Always Sinful to Wage War? To this question, St. Thomas replies, "Secondly, a just cause is required, namely that those who are attacked, should be attacked because they deserve it, on account of some fault."

military targets would be like using a sledgehammer to kill a fly on someone's head, and when a fly swatter is handy.

Fr. Connell, of course, also employs the principle of proportionality in the rule of double effect; and this begins to introduce greater limits upon what is morally permissible. The condition that the killing of noncombatants can be permitted as an indirect effect only "when the immediate effect, the military gain, is sufficiently important to justify the attackers in permitting the bad effect, the harm done to the noncombatants," notably affects his answer to this further question concerning use of the H-bomb: Would it ever be lawful to use the H-bomb on a military target in the vicinity of a large city, when it could be foreseen that many thousands—perhaps even hundreds of thousands—of noncombatants would be killed or severely wounded?"

The answer is: "No, unless the target is one of supreme importance, such as the only factory in which the enemy is making his own superbombs, or the building in which all the warlords of the enemy are assembled." This leads to the further question whether, when the military target is not of such "supreme importance," the H-bomb may "be lawfully used in the vicinity of a large city if the civilians are warned of the coming attack?" "Yes," Connell answers, "if these persons are given sufficient opportunity to leave the city and to find adequate shelter elsewhere." But, if it is that important to knock an industrial center out of the war, and unavoidably its residential section, the specific city or a few cities must be named, because a blanket warning to the vast majority of noncombatants in an industrial nation to take to the fields would produce such death, disease, and starvation as to be the equivalent of a direct attack upon them as a means of hitting the military targets. Finally, the question may be asked whether, under these severe limitations as to the morality of its use, "the President's decision to proceed with the manufacture of the H-bomb can be harmonized with the principles of God's law as the Catholic Church propounds them." To this "an affirmative answer seems called for. Since the bombs can be lawfully used in warfare under certain conditions, they can be lawfully manufactured." We have already seen that a war in which some unjust means are used may nevertheless be just, as long as some possibly lawful use is made of the H-bomb; and meantime even these terrible instruments may help to keep the peace. Moreover, the maximum deterrence may be sought by means of the possession of this weapon, even though its rightful use is severely limited, because, as Connell goes on to remark (perhaps taking his cue from Thomas Aquinas' assertion that while it is not unlawful for a commander to have military secrets it would be dishonorable for him to pretend that he had none!),[40] "we surely have no obligation to proclaim to the world just how we would use the H-bomb in the event of a future war."

In his Christmas message, 1948, Pope Pius XII condemned "aggressive" war as "a sin, an offense, and an outrage against the majesty of God"; and "modern total war, and ABC warfare in particular," unless this could be clearly in self-defense, as "a crime worthy of the most severe national and international sanctions." He had earlier placed upon the conscience of all Roman Catholic Christians "the duty to do everything to ban, once and for all, wars of aggression as a legitimate solution for international disputes and a means towards the realization of national aspira-

[40] S-T, II-II, Q. 40, art. 3: Whether It is Lawful to Lay Ambushes in War? To this question, St. Thomas responds by distinguishing two ways of deceiving an enemy—one being the breaking of an expressed promise, which is "always unlawful," and another manner of deception, described as follows: "A man may be deceived by what we say or do, because we do not declare our purpose or meaning to him. Now we are not always bound to do this. . . . Wherefore much more ought the plan of campaign to be hidden from the enemy. . . . For a man would have an inordinate will if he were unwilling that others should hide anything from him."

tions.... The theory of war as an apt and proportionate means of solving international conflicts is now out of date."[41] On any interpretation, an important modification of the church's doctrine of war has been made for Roman Catholics by these positive teachings, which single out wars of aggression for sweeping condemnation. Since the Holy Father did not define what he meant by a war of "aggression," this teaching seems to trouble Fr. John Courtney Murray.[42] He thinks that the Pope meant to deny to individual states, in this historical moment, the competence to make war, on their sovereign judgment alone, for the vindication of what they regard as their legal rights and legitimate interests. "The use of force," Fr. Murray writes in interpretation of the Pope's words, "is not now a moral means for the redress of violated legal rights. The justness of the cause is irrelevant; there simply is no longer a right of self-redress; no individual state may presume to take even the cause of justice into its own hands. Whatever the grievance of the state may be, and however objectionable it may find the *status quo*, warfare undertaken on the sovereign decision of the national state is an immoral means for settling the grievance and for altering existing conditions."[43] The *historical* explanations of this radical modification of traditional teachings are two: (1) "the immeasurably increased violence of war today disqualifies it as an apt and proportionate means ... even for the redress of just grievances"; and (2) to admit the right of just aggressive war would seriously impede the development of the judicial organization of the world community for the settlement of disputes and the correction of just grievances, which Pius XII regarded as the only

[41] Christmas message, 1944.
[42] "Remarks on the Moral Problem of War," *Theological Studies*, XX, 1 (March, 1959), 45-47. Reprinted as "Morality and Modern War," by the Church Peace Union, 1959; and in part by *Worldview*, Dec., 1958, pp. 3-7.
[43] *Ibid.*, p. 46.

means of outlawing all war. In other words, it may be said
that, because the only legitimate reason for the right of war
is the unorganized state of international relations, the Pope
hoped to further international organization by verbally withdrawing that right. This may invidiously be compared to
the way in which Protestants often seem to suppose that the
way to "strengthen the U.N." is to speak as if it already had
the strength and therefore no nation the right of war. This
procedure should trouble us as much as Fr. Murray, I must
say, seems to be troubled by the apparent teaching of the
Roman Catholic Church since these messages. How can this
sin in the moral order, now defined by the Pope, be trans-
posed into a crime in the international legal order? "Pius
XII did not enter the formidable technical problem, how
this legal transcription of a moral principle is to be effected,"
Fr. Murray comments, and he adds: "This problem has
hitherto been insoluble."[44]

Courtney Murray himself offers two systematic explanations of the Pope's proscription of aggressive war, each designed to render this more acceptable, intrinsically and to
himself. The first is this: Pius XII "seems to want to move
back into the center of Catholic thought the older broader
Augustinian concept of *causa iusta.* War is not simply a
problem of aggression; more fundamentally it is a problem of
injustice. It is the concept of justice that links the use of

---

[44] *Ibid.*, p. 47. The "veteran Dominican theologian of the just war," Fr.
Franziskus Stratmann, of Great Britain, makes comment upon these Christmas messages that obviously follows to greater extent the tendency of Pius'
thinking: he, too, assumes that the desired organization of mankind has
come to pass, or may be best assisted by moral pronouncements against the
right of war ("War and Christian Conscience," in *Morals and Missiles*, pp.
21-23).   In the relations between nations, as in the domestic life of any
state, defense, as far as possible, should "be raised from the primitive state
of guarding yourself to the legally sanctioned guarding of justice;" "we are
on the way towards withholding the right of self-defense from individual
nations in order to assign it to the organized international community;"
"with this development of law, the defensive war in its earlier single-State
pattern *would* in principle *be superseded"* (italics added).

force with the moral order. Would it be correct to say that Pius XII represents an effort to return Catholic thought to more traditional and more fruitful premises? If there is a way out of the present impasse created by the outworn concept of aggression in the modern sense, it can only be a return to the concept of justice."[45] This seems on its face an unlikely explanation. How is a *concept* of just war and of justice to be restored by condemning aggressive *war*, and not the concept? And, if the concept of the "aggressor-defender" war is to be criticized, how is this done by seeming to condemn only one aspect of this concept? Fr. Murray himself moves in exactly the opposite direction when he also wishes to oppose this notion. The idea of an aggressor-defender war, he writes, is a "military transcription of a basically moral concept" that is "of little, if any, use in our contemporary situation." Then, in order to call for a restoration of the traditional concept of the just war, and in course of contending that "the use of force can no longer be linked to the moral order merely by the concept of aggression, in the modern understanding of the concept," he does not follow the lead he attributes to Pius XII or condemn aggressive war as a means of undermining such unsatisfactory doctrine. Instead he writes, "There is urgent need for a thorough moral re-examination of the basic American policy of 'we will never shoot first.' Under contemporary circumstances, viewed in their entirety, is this really a *dictamen rationis?*"[46] Elsewhere he scathingly denounces the U. S. Department of Defense and its allied agencies for finding "sufficient moral warrant for their policies in their loyalty to the good old Western-story maxim 'Don't shoot first.' With the moral issue thus summarily disposed of, they set policy under the primatial control of that powerful dyarchy, technology and

[45] *Ibid.,* p. 46 n. 13.
[46] *Ibid.,* p. 45 n. 10.

the budget, which conspire to accumulate weapons that, from the moral point of view, are *unshootable, no matter who shoots first.* Those who are disquieted by this situation—which is not ambiguous but simply wrong—are invited to find comfort in the emanations of crypto-pacifism from the White House, which seems to hold that we shall never shoot at all."[47]

The other systematic explanation of the Pope's teaching offered by Fr. Murray is that he meant to proscribe two of the three traditional reasons for recourse to war by a sovereign state—*ad vindicandas offensiones* (to gain vindication against an offense, e.g., to national honor) and *ad repetendas res* (to retake the thing, e.g., to recapture territory)—but to leave standing the third: *ad repellendas iniurias* (to repel injury). This distinction forms the backbone of his own treatment of the problem of war today, under these two heads: "All wars of aggression, whether just or unjust, fall under the ban of moral proscription" and "A defensive war to repress injustice is morally admissible both in principle and in fact." But it is plain that "to repress injustice," to repel injury, may easily burst the bonds of the aggressor-defender terminology within which he is forced to operate by the church's positive teaching. And having offered the explanation that by condemning aggressive war the Pope meant to withdraw from States the right of war, except *ad repellendas iniurias,* Fr. Murray concludes: "At that, the main thrust of his thought on war, viewed in the context of his dominant concern with international organization, goes against the modern notion of the *ius belli* as an inherent attribute of national sovereignty."[48]

We are left with the historical explanation of this teaching, in fundamental condemnation of all "wars of aggres-

[47] "Morality and Foreign Policy: II," *America*, CII, 25 (March 26, 1960), 766; or in *Worldview*, May, 1960, p. 8.
[48] *Ibid.*, p. 46 n. 12.

sion" however just the grievance, that it now may be the
teaching of the Catholic Church that recourse to armed
force, initiated by any nation, is wholly disqualified as a proportionate means for the redress even of just grievances, because of the awful force of modern weapons.   An emphasis
comparable to this has, of course, been made in Protestant
circles.   An example of this, short of the so-called "nuclear
pacifism," may be given before concluding this chapter.   In
a statement drawn up by Angus Dun and Reinhold Niebuhr,
in reply to the statement of the Historic Peace Churches entitled "Peace is the Will of God," the position taken was in
general that of the just-war theory.[49]   "The notion that the
excessive violence of atomic warfare has ended the possibility of a just war does not stand up," the authors declared,
and they proceeded to elaborate their point of view by making large use of ecumenical pronouncements on the problem of war.   The one which seemed to them most acceptable
was the statement of the Oxford Conference that Christians
have the duty to participate in war "waged to vindicate what
they believe to be an essential Christian principle: to defend the victims of wanton aggression, or to secure freedom
for the oppressed."   But then the difference between these
two expressions of a possible justification for war begins to
loom large under the conditions of modern warfare, and increasingly so since the Oxford Conference met.   Defense
against aggression seems a safer and saner justification than
securing the freedom of those already oppressed.   Because of
the consequences war today may entail, only the most imperative demands of justice should be honored.   "For this
reason the occasions to which the concept of the just war
can be rightly applied have become highly restricted.   A
war to 'defend the victims of wanton aggression' where the

[49] "God Wills Both Justice and Peace," *Christianity and Crisis*, XV, No.
10 (June 13, 1955).

demands of justice join the demands of order, is today the clearer case of a just war. But where the immediate claims of order and justice conflict, as in a war initiated 'to secure freedom for the oppressed,' the case is now much less clear. . . . Although oppression was never more abhorrent to the Christian conscience or more dangerous to the longer-range prospects of peace than today, the concept of a just war does not provide moral justification for initiating a war of incalculable consequences to end such oppression." Since the Dun-Niebuhr statement, however, the Hungarian revolution has shown that sometimes the obligation to restrict action in face of more serious consequences, or the consideration of order as well as justice that was mentioned, cuts right across the distinction between defense against aggression and securing the freedom of the oppressed. To state the prudential calculation that should be made in any use of force for the sake of justice in terms merely of a distinction between aggression and defense (or moving any further in that direction than Dun and Niebuhr do) does not seem a very rational dictum; and often it does not have the advantage of actually clarifying how and when force may be applied in situations that are all exceedingly complex, and "aggression" as difficult to determine as "justice" is, to compensate for apparently replacing the just-war doctrine by a concept of aggressor-defender war. No sweeping proscription of "aggressive" war can hope to stand, based as it is on the assumption that history can be frozen where we are, i.e., always in a relatively unjust *pax-ordo* or on the entirely erroneous assumption that any existing international organization is capable of introducing *fundamental* changes into this order but in an entirely orderly fashion and by mutual consent. And in any case, aggression has to be defined so as to include within its meaning, not only the first resort to arms, but also any basic challenge to the security position of a rival nation, to its *pax-ordo-justitia* and the laws of its peace, against which the only effective defense may be, and is known to be, a resort to armed force.

In ensuing chapters, we shall consider the just war in contemporary Protestant thought, where it is both effectively present and a conclusion yet to be reached again. In this connection, it seems well for us to consider first a recent document of world-wide significance for study and discussion among the members and theological leaders of the Protestant, Anglican, and Orthodox churches associated together in the World Council of Churches.

Chapter Five

THE WORLD COUNCIL OF CHURCHES STUDY DOCUMENT ON "CHRISTIANS AND THE PREVENTION OF WAR IN AN ATOMIC AGE"

The Provisional Study Document on "Christians and the Prevention of War in an Atomic Age—A Theological Discussion," issued by the Division of Studies by action of the Central Committee of the World Council of Churches, August 27, 1958, is in many ways astonishing, both in what it says and in how it came to be uttered (i.e., issued). The document was written by a committee of distinguished scholars and churchmen[1] who four or five years ago were asked to prepare a statement upon the subject assigned them and who meet from time to time laboring together to discover the wisdom that Christians and men generally need in this new age of potential nuclear war. It is no reflection on the distinguished members of this committee, but upon the enormity of their problem and the intrinsic limits in the

[1] Sir Thomas Murray Taylor, Principal and Vice Chancellor, University of Aberdeen, *Chairman;* Prof. Herbert Butterfield, Master of Peterhouse College, Cambridge; Rear Admiral Sir Anthony Buzzard, London; the Rt. Rev. Robert Cecil Mortimer, Bishop of Exeter; Prof. J. de Graaf, Professor of Theology, University of Utrecht; Prof. George D. Kelsey, Professor of Christian Ethics, Drew University; Prof. Henry Margenau, Professor of Physics, Yale University; Dr. C. L. Patijn, member of Parliament, the Netherlands; Prof. Mario Albert Rollier, Department of General and Inorganic Chemistry, University of Cagliari, Prof. N. H. Söe, Professor of Theology, Copenhagen; Prof. Douglas V. Steere, Professor of Philosophy, Haverford College; Prof. Helmut Theilicke, Professor of Theology, University of Hamburg; Prof. Etienne Trocmé, Professor of New Testament, University of Strasbourg; Prof. Carl F. von Weizsäcker, Professor of Philosophy, University of Hamburg.

results to be expected from any committee, to say that they did not succeed; and to add that even for an ecumenical document there are glaring defects in its workmanship.

When this document was presented to the Central Committee for action, two members of the commission, Dr. C. L. Patijn and Prof. C. F. von Weizsäcker, made statements in explanation of it. A prior critique by the C. C. I. A. Executive Committee (Nyberg, 1958) was entered in the record. "Dr. Baillie said he was less sure of the validity of the criticisms of the report offered by the C. C. I. A. after having heard Dr. von Weizsäcker expound it." Two pages in "brief explanation of the basic trend of thought of this chapter" were introduced into the document just before its most controversial Chapter V, "The Prevention of War: Discipline in Reference to Warfare." I think it is fair to say in both these cases that the explanations do not fully explain. The Reference Committee did not wish the document released in its present form to the churches for study. On motion by Dr. Pope it was so released as a *Provisional* Study Document, with a statement to be printed on its face specifying that this is only "a first step in a continuing study process" and with the warning that "no point here expressed is to be understood as an official view of the World Council of Churches. This document is in no sense a statement of World Council policy." A motion to substitute the words "does not constitute" for "in no wise constitutes" a formulation of World Council policy was defeated; and instead it was resolved to *underline* this statement to be reproduced on the cover page of the document, and to introduce it with "N. B." This seems an undue amount of official caution in an age when almost any fresh thought about the problem of nuclear warfare is better than none at all. And so, fortunately, the document is before us. What may provisionally be said about it?

In a curious way this document stands squarely within the tradition of just-war theory, and yet not so squarely there, because of an unsureness and ambiguity introduced throughout, I can only say, by the Calvinistic impulse to transform the world gone to seed in an inarticulate pacifism that has in mind at every point the final and complete prevention of war. It stands squarely within the modern Protestant movement to "renounce" war altogether (whatever that may mean), yet not so squarely there because of the lingering force exerted by the rightfulness under certain circumstances of the just or limited war.

The present situation, it should be clearly recognized, is one in which "mankind permanently possesses the capacity of nuclear destructiveness" (#9). These weapons, then, "are a permanent possession of mankind," whether stockpiled in underground warehouses or stored in the human mind. "The knowledge of how to produce the weapons will remain with us always, and . . . mankind is therefore less secure than it was before it had this knowledge. Thus the full force of our situation must be emphasized. We now possess the actual weapons, and we shall always possess the knowledge of how to produce them. They have become *a permanent aspect of human culture*" (#65, italics added).

At the outset, the Commission decided not to discuss the problem of war in general but to confine itself, in accord with its mandate, to war in the atomic age; and it stipulated that "in this paper, the term 'all out war' means a war in which the most destructive weapons are used to the full" (#10). This definition of terms should be kept in mind when, in the course of the document, one comes upon such expressions as "to use nuclear weapons all out." Already, here at the beginning, the analysis is that with which we are familiar from the traditional theory of justified warfare: "It is not possible to use nuclear weapons all out and to select and destroy physical objectives with discrimination. In all-out nuclear war one cannot 'get' merely the armed forces and the war-making class, or the centres of production, or military installations" (#11). Unfortunately, the principal limitation this Commission seems to have explicitly in mind is only the principle of proportion, or a calculus which requires ever more evident good to be obtainable (or evil restrained) to balance the increasing devastation of modern war. Merged with concern over the vastly greater evil that war now entails is, of course, the wrong of the indiscriminate killing of people; but these are *merged* together as the problem of disproportionate devastation. It seems to be only a matter of killing "more" people; and not the separate, absolute moral limit that prohibits the *direct* killing of noncombatants, few or many. The effort to keep destruction proportionate to the end of upholding justice, this document states, "has led Christians in the past to formulate guiding rules regarding their participation in war. Not every means of warfare was deemed legitimate. A means and scale of warfare which were destructive of the end in view, e.g. the maintenance of order and justice, could not be justified. This insight has particular relevance to the present situation and in our view has fresh importance and validity. We call attention to the fact that the use of nuclear weapons can certainly more than ever before cause such a scale of devastation and consequences so incalculable that they cannot be balanced by any conceivable advantage to mankind" (#23). Can it be that, on account of the awful destructiveness of the existing weapons of war, this Commission is convinced that the church in its teachings can now derive adequate moral immunity for noncombatants, and its statement of the principles of limited warfare that is at all possibly a purposive human activity on the part of civil society, merely from balancing conceivable advantages to mankind?

The main body of the document consists of three chapters (III, IV, and V) in which the key word is "discipline." Each is entitled "The Prevention of War"; and Chapter III bears the subtitle "Discipline in Reference to Technological Factors"; Chapter IV, the subtitle "Discipline in Reference to Political Factors." The tone of the whole is set by the assertion that "it is in a certain sense non-technical to use technics to the full,"[2] and in terms of this statement the Commission measures as in need of greater "discipline" the discernible "tendency toward an all-out use of science and technology" or "a certain indiscriminateness in the use of technology" in present-day society (#35). Technics as a whole need to be kept subordinate to truly human ends; and, at the least, the same is the case with regard to weapons technology. A discipline of limited use should begin to be consciously imposed all along the line. Yet the goal of discipline and limitation in the use of economic and political means is not a comparable limitation of war as such, but its entire elimination. The topic sentences of these two sections affirm: *"If war is to be prevented,* there must be developed within technological civilization as a whole a spiritual discipline which is capable of using technological achievements in responsible and ethical fashion," *"If war is to be pre-*

[2] C. F. von Weizsäcker explains this in terms of a car capable of being driven 60 miles an hour, and the intrinsic morality of sometimes doing so. "But it becomes not only immoral, it becomes non-sensical if I try to drive the car through a crowded street in a city at 60 miles an hour. This would be a misunderstanding of technology in itself, it would be a non-technical behavior. So the meaning of technology in itself contains and must contain the idea that we should not use technical means to the utmost." This conclusion is sound, but it is hardly a technical limit to be found within technology itself. "There are and ever will be," his explanation continues, "technical possibilities from whose use we must refrain in order not to destroy the ends of technology itself." Similarly, the limitations upon warfare arise from an analysis of war as a purposive human activity, not from any intrinsic self-limiting ground in the weapons themselves. *Provisional Study Document,* W. C. C., Aug. 27, 1958, p. 11.

vented, a first and foremost need is for a special discipline in the conduct of political affairs" (## 34, 45, italics added).

The most significant and most controversial section of this document in Chapter V, which bears the title and subtitle: "The Prevention of War: Discipline in Reference to Warfare," and which consists of argument in support of two propositions. *"A first requirement is for a discipline which is capable of possessing nuclear weapons and the means of their delivery, but of never using them in all out warfare"* (#64). Concerning this first proposition, it should be remembered that "possession" means something that can now not cease to be the case (merely by destroying the stockpiles, factories, and laboratories),[3] and that "all out" means quite limitless use. This last, especially, must be held in mind when we read the Commission's statement that, on the expectation that human conflict and open fighting will continue, this "must not be allowed to develop into all out war. . . . Christians must never consent to [the] use [of nuclear armaments] in all-out war. . . . We are agreed on one point: This is that Christians should openly declare that the all out use of these weapons should never be resorted to. Moreover, that Christians must oppose all policies which give evidence of leading to all-out war. Finally, if all-out war should occur, *Christians should urge a cease fire, if necessary, on the enemy's terms,* and resort to non-violent resistance. We purposely refrain from defining the stage at which all-out war may be reached" (66, italics added).[4]

---

[3] Even if the difficulties of an inspection system and international suspicion were "somehow overcome and if the bombs should have disappeared materially from the earth, they would stay with us intellectually, so to speak in the level of potential existence. During these last twenty years the knowledge how to make atomic bombs has become an integrating factor of our technical civilization. I do not see how it could disappear again except by a complete destruction of that civilization. Every future war between major powers therefore will renew the temptation to build those bombs even if they have been destroyed in peace time." C. F. von Weizsäcker, *op, cit.,* p. 13.

[4] This "first proposal should also be appraised in terms of possibility of

Nevertheless "a limit must be consciously set at some point" (#68). The megaton weapon includes a fusion reaction that is technologically open ended. There is now no limit to the power of the explosions that are possible. *"Since this limit is not now set by the limits of technological knowledge, it must be set by a decision of mind and will. The decision not to resort to these weapons in all-out war [sic!] is therefore a relevant decision."* It would be irresponsible simply to rely on the mutually deterrent effect of these weapons (♯69). It is worth pointing out again that the conditions requiring a decision not to make all-out use of the H-bomb are primarily the limitless amount of devastation; it is not, at least not explicitly, that their direct and limitless use meets the limit which prohibits the direct slaying of civilian populations, in all-out war or not.

At this point certain members of the commission insert a reservation that extends to four paragraphs (#69 a-d). They regard *any* use of the H-bomb as itself "an atrocity." "The use of the H-bomb constitutes an atrocity not to be justified in a belligerent even if the enemy is guilty of it." We have seen that Roman Catholic moral theologians reach this same parting of the ways, some finding a possible use of the H-bomb within the limits of the traditional immunities and proportionality, others finding that these criteria are no longer capable of being applied in the use of such a weapon. The minority of this Commission, however, do not rule out the H-bomb because it goes beyond these limits. The reason given is that "in the case of the H-bomb this contradiction [between war and the Divine Commandment of Love] is so great and palpable that it raises serious doubts of the validity of any line of reasoning which may be invoked to sanction the use of such weapons, even if it has a thousand years of ec-

---

performance." Critique submitted by the C. C. I. A. Executive Committee, #9, p. 38.

clesiastical history behind it" (69d). In other words, the two pacifist members of the Commission found it possible to agree with the majority statement that all-out nuclear warfare should be renounced, a cease fire on enemy terms being preferable to such incommensurate devastation and such a departure from the love-commandment; and they then applied the absolute pacifist position (which always finds a "great and palpable" contradiction between war and the Divine Commandment of Love) to reach a proximate disagreement with their colleagues over *any* use of the H-bomb, which the majority seemed still to allow. They were joined by two non-pacifist members of the Commission, who at this point should have written a separate "reservation" based on the prudential considerations of the majority (if these are only such), simply drawing the line *before* any use at all of megaton weapons and stating their conviction that the use of weapons beyond atomic ones in itself exceeds the limits of permissible violence or the purposive, controlled use of force and that the evil of surrender to any injustice is bound to be less than the evil wrought by such extensive destruction. In short, these Commissioners wandered about within the contradiction between war and the Divine Command of Love, forming first one and then another unstable coalition based on insufficient analysis of the morality of war. No spokesman gave voice to the view that a realistic and in-principled love, on going into political action, fashions the limits of justifiable warfare, lessening the distance between war and the Divine Command by both justifying war on occasion and always setting moral limits upon its conduct. If this was in mind, it remained inarticulate, or rather, as we shall see, this was explicitly refused in their rejection of the option of making living contact again with just-war theory.

The second, main proposition is that *"the discipline of possessing nuclear armaments but of not using them in all-out war must be a part of, and grow out of, a second and broader discipline, namely that discipline which is capable of using armaments, whether conventional or nuclear, if at all, in a radically limited war only"* (#70). The discipline of using nuclear armaments as though not having them requires the further restraint of being willing to fight even a small war with an eye to preventing its escalation into a big one. This requires a prior decision, even in small wars, which would severely limit them; and, in fact, it is logically the same decision as that stated in the first proposition. There must be developed a "discipline among the peoples and their leaders which will enable them to stop, even if necessary on the enemy's terms, rather than embark on all-out war. It is not necessary for a nation or a group of nations, to announce in advance the precise point at which they will stop. This might tempt a hard pressed enemy to test that point. It is necessary for them to possess a plan whereby they can stop, and to have the will to carry it through" (#79).

There is here some apparent confusion. A military command may with honor keep its plans secret among options of strategy that are morally licit or in accord with the nature of justified warfare; but it may be questioned whether it would be lawful to deter an enemy by the threat of an action (the *all-out* use of megaton weapons) that is intrinsically immoral and judged to be beyond reason and one which a nation is already resolved not to employ. By the same token, if the H-bomb as such cannot under any circumstances have any licit use, the possession and threat to use it would itself be immoral—and more than likely, ineffective in deterring an enemy who may believe he can risk (even without public announcement of it) testing the point beyond which we are resolved not to go. Moreover, unless this Commission in its probing strikes some more intrinsically moral reason for prohibiting indiscriminate bombing than the proportion of devastation, unless it in short has resort to the traditional immunity of noncombatants from direct attack, the limitation of war in an atomic age which it is seeking to establish is liable to go to pieces upon the objection offered by the C. C. I. A. Executive Committee (#9): "In so far as the balance of deterrence does in fact today inhibit war-making, is it not a threat, at least psychologically and politically, to that balance to state in advance that there are limits—without specifying what they are—beyond which the enemy can go without disaster to himself?"

Still this second proposition of the Commission yields specific limitations, upon all wars in the atomic age, which are worth noting. "First, . . . the use of armaments should be separated from ideological systems." Especially, the possession of nuclear armaments should not be used to impose or further ideological systems. "A supreme effort of discipline is required so that ideological battles are fought by means other than military, and so that the military policies of nations do not have the ideological impetus behind them which results in indiscriminate destruction" (#76). "Second, there is no ground for Christians to support a war for the objective of unconditional surrender" (#77). "Thirdly, if ideological causes and unconditional surrender are removed as legitimate objectives, there remains the possibility of using armaments in order to push an aggressor to the point where he is willing to negotiate. . . . In the present situation this is the only use of armament which we can see as supportable, and consonant with the preservation of order and justice." At this point, the Commission limits its proposed limitations, and disciplines its discipline: "It is hard to see how the objectives of war can be further limited without

disregarding all legitimate considerations of defense and order within the world of nations" (#78). In other words, at
this point the Commission finds itself unable to reject the
basic principle of the traditional theory of justified warfare,
namely, that force may be morally obligatory *ad repellendam
iniurium.* All its reservations and limitations have been
limits by which the exercise of this right is sought to be surrounded. In this way we are to understand the statement
that "there must be a discipline which is determined to use
the possession of megaton weapons and the upper ranges
of kiloton weapons as deterrents only, and only in a discriminating way.... This deterrent power ... should not
be used for the defense of ideological systems.... At least
it is not permissible to use them before the other party has
used them [i.e., even in case of use that is *not* going to be
"all out"], or to take any advantage from their possession,
except to deter other parties from using them" (#81). The
lack of prominence given by the Commission's statement to
the duty of the State to repel injury seems to be the basis
of paragraphs 6, 7, and 9 of the Critique Submitted by the
C. C. I. A. Executive Committee. They speak of "the main
political conflict of today" as more than a matter of mutual
"hostility"; of "our duty to use power responsibly in the
service of law and justice"; and they raise the question,
"Can ideological systems be entirely separated from the use
of armaments?" While those objections are pertinent to
the Commission's omission *in emphasis,* they seem to display
the same lack of understanding that a just war, in the traditional theory which relatively unbeknownst to itself the
Commission was at work re-establishing, is not the same as
an idea-war.

The second proposition of Chapter V, which we have
sketched above, is introduced in a way that is worth no-
ticing, because here it is that the ambiguity and unsureness

of which I have spoken radically affect this document, and set it significantly apart from the doctrine of the just war. Before taking a single step beyond "the highest limit" of renouncing the all-out use of megaton weapons, and before specifying any further limits upon warfare which the Christian should uphold, this document wants it clearly understood that these restrictions are *"for the time being, as safeguards in the present dangerous situation."* Presumably war itself is such an evil thing that a Christian would not have sufficient reason to try to limit its conduct, its goals and its effects, if he lives not in hope that war can be abolished altogether. According to the Commission's own self-understanding of the matter, this is what separates their endeavor from the church's doctrine of war in the past, and from most of the doctrines of limited war that have been produced in the present day. *"As such, these first steps for the limitation of war* [i.e., going beyond "the highest limit"] *are not to be compared with traditional Christian ideas for the control of warfare.* The abolition of *war* is the goal which we must achieve lest the powers of the atomic age destroy us, and these first steps are linked with the achievement of that end. Unless that goal is in mind, these first limitations have little meaning" (#71). The reader may well regard this as an astonishing expression of hope on the part of a Commission which defined the "possession" of nuclear armaments as intrinsically irrevocable. The document, however, correctly appraises the fact that the church's teachings about war have not in the past been regarded as meaningless without the arrival of peace in everlasting earthly life or earthly life in peace. That, I take it, was not the meaning of Courtney Murray's stipulation that "it is true that the traditional doctrine of war looks forward to its own disappearance as a chapter in Catholic moral theology," or of his acknowledgment that, at best, the work of intelligence in making war possible is "paradoxical enough," particularly when "this effort takes place at the interior of the Christian religion of love"; for he goes on to say, "the principles of the doctrine themselves make clear that our historical moment is not destined to see a moral doctrine of war discarded as unnecessary. War is still the possibility, not to be exorcised even by prayer and fasting. The Church does not look immediately to the abolition of war. Her doctrine still seeks to fulfill its triple traditional function: to condemn war as evil, to limit the evil it entails, and to humanize its conduct as far as possible."[5] The question may be posed with all urgency whether this is not the hour for Christians of all denominations to make common cause to bring to an effectiveness it has not had for many decades the common Christian doctrine of war. More than this as a goal (if not, alas, this also) must surely be appraised in terms of the impossibility of performance.

Instead, the Commission finds it "necessary for Christians to disavow at once" a "disturbing tendency" at the heart of the present-day discussion concerning limited war. "This is the tendency to assume that nations cannot engage in full scale war because the attendant destructiveness involved will not pay. . . ." That, so far, is truly a complacent assumption, to which the Commission's words are pertinent, when they state that the proposed "highest limitation" upon war will not come to pass without a resolute decision of mind and will. But the foregoing sentence continues by describing a coequal part of that disturbing tendency which Christians should disavow at once, in the following words: "and that the only way, therefore, in which to make warfare an instrument of policy is to limit it."

This tends to be an argument which tries to save warfare for the use of nations in the pursuit of their aims in a situation in

[5] "Remarks on the Moral Problem of War," *loc. cit.*, p. 57.

which they realize that full use of warfare is self-destructive. The Christian cannot accept this justification of limited war. It is not our purpose to preserve warfare. It is our purpose to limit war as a first step in getting rid of it.

This paragraph (#72) concludes with a necessarily confused statement of the Commission's conclusion from this as to the only use that should be made of limited war (in their sense): to deter all-out war, and to deter even limited war from breaking out. Then the last sentence opens the back door for a return of the just- or limited-war doctrine: "It should never be resorted to for the pursuit of merely nationalistic ends, but only as a last resort *to preserve justice and order"* (italics added). Is it not obvious that the doctrine, latterly introduced, makes clear that our historical moment is not destined to see a moral doctrine of war discarded as unnecessary; and that in the end the Commission contradicts its own assertion that there is no meaning to be found in the limitation of warfare except as a step believed to be toward the abolition of war altogether? And what is the forcible repulsion of injustice and disorder but the pursuit of a national—if not a nationalistic—end?

The pages (29a, 29b) inserted in explanation of the course of the argument in Chapter V emphasize the brackets within which is to be understood this Commission's consideration of the limitation of warfare. The new order of magnitude of the largest war possible today forces upon our century the necessity of abolishing war altogether. Only because "we felt a discussion of means to prevent war only would be too weak" did the document not confine itself to this paramount issue. The bracketed discussion of limited war "certainly could be misunderstood to mean a justification of war, if limited; but we hope to have made clear ... that the only final goal of such a discipline can be the total abolition of war *which must be achieved not in the distant future but must be envisaged now.*"[6]

The insert then explains that the proposal that a nation, rather than defend itself by the use of megaton weapons *in all-out fashion,* sue for peace on the enemy's terms and resort to non-violent resistance was not put forward as "an appropriate solution" of the crisis that would then be upon it. Instead, if this action is taken it may mean "decades of tyranny and suffering." The Commission's reasoning is only an "alternative of horrors," or the judgment that "the killing and, what may actually be more abominable, the mutilation of whole populations by all-out war, could mean worse suffering and might be less justifiable than even the acceptance of defeat under the conditions imposed by a tyrannic victor." In other words, there would be no proportionate grave reason in the good to be obtained or the evil to be avoided for permitting such killing and mutilation to take place. Here, where the slaying and maiming of human beings is most expressly mentioned in this document, would have been the place to state the principle that this cannot rightfully ever be done as an end or as a means to some good end, but only as an indirect effect unavoidably forthcoming from an action from which also proceeds the good effect, proportionate to it—if such a moral limit upon the conduct of warfare was in the minds of its authors, and not only a balancing of horrors. By contrast, the traditional

---

[6] It is impossible to determine the main intention behind the following criticism offered by the C. C. I. A. Executive Committee: "The study centers chiefly on the prevention of atomic war, rather than the prevention of war in an atomic age, and therefore naturally discusses the limitation of war. We ask whether this extension of its terms of reference was perhaps inevitable or represents too great a departure from the original mandate" (#1). On its face, this seems to ask for a discussion of the abolition of war to the exclusion of its limitation; and this objection may be the reason the goal of preventing all war is placed *first* in the explanatory insert, instead of in the middle, as in the text of chap. v. On the other hand, objections 6, 7, and 9, as we have seen, would require that greater prominence be given to the justification of war *ad repellendam iniuriam.*

theory was never reducible to calculus; and its formulators were more concerned to "weigh" the vast immorality of the act of directly depriving the innocent of life, limb, or property than to count the number dead or the extent of the mutilation (which if incidental to a proportionate defense was justifiable; and if not, a little murder was still murder). If the Commission supposed that obviously the all-out use of H-bombs is bound always to be murderous, in the real meaning of that word, and not just exceptionally destructive, it should have said so. The destructiveness is obvious, but perhaps not so obvious is the exact moral boundary that has been overstepped.

As for the proposed limits less than the renunciation of *all-out* use of megaton weapons, the insertion attempts to answer objections that may be made from opposite sides to its proposal that nations discipline themselves "to decide and to announce that no nation can be justified which, under whatever pressure, uses megaton weapons [still, of course, with the resolve not to go all out] before the enemy has done so." To the objection that this limit unduly restricts freedom of military action and the power of deterrence against attack, the reply is that "a deterrent is more efficient as a deterrent if, being limited, it will be applied with a higher degree of certainty than an unlimited threat which we will not dare to carry out." Thus, the first blow may as well be granted even in the limited use of megaton weapons, since an enemy will suspect that the first strike will not actually be made anyway, because of fear of the consequences or other reluctance to initiate the use of these weapons. If it is reasonable to announce renunciation of the first blow in limited use of megaton weapons, the question may be asked why should the point not be announced at which a people is resolved to capitulate in order to keep themselves and the world from all-out megaton warfare?

If the enemy is likely to be deterred only by deterrents we are more certain to use (i.e., weapons short of H-bombs), why should our announcement that we will not engage in such all-out war, and of the point beyond which resistance will no longer be worth the cost, be the thing that may tempt him to test that point? (Cf. #79). These are quandaries not only of this Commission,[7] but of our age.

To the objection that publicly to prohibit ourselves the first megaton blow implies "a tacit consent to the use of smaller atomic weapons," the reply is that this proposal "goes as far as there is any hope of acceptance by the great powers now and that further steps must follow if the envisaged discipline is to be realized." Presumably the same answer would have been given to the same objection against proposals to limit the use of smaller atomic weapons; and then to limits proposed on the use of gunpowder, or to any proposed for that "right devilish weapon," the crossbow. And so we return in rapid strides to one main thread in the argument of this document, the contention that limitations upon warfare have little meaning unless the total abolition of war is *envisaged* here and now. This, I suggest, is more the quandary of this Commission than of our age. The only kind of limited war, if any limits are possible, which the nations are likely to accept, is the just-war

[7] C. F. von Weizsäcker seems to see an advantage to be gained from making public both renunciations, of all-out use and of the first blow even in limited use: "To make these clear statements about what one will not do, as a powerfully atomically armed nation, makes also clear what one will do short of this. The potential enemy knows then not only what he has not to fear, but what he has to reckon with before that point is reached" (*op. cit.* p. 13). C. L. Patijn appears to stress more the dangers: "It cannot be denied that there would be risks involved in declarations which would state in advance that there are limits beyond which an enemy can press with impunity. I therefore do not believe that the World Council of Churches could ever make a policy statement of this kind. But in facing the awful possibility of all out atomic war there is no escape from the question whether Christians should not have a duty to stop, rather than embark on all out war if the situation is getting out of control. This is, therefore, not a rule which can be fixed in advance and in general, but a serious question for further consideration and further study" (*op. cit.*, p. 7).

doctrine; and this is not due to obduracy but to their responsibility for the repulsion of injury. It would be deplorable if the church's word to the nations concerns only the alternative of horrors, if in the midst of this potential devastation we do not represent what is more horrible still (the direct killing of even one innocent *or* the surrender to tyranny of the *pax-ordo-justitia* that still endures), and if we speak only of limits whose real meaning (apart from the details) can be accepted only if nations cease to be nations.

Still, within limits, and "for the time being," this is a just-war document. As the Hon. C. L. Patijn said in his opening comment, citing ##22 and 81, "It is recognized that power must be used only in the service of justice and order, that even war can be necessary for the preservation of justice and order." The new weapons have not changed that. "Our obligations—whether political, legal, moral or ideological—remain the same, but we need a new restraint, a new discipline in our conduct in carrying out these obligations" (p. 5).

Prof. C. F. von Weizsäcker makes it clear that there was ample discussion among the committee whether they should not begin with the concept of the just war. "The theological intention under which the Commission was established contained the question whether dogmatic concepts like creation and eschatology or concepts of moral theology like that of the just war could give us guidance in the problem of war in the atomic age," he writes; but then he reports the judgment they reached: "After long discussion we came to the conclusion that these concepts would not be helpful." This was unfortunate, both because to attempt then to speak of war as under any circumstances warranted inevitably meant to deny themselves some part of the wisdom of past reflection on this problem, and chiefly because of the impulse which ruled out this doctrine. The following comment is significant in this regard:

> Our extensive discussion of the concept of a just war you will see mirrored in many parts of the document, but we did not accept that concept as a starting point either. Even the words "just war" do not sound very acceptable to people of our time. This fact in itself shows how far our views have moved under the impact of modern technology and especially the atomic age, because the idea of a just war has been a very common one during most of the Christian era. Still it cannot be denied that our considerations about limited war have not been far from the old discussions about the just war. For just war never should have meant the justification of war as such but precisely its limitation in ends and means to such fields where a just cause and a just behaviour of the belligerent might make war the lesser of two evils. Yet I feel we were right in not using the term just war, partly because it is open to so many interpretations which are not and never were Christian interpretations, and partly because our discussion of limited war *most definitely intends the abolition of all war and not the establishment of a permitted range of warmaking* [p. 10, italics added].

The concern most prominent was that of providing an "answer to those who claim that by limiting war we make it possible once more, after the fear of total war had eliminated the possibility" (p. 13). Instead of undertaking directly the intellectual work of considering how war may be made morally possible, because it is not improbable, the approach taken was that of a modified nuclear pacifism which undertakes this gingerly and reluctantly and with all kinds of unearthly qualifications. "We are confronted with a military theory" of limited warfare, von Weizsäcker sums up, with the air of a man coming to terms with the world he lives in; we had to understand it, and "it is true that our report gives positive support to some elements of this military theory. *I feel that this would have been impossible* were it not for two reasons" (pp. 13-14, italics added). One of these reasons is simply the admission that, "since limited wars are still a fact of our time, Christians will come into situations in which they must know how to behave in the midst of them. I am unable to blame him who refrains from any participation. . . . But I am equally unable to blame him who tries to apply discipline and discrimination to the warfare itself and thereby to minimize both its horrors and the danger of its escalating into an all out war." The second reason which according to this interpreter alone made it possible for this Commission to give support to certain elements of the theory of limited war with which they were "confronted" (confronted, as by an alien theory, only because they began by ruling out the concept of a just war as the point at which to begin), was that they "agreed with the interpretation of the military theory referred to which understands it to be a contribution to the abolition of all wars." And then his final statement: "These two reasons constitute *the thin thread* linking the prudential considerations on the limitation of war with our attempt to bring the Gospel to bear on the actual life of the world" (p. 14). This "thin thread" in the here and now—through what is here and now envisaged for the there and then of some immediate future historical era in which Christian hope is concentrated, and which retrospectively gives the only meaning and justification of the limited actions through which we now must pass—becomes a woven texture of connection between the Gospel and the actual life of the world. It threatens to identify the sphere of the Gospel with the sphere of the State, in so far as while commingling with the latter Christian responsibility receives its justification only proleptically from a quite transformed state of affairs in the there and then.

One can improve on Augustine's doctrine of the Two Cities, and perhaps his analysis of secular justice is in need of correction, especially as regards the justice that may be achieved within the domestic order of the State. But this alteration can be made without abolishing the duality of the cities in which Christians dwell. Perhaps there are objections to the hierarchical synthesis of natural justice and supernatural charity in the Roman Catholic view. But that viewpoint was at least in no danger of historically collapsing this distinction, and it had room for a necessary and temporally interminable work of justice in its own right. The elevation of justice by charity, not lacking here and now, was yet an elevation into identity only beyond the historical plane, when faith disappears in sight, hope in attainment, and justice in charity (which was unfortunately sometimes expressed as rendering God his due). Doubtless Luther's doctrine of the Two Realms can also be improved upon—beginning, however, with the acknowledgment that the "natural law" governs the realm on the left hand of God, and that this was not merely a vestigial remain in Luther's thinking, and also that there was for him a dynamic duality and not only a static parallelism between the Two Realms, indeed that the Christian was bound by love to do what his office required. It is puzzling to me how Reinhold Niebuhr can continue to castigate Luther for this doctrine even in his latest book on *The Structure of Nations and Empires*,[8] especially when we remember that Niebuhr's social ethics has, with the gradual expulsion of liberal or semi-Marxist programs from his mind, become more and more pragmatic; i.e., it follows the grain which wisdom in this world must needs follow, and when we also notice that in this latest book he plainly does not expect the structure of nations and empires to become anything other than what it was, is, and ever shall be—except for an occasional hypothetical concession that "if" under the impact of modern weaponry na-

[8] New York: Charles Scribner's Sons, 1959.

tions and empires become radically different, things, of course, will be different from what they were in the past.

On this matter, I have come to agree with Joseph Sittler that Luther "had an understanding of the function of the state as a 'mask of God' which far transcends his practical conclusions from princely-state circumstances of the sixteenth century, and is intrinsically more inclusive of the facts of human evil and political creativity than the state-view of either Geneva or Rome";[9] and with Werner Elert's ironic remark, in reply to Troeltsch's description of the "dichotomy" in Lutheran social ethics as an "attempt at a solution," that "if it be such, this 'attempt' incorporates as an essential element an analysis of the total human situation which is not the product of our imagination but the statement of a reality which we cannot escape under the judgment of God. If there is an ambiguity in our procedure it can only originate in the ambiguity of God's design."[10] In speaking of Christ's way with men we should always strive to tell the truth about the nature of the world and of human history. It is difficult to speak with sobriety about "Christ transforming culture" and converting the works of men. This I have learned from attempting these last several years to teach H. Richard Niebuhr's *Christ and Culture* to my students: they can never quite understand why Augustine and Calvin belong under the type "Christ transforming Culture." That this is not simply a function of their lack of information or their immaturity, or their teacher's lack of aptitude, seems to me to be indicated by the fact that when Richard Niebuhr's book first appeared almost everyone in American Christendom rushed to locate himself among the "transformists": naturalists, process theologians, personalists, idealists, Lutherans and Anglicans who were sometime

---

[9] *The Structure of Christain Ethics* (Baton Rouge: Louisiana State University Press, 1958), p. 80.
[10] *The Christian Ethos* (Philadelphia: Muhlenberg Press, 1957), p. 409.

Thomists, as well as those you would have expected. It was as if the "typology" or clustering of Christian approaches to man's work in culture and history had suddenly collapsed in 1951, so universal was the conviction that, of course, the Christian always joins in the transformation of the world whenever this is proposed. At least as a corrective, it is of first importance to maintain a clear distinction between loyalty to Christ and our responsibility to uphold the orders of society, especially if it is our view that it is precisely Jesus Christ through whom we can and may and must act within the world. That seems to be dropped from view when we set about "preventing" war as the exclusive goal (by whatever remote steps) of Christian action in international affairs. The magnificent and terrible spectacle of man's life in history is not apt to peter out into the bourgeois image we saw for a moment when Vice-president Nixon and Khrushchev were talking like Fuller Brush salesmen in the kitchen of the model home in the American Exhibition in Moscow. (This last statement was written *during* the recent "thaw" in international relations, not when the weather turned cold again.)

Chapter Six

JUSTIFIABLE REVOLUTION

Before we "prevent" war altogether, there is another chapter in the history of the just-war theory that should be taken into account. This is the transformation of justified war into justified revolution; and the inherently improbable fact that this took place by means of an extension of that condition of the just war which, by requiring official declaration and initiation of war only by legitimate political authority, was designed to prevent the use of, or responsibility for determining the use of, armed force by private persons or groups within a nation. During the early centuries of the just-war tradition, along with the prohibition of private defense even against an unjust aggressor, lest a Christian wound the man whom by His wounds Christ died to save, the entire responsibility for estimating the cause, aiming at the right end, counting the cost, and officially declaring war or initiating the use of armed violence in defense of the public good was placed on the topmost legitimate political authority. The private citizen in his soldiering had not to reason why. St. Peter did wrong in cutting off the ear of the high priest because he had not been ordered to do so; and—to the extent that we may describe Jesus' action in this-wordly terms—he did not resist, even by means of legions of angels, not because he was a pacifist, but because he recognized that those who came to arrest him had the sole authority to use armed violence, justly or unjustly. "The natural order which seeks the peace of mankind, ordains that the monarch should have the power of undertaking war if he thinks it advisable and that soldiers should perform their military duties in behalf of the peace and safety of the community" (Augustine).

Down to approximately A.D. 1000 a private soldier had to do forty days' penance for fighting in any war, however just. I suppose this was for any private animosity that may have arisen in him, and also as a precaution in case he had been involved in doing an injustice which, however, he had not to determine.[1] After A.D. 1000 this requirement began to lapse, probably for two reasons. In the first place, the just war became a holy war, gradually at first, then with increasing rapidity, fought under the aegis of the church. In the second place, the private person was given, at least theoretically, responsibility for *not* fighting in a palpably unjust cause. This was, for example, the teaching of Thomas Aquinas. A Christian is not bound to follow his prince in every case, provided he knows or can know that the cause is unjust or that the war will not help to produce a better peace. When it was a question of private action going beyond trying to persuade the prince or conscientious refusal to obey, and suffering punishment for it, the presumption was still in favor of the public decision to go to war. And even the theoretical possibility of resisting the prince's official decision did not mean that fully legitimate authority for initiating the use of armed force rested with private individuals, or any group of them.[2]

[1] ". . . the axiom 'the Church shrinks from bloodshed' was taken so seriously throughout the first thousand years of the Christian era that numerous ecclesiastical synods imposed severe penances on killing in war. The penances had plainly more of a purifying than any special punitive character, but *a purifying did seem necessary*." Fr. Franziskus Stratmann, "War and Christian Conscience," in *Morals and Missiles*, p. 19 (italics added).

[2] While the above is a generally valid interpretation of the requirement of legitimate, official declaration in the just-war theory, it may not be an entirely adequate representation of Aquinas' views. It is true that, in answer to the question, Whether It is Always Sinful to Wage War? (*S-T*, II-II, Q.

Luther took over the just-war theory in the conservative shape he found it. He asserts both the right of private resistance and a conservative (but not necessarily for that reason an improper) interpretation of the exercise of this right. "When a prince is in the wrong, are his people bound to follow him too? I answer, No, for it is no one's duty to do wrong; we ought to obey God Who desires the right, rather than men." But then Luther continues: "How is it, when the subjects do not know whether the prince is in the right or not? I answer, as long as they cannot know, nor find out by any possible means, they may obey without peril to their souls."[3] I think he means that not to obey where they do not know will imperil their souls.

40, art. 1), St. Thomas severely distinguishes between the private person and the public official: "For it is not the business of a private individual to declare war, because he can seek for redress of his rights from the tribunal of his superior. Moreover, it is not the business of a private individual to summon together the people, which has to be done in wartime. And as the care of the common weal is committed to those who are in authority, it is their business to watch over the common weal of the city, kingdom or province subject to them. . . . So too, it is their business to have recourse to the sword of war in defending the common weal against external enemies." Moreover, even the topmost earthly prince takes the sword without violating the Gospel command that no Christian do so, because even he does this by the authority of Another that is higher than he: ". . . to have recourse to the sword (as a private person) by the authority of the sovereign or judge, or (as a public person) through zeal for justice, and by the authority, so to speak, of God, is not to *take the sword,* but to use it as commissioned by another, wherefore it does not deserve punishment."

Still, the foregoing are the just rules of war against an external enemy. The question of internal revolution is the issue there where Aquinas significantly qualifies his condemnation of "sedition" as always a mortal sin, by the following words: "A tyrannical government is not just, because it is directed, not to the common good, but to the private good of the ruler. . . . Consequently there is no sedition in disturbing a government of this kind, unless indeed the tyrants rule be disturbed so inordinately, that his subject suffer greater harm from the subsequent disturbance than from the tyrant's government. Indeed, it is the tyrant rather that is guilty of sedition, since he encourages discord and sedition among his subjects, that he may lord over them more securely; for this is tyranny, being conducive to the private good of the ruler, and to the injury of the multitude" (*S-T,* II-II, Q. 42, art. 2, Reply to Obj. 3). Still, it was Calvinism which finally attached to an act of "summoning the people" for internal revolution the force of legitimacy in declaring war on an external enemy that had been reserved for centuries to the highest prince.

[3] *Secular Authority: To What Extent It May be Obeyed, Works* (Muhlenberg Press), III, 270.

The development of the principle of official declaration or legitimate initiation of the use of armed force that was to sway the future came in answer to the question: Who may resist and what form of resistance may be used against an higher authority? In the political situation of that day, this question had to be asked of the people's relation to their prince, and of the prince's relation to his overlord, the Emperor. In his *Secular Authority,* Luther addressed himself to both instances of this one issue. For the people he framed a reply to be used when they were required to do an unjust thing: "If you command me to believe and to put away books, I will not obey; for in this instance you are a tyrant and overreach yourself, and command where you have neither right nor power"; and he adds, "For I tell you, if you do not resist him but give him his way, and let him take your faith or your books, you have really denied God." The resistance Luther approved was plainly only passive resistance, or non-violent co-operation, together with a hearty willingness to suffer for it: "The tyrants have issued an order that the New Testaments be delivered to the courts everywhere. In this case their subjects ought not deliver a page or a letter, at risk of their salvation.... But if their houses are ordered searched and books and goods taken by force they should suffer it to be done. Outrage is not to be resisted [i.e., by force] but endured, yet they should not sanction it, nor serve or obey or follow by moving foot or finger."[4]

Ibid., III, 257-258. True, only religious liberty was at issue here, or the freedom of inner faith. This may be compared with one of the earliest modern delimitations of tyranny in the tradition of rationalism, Spinoza's *Tractatus Theologico-Politicus,* where for tyranny to touch inner thoughts is said to be both improper and beyond the capacity of government (without creating for itself unreliable citizens whose words do not mean what they think); and in both Luther and Spinoza an inseverable connection between inner faith or thought and the freedom to possess books is established. It is a great pity that standard anthologies of Western political writings always reprint Luther's *Address to the Nobility of Germany* and not also, or instead, his *Secular Authority,* which Luther himself understood to be a corrective of his earlier work.

Turning to the other form of the question (the relation of the German princes to the legitimate authority over them, in 1523, the date of this treatise, Luther gave them the same counsel he gave to the people. Non-violent resistance, and sturdy refusal to carry out unjust orders that descend from above, alone are the means Luther allows even a prince to exercise in attempting to frustrate the action, however unjust, of legitimate authority. "To act here as a Christian, I say, a prince should not wage war against his overlord—the king, emperor, or other liege—but should let him who takes take. For one must not resist the government with force, but only with knowledge of the truth; if it is influenced by it, well; if not, you are innocent, and suffer wrong for God's sake."[5]

So Luther submitted to be hidden, and his prince ranged himself on the side of the Lord and Luther by resisting by all means short of a war of rebellion. Besides, the Emperor was engaged in Spanish-French-Austrian conflicts. The year before the *Secular Authority* was published, Luther disinterestedly advised his own immediate overlord that his opposition to the Emperor, and protection of Luther's person, should be confined to neglecting to execute imperial decrees, while he still ought forcefully to restrain, within his kingdom, the riots at Wittenberg. In 1525 he called for arms against the peasant uprisings led by the Münzer prophets. At the beginning of the next decade, however, the Emperor was perhaps in a position to concentrate his forces against the political, economic, and above all the religious reform in northern Europe. More now seemed to be at stake than private conscience and books and one lone ex-monk. In 1531 Luther became convinced of the princes' right to use arms in resisting the legitimate imperial power when this might be unjustly ranged against them. He was

[5] *Ibid.,* III, 269.

convinced not so much by the exigencies of that historical moment, which was to lead to the formation of the League of Schmalkald, as by the arguments the jurists were able to marshall from an appeal to the more or less unwritten constitution of the Empire. Luther himself explained and defended his adoption of this new viewpoint, in answer to the charge that he had merely recanted his former opinion that resistance to the Emperor was wrong:

> I am not conscious of any inconsistency.... The jurists first alleged the maxim that force might be repelled with force, which did not satisfy me; then they pointed out that it was a positive imperial law that "in cases of notorious injustice the government might be resisted by force," to which I merely replied that I did not know whether this was the law or not, but that if the Emperor *had* thus limited himself we might let him remain so ... and, as the law commands, resist him by force."[6]

Luther's final position, therefore, permitted the princes to use armed resistance. "Lawful" resistance was not the same as rebellion or treason. He was instructed in this by the Saxon jurists; and because of a certain ambiguity in the word "lawful," this step taken by Luther was to have decisive importance in the Protestant cultures in the future, leading finally to a doctrine of legitimate revolution led even by private persons. The fact, however, that Luther never changed his mind about the sole means a people may employ to repel injustice, in combination with his vesting the head of a mere principality with the ancient legitimate authority to determine the cause and himself alone declare a just war, constitutes the heritage of "statism" Luther is said to have bequeathed to the German nation. The most famous, or infamous, example was Luther's call to the princes during

[6] Letter to Spengler, Feb. 12, 1531. Preserved Smith: *The Life and Letters of Martin Luther* (Boston and New York: Houghton Mifflin Co., 1911), p. 217. Cf. also James Mackinnon: *Luther and the Reformation* (Four vols. New York: Longmans, Green & Co., 1930), IV, pp. 22-28.

the peasant uprising of 1525: "Dear lords, save us, help us, have pity on poor folk; use your swords, your bludgeons and your daggers as much as you can. If you die, it is well, you cannot die a happier death, for you die in obedience to God and in the service of love."

These blood-curdling words ought, however, to be understood with more historical knowledge and imagination than has usually greeted them. Even Luther was not without his moments of consistency. It was not only that the peasants and their leaders were confusing the realm of Christ with the realm of the State, the peace of God with earthly peace, and His righteousness with achievable justice. It was also that within the realm of political action they were incompetent to take direct, armed action no matter how just their cause may have been, according to an ancient theory of which Luther was not the author. Theirs was not the charge of law courts and armies; they had not the majesty of magistrates, the power to promulgate edicts, or responsibility for the public good in such a way that they could be supposed able to change its institutions responsibly. Doubtless the suffering of the economic refugees of the sixteenth century was enormous, and the injustice they suffered gravely in need of correction. But that alone was never sufficient to justify war. The necessity of preserving or improving *pax-ordo,* and consequently the legitimate representation of this *pax-ordo,* also were indispensable ever to justify recourse to violence. Not discerning the possibility of limited revolution, a revolution with limited aims and responsible means, Luther always sided with those who condemn rebellion and against those who cause it.

Yet he brought the legitimate authority to declare war one rung down the ladder. The next step was taken, theoretically, by Calvin, and in practice by second- and third-generation Calvinists. Calvin granted that a use of force might justly be initiated by officials within a nation besides the prince or king in topmost authority, provided only that they were in established positions within the internal organization of the State. In his celebrated "lesser" or "minor magistrates" passage, it is significant to note, Calvin speaks explicitly of the continuing duty to obey legitimate authority and wait on his word; and as against tyranny he, too, seems to allow only the acceptance of suffering and passive resistance. Yet, as Woodhouse points out,[7] Calvin fixes limits to obedience, and *between the lines* writes a charter for justifiable revolution that was to send a tremor through the established orders of society. This passage from the *Institutes* is worth quoting in full:

But whatever opinion be formed of the acts of men, yet the Lord equally executed his work by them, when he broke the sanguinary scepters of insolent kings and overturned tyrannical governments. Let princes hear and fear. But, in the meanwhile, it behooves us to use the greatest caution, that we do not despise or violate that authority of magistrates, which is entitled to the greatest veneration, which God has established by the most solemn commands, even though it reside in those who are unworthy of it, and who as far as in them lies, pollute it by their iniquity, for though the correction of tyrannical domination is the vengeance of God, we are not, therefore, to conclude that it is committed to us, who have received no other command than to obey and suffer. This observation I have already applied to *private persons*. For, if there be, in the present day, any *magistrates appointed for the protection of the people and the moderation of the power of kings,* such as were, in ancient times, the Ephori, who were a check upon the kings among the Lacedaemonians, or the popular tribunes upon the consuls among the Romans, or the Demarchi upon the senate among the Athenians; *or with power such as perhaps is now possessed by the three estates in every kingdom when they are assembled;* I am so far from prohibiting them in the discharge of their duty, to oppose the violence or cruelty of kings, that I affirm,

[7] A. S. P. Woodhouse: *Puritanism and Liberty* (Dent, 1938), Introduction, p. 61.

that if they connive at kings in their oppression of their people, such forebearance involves the most nefarious perfidy, because they fraudulently betray the liberty of the people, of which they know that they have been appointed protectors by the ordinance of God.[8]

This strong language could quite easily pass over into a theory of justified revolution. One thing, however, it was not: it was not an incitement *to riot* or to unlimited revolution. The limits are fixed by the principle of legitimacy determining who may rightfully initiate action "to oppose the violence or cruelty of kings." The final test necessary to justify war, namely, that the topmost official must alone exercise this responsibility for resort to arms, now comes to rest upon "lesser magistrates" within any nation. Calvin, of course, hedged this possibility with impossible conditions. Over twenty years after that passage was first written, his advice to the Huguenots was: "Better that all the children of God in France should perish than that the Gospel be dishonored by the bloodshed of resistance, unless Princes took action to maintain legal rights *and parliament as a whole act with them*. It is not sufficient that a single Prince should lead them."

This requirement of unanimity among the "minor magistrates" did not much affect the course of subsequent events (no more than did all the Puritan sermons on asceticism and the simple life affect the dynamism of economic life once the principle of serving God *per vocationem* had been let loose in the world). Some magistrates were bound to range themselves on the side of the Lord and his people and issue a call to revolution to oppose the cruelty of kings. When they did, they acted by virtue of their office as magistrates, on behalf of the *pax-ordo-justitia* of their nation. This was then justified revolution, derived from the theory of *justum*

[8] Bk. IV, chap. xx, #xxi (italics added). Tr. John Allen. Published 1936 by the Presbyterian Board of Christian Education, Philadelphia, Penn. Used by permission.

bellum by turning full-circle upon itself the restrictive provision that only the monarch could start the use of violence.
Thus, what was originally an entire proscription of private
initiative in taking up arms became the prescription for
doing so. For only one more small step had to be taken,
and not only could any first-class sheriff or justice of the
peace lead a revolution, but any heretofore purely private
person as well, so long as he acted "in a magisterial capacity." Whoever regards this as a bit of an excuse for em-
powering a private faction should remind himself of the
meaning and validity of what we call a "citizen's arrest."
Here too a private person clothes himself for a moment with
the majesty of public order and he acts on behalf of society
as a whole; and moreover, in arresting someone, he assumes
all the limits and liabilities upon the arresting power with
which this has been surrounded for the good of the people
individually and collectively. In a similar fashion, justifiable
revolution is revolution within responsible limits.

Woodhouse has written that "nothing could dissipate the
divinity that hedged a king save the divinity of religion itself when religion was ranged against him."[9] Leaving aside
the brief period of the so-called divine right of kings which
this commentator may have had mainly in mind, the most
ancient divinity that hedged kings was the sole authority to
declare war and take sole initiative in the use of armed force,
according to the church's theory of just war; and, against
that background, historically speaking, only this same principle of legitimacy, brought down to the level of the people
generally, acting magisterically, could unhedge a king or the
standing order. This is not to say that there were not other
forces acting also in this direction. King John's noblemen
found in their own interests sufficient reason to wrest Magna
Carta from him. They had not to ask Luther, who brought
the right of political and military initiative down to about

[9] *Op. cit.,* p. 61.

the same rank in the social hierarchy. It is only to say that, given the requirement that war should be declared in the right manner (itself a product of the church's effort to limit the use of force), it was necessary, as one among many influences at work, that there be a comparable stipulation in a theory of revolution, setting the call to arms within responsible limits, before the Christian conscience of the West could give its full approval to military action from below on behalf of a more just order of society.

This theory of "constitutional" or "official" revolution is of the very greatest importance. It means that an abstract and universal justice, or its serious violation within a nation, is never sufficient to warrant an appeal to arms. Rebellion based on such grounds alone would lead to civil war for an infinite end, on an infinite number of occasions, and probably by the use of limitless means. Instead, one must wait—long past the point where simple justice began to be violated—until there arises someone or some group capable of representing a better *pax-ordo,* and capable of bringing this to pass without letting worse befall. But this was not to side with those who always condemn revolution; for the principle of legitimacy limiting the use of force to situations in which it can be employed responsibly was coupled in Calvinism with the service of God *per vocationem* as magistrate or citizen; and with the view, born of a mighty conviction as to the sovereignty of God, that His sway should be felt in every crevice of the kingdom. Consequently, not only inner faith and books but social relationships and social justice are religious matters and just as important as the freedom of faith.

Looking back to sum up, we may characterize the medieval, feudal order as an hierarchical arrangement of the social classes, tier on tier, with provision for the payment of duties and the possession of rights flowing between them.

A man's duty was to his liege-lord above him, but at the same time his rights came from what the lord was understood to owe him in return. It was difficult to tell whether a man was bound to his lord more than his lord was bound to him. This nicely balanced scheme of reciprocal duties and rights, however, had one grave defect which made the whole arrangement unstable, and insured that feudal institutions were finally destined to topple over one way or another. The unresolved problem was that, while everyone knew what his duties and rights were, no one knew who was responsible for determining whether dues were paid or not, or rights arrogantly violated. Who had this remaining and decisive right, namely, the right to hold the others accountable?

The question, Who holds whom accountable? could be answered by moving in either of two directions as the Western World emerged out of feudalism. It could be said that the top rank holds people below them responsible for the payment or non-payment of what is due, while they themselves (still duty-bound to those in the lower ranks) are nevertheless accountable to none. Or this question could be answered by saying that the people below possess the right to call to account those who are above. The conciliary reform of the medieval church attempted to institutionalize this answer within the ecclesiastical order: it attempted to hold the Popes accountable to Councils. When this did not succeed, this institution went more decisively in the other direction. The Papacy itself may not be called to account, although it is still as true as it ever was that the Pope is only the servant of the servants of God; i.e., he is morally and spiritually bound to the whole body of spiritual society below him. For a brief moment, during the period of the divine right of kings, medieval political institutions toppled over in this same direction: a divine-right king was not a monarch who owed no duties but to God, his duties were toward the entire nation; he was one who was accountable only to God, not to them.

Against this background, it must be said that the history we have traced of the development of the theory of just revolution provided powerful impetus in the direction of locating in the people themselves the power and right to hold princes and governments politically accountable. Obviously, the justification of revolutionary change in government, by means of violence if need be, surpasses and includes within itself a justification of revolutionary change by political action short of the use of arms. Giving the people on occasion legitimate military initiative at once grants them on more, most, or all occasions legitimate political initiative. Thus did the private consciences of free men become the fundamental source of political authority, as only the practical extension of the priesthood of all believers, it is true, but this by way of the magisterial capacity assigned to every citizen's role in society, with all the dignity and responsibility that formerly hedged a king. The importance of Calvinism was that it provided the ground for political and revolutionary initiative to be taken by the common man (though, after that was done and the result accomplished, a Maritain can very well assert that while the Pope is the vicar of Christ, the king or government is the "vicar of the multitude"[10]). At the same time, the continuing importance of Roman Catholicism is that, with its tradition of natural law still intact, it instructs these new magistrates as it did the old ones in what is just and not alterable merely by their "sovereign" will, and in the law to which their decisions should conform.

What, then, is democracy but *justum bellum?* No Teacher in Galilee taught his disciples to resist evil by ballots. In

[10] *Man and the State* (Chicago: The University of Chicago Press, 1951), pp. 36, 49-50.

this, as with other forms of resistance or means for gaining the victory, the Christian, who himself alone should be willing to suffer deprivation of rights, still governs himself by love and uses the institutions of the State to suffer no injustice to be done. In this form, too, the use of force to accomplish desired and desirable ends must, if justified for the Christian, be limited: limited as to ends, a requirement which rules out an abstract and universal justice as a false infinite and which therefore seeks only a relative justice within realizable peace and order; and limited also as to means, a second requirement which seeks not to destroy but to maintain the opposition alive, refuses to politicize the whole of life but instead maintains the distinction between the political combatant and the independent noncombatant areas of life to which political encounter should be kept subordinate—holding, indeed, that within the nation men live in Two Cities and not in the one unified commonwealth of classical times.

Who can look out upon the world in this or any other historical era and *not* say, in an imperative statement, the problem today and in the future is limited war, the problem today and in the future is limited revolution? This has to be said of the use of any form of power with purpose— as this is attenuated and moderated in the normal conflicts of domestic politics in the democracies, in the ever-changing emergence of peoples or repressed classes the world over to new power, by violence if necessary, and in the ever-changing balance of power among nations. Who expects the domestic life of all the nations, with but a few possible exceptions, to be a changing order changing orderly? Or who expects this in any nation forever? And who expects international relations likewise to be a changing order changing orderly? One can only conclude that the "prevention of war" is based on an unhistorical expectation of the cessation of change; it is a naturalization of the kingdom of God to the dimension of time. The *highest* end we can actually aim at is the limited use of limited force; and, God knows, that is utopian enough.

If this is the case, then there is a decision of major consequence that must be made at once. The church must decide now whether its doctrine of war is only meant to be teaching addressed to the leaders of a nation and to the military command in warfare, and to the leaders of revolution, or whether this doctrine, with its limits, is also addressed to the people who participate in justified war or justified revolution. It cannot be said that this question has been settled in principle since the Middle Ages, when it came to be allowed that a Christian ought *not* to yield to the command of his political superiors and fight in a palpably unjust war or engage in the use of immoral means. Nor, on the other hand, is it easy to call in question the conservative interpretation of the Christian duty to resist, which favors what his leaders say over his own judgment unless he is absolutely sure in his own conscience. In an age when war is apt to be total, and therefore, unjust, will it be sufficient to limit war for the church to address its teaching to the leaders of nations; or must not, as the Provisional Study Document of the W. C. C. seems to envisage, this discipline be addressed and inculcated so far as the church finds possible in the people generally?

But it does not seem possible *responsibly* to call for a general discipline to limit the use of force unless the church at the same time makes the decision to support its members who refuse to fight because they believe a particular war to be unjust with the same vigor with which it has in recent years supported the pacifist witness within its ranks and within the nation. This would mean that the church will consciously attempt to obtain in military draft laws some status for those who refuse to fight unjustly as well as for those who have conscientious objection to all war. Perhaps the time has now come to accept with all seriousness the rejection by pacifists themselves of the concept of "vocational pacifism" (for it is this the churches in their main emphasis have endeavored to get incorporated in legal structures). Perhaps we need to take more at face value the statement that "we therefore reject the concept of vocational pacifism. . . . We must maintain firmly that to put pacifism aside as a special 'calling' for a few to keep the conscience of Christendom alive is a misinterpretation of the Gospel ethic."[11] That, in fact, should seem not only to the peace churches but to the major tradition of Christian teaching on war a strange way to keep the conscience of Christendon alive, when the conscience most sorely in need of being kept alive, after first restoring its now nearly completely lost effectiveness, first among Christians and then among the nations, is the doctrine of just or limited war. Here effective witness may be made; but to do this requires not only discipline but action, political action.

[11] *Peace Is the Will of God: A Testimony to the World Council of Churches,* A Statement Prepared by the Historic Peace Churches and the International Fellowship of Reconciliation, October, 1953, pp. 10-11. That "vocational pacifism" was always only a Catholic notion is made strikingly clear by *Morals and Missiles: Catholic Essays on the Problem of War Today* (James Clarke, 1959), where it is proposed that pacifism now come out of the monasteries, and that "the ideal of non-violence" be placed before all Christians, "not as a Christian *precept,* but as a *counsel* offered to all who have the vision and courage to accept" (p. 11). "Voluntary renunciation of arms is not included in the three recognized counsels; however since Christ observed it . . . it belongs to the Christian ideal" (Franziskus Stratmann, *ibid.,* p. 33). "Until now it has been a matter of debate whether it is legitimate for a Christian to refuse to fight, but now the question must be whether it is legitimate for him to fight at all. . . . Moral theologians tend to be concerned with finding how far it is possible to go in any particular direction without actually committing sin. But the Gospel of Christ is not at all concerned merely with the avoidance of sin; . . . it is concerned to show the ideal of life which Christ sets before His disciples. . . . It is not a question whether it is 'legitimate' to fight in a war, but whether the world has not reached a point where we may be called upon to renounce this very 'right'" (Dom Bede Griffiths, *ibid.,* pp. 69, 71).

Before undertaking such a campaign of responsibly disciplining ourselves and Christians generally to the severe limits of just war, we in the United States need to take notice of certain principles operative in the way in which consientious refusal to fight has been allowed by our Selective Service laws. This has been wholly at the grace of Congress in legislating the conduct of war. Doubtless for these our leaders to allow status to the pacifist was, in some sort, a recognition of higher principle; but it was not a recognition of higher *constitutional principle.* Therefore, the exemption accorded might have been refused, and may be revoked or modified by Congress in its discretion. In other words, the war-making power still today basically assumes that the topmost leaders estimate the cause, count the cost, and declare justified war; and it is assumed even when granting exemption for conscientious objection that no private citizen has any constitutional right but to obey, if Congress so decrees. The Supreme Court in the D. C. Macintosh case rejected the astonishing assertion that it is a "fixed principle of our Constitution, zealously guarded by our laws, that a citizen cannot be forced and need not bear arms in a war if he has conscientious religious scruples against doing so." The court said further:

Of course, there is no such principle of the Constitution, fixed or otherwise. The conscientious objector is relieved from the obligation to bear arms in obedience to no constitutional provision, expressed or implied; but because, and only because, it has accorded with the policy of Congress thus to relieve him.... The privilege of the ... conscientious objector to avoid bearing arms comes not from the Constitution but from acts of Congress.[12]

This decision of the court seems to have been overruled by the court in the Girouard case;[13] but what the court said in

[12] United States vs. Macintosh, 283 U.S. 605 (1931).
[13] Girouard vs. United States, 328 U.S. 61 (1946).

this 1946 case was that in our naturalization laws Congress had not indicated an intention to disqualify from citizenship aliens whose religious convictions barred them from combatant service. Presumably it might have done this and would have done so if that was in fact its intention; but the court refused to attribute to Congress any such intention. This does mean that, on the Girouard ruling, Professor Macintosh might have become a citizen, even though there was this difference that Macintosh was a just-war Christian, Girouard, a pacifist; and Congress in making laws governing the participation of citizens in warfare has sometimes granted exemption to the latter, never as such to the former. But the Girouard ruling certainly did not reverse the ruling, quoted above from the Macintosh decision, that in these matters Congress is the supreme arbiter on earth of who among United States citizens must go to war and who may not. It did not accept as its ruling opinion the words of Chief Justice Hughes in his dissent in the Macintosh case. It did not establish as a matter of *constitutional* principle that "When one's belief collides with the power of the state, the latter is supreme within its sphere and submission to punishment follows. But, in the forum of conscience, duty to a moral power higher than the state has always been maintained."[14]

This means that in disciplining ourselves and people generally to the requirements of just or limited war we have to apply to Congress; i.e., this will be a doctrine addressed after all primarily to the leaders of government. This does not mean that just-war refusal to fight in unjust war or in one that makes unlimited use of immoral means may not be the way to address them, nor that this may not be the discipline needed to bring about the needed limitation of war-

[14] Here, I believe, Professor John Bennett, *Christians and the State* (New York: Charles Scribner's Sons, 1958), p. 113 and n. 30, is in error as to the law in these cases.

fare, or what the Christian must do in any case. But it may mean the acceptance of a state of affairs like that of 1944 when one out of every six persons in Federal prisons had been incarcerated for violation of the Selective Service Act because of his religious convictions;[15] but this time mainly on account of objection to the use of unlimited weapons of war, and not mainly to war as such. The appeal to Congress would have to be for a distinct classification of religious objection upon just-war grounds in place of the denial of this today as "political objection" to a particular war, or the lumping together of objectors of this sort with pacifist objectors, much as sometimes the latter are now classified as preachers by hard-pressed draft boards. I do not necessarily advocate this. It may be that a searching examination of the problems which would be raised by the just-war doctrine, if it became operative at all as a matter of private judgment, would cause us to draw back on the ground that this would seriously impair the government's power and right to repel injury (also the heart of the just-war theory); and that instead we would be forced to see the wisdom of the ancient tradition, and still largely the emphasis in the Roman Catholic interpretation of it, which held this doctrine to be primarily addressed to the leaders of nations, and which still today requires the private citizen to serve in a war in which unjust means are used, provided that just means are also used. This, then, raises the question of a Christian's action as a soldier during wartime in refusing to participate in the use of immoral means. I say only that such questions as these have to be faced, and frankly and openly debated in the churches, at the same time that any discipline as to warfare is undertaken; and in these deliberations may the Holy

---

[15] Leo Pfeffer: *Church, State and Freedom* (Boston: The Beacon Press, 1953), p. 508. See pp. 505-507 for a discussion of the Macintosh, Girouard, and other comparable cases.

Spirit be more than the odd man! If the decision is reached that the church's doctrine of just or limited war is *not* addressed to private citizens and soldiers, then, if also penance is good for anything, consideration should be given to reviving the requirement of forty days' penance following participation in any war.

Chapter Seven

THE JUST WAR IN CONTEMPORARY AMERICAN PROTESTANT THOUGHT
Some Conclusions and a Conclusion To Be Reached

We now ask: What decision should be made with regard to the line of reflection upon the problem of war which we have passed in review? Shall the common Christian, and now peculiarly the Roman Catholic, doctrine be dismissed as "taxinomical endeavors in the field of military morality,"[1] specifically lacking in "the quality of moral revulsion?" The latter is professedly not allowed to govern; but is the rational analysis any longer valid? A negative answer will be given to this question by two different groups of people. Those who give in to the crypto-pacifism in the atmosphere will define war itself as the problem and refuse to think seriously about the morality of war itself. They will declare the church's doctrine of civilized warfare to be fundamentally morally defective, adding perhaps that it is now useless. On the other hand, those who are resolved to run with our galloping weapons technology will define war as a problem for technical reason alone. These will declare the just-war doctrine to be wholly irrelevant and useless, adding perhaps that the people's morality enters in only as a factor to be taken into account by the "artistic" planners of mili-

[1] Steven S. Schwarzschild: "Theologians and the Bomb," *Worldview*, May, 1959, p. 7, commenting on the article by John Courtney Murray.

tary policy. The truth will not be found dwelling in either of these extremes.

a. Is the Traditional Moral Immunity of Noncombatants Still Valid?

First it should be pointed out that all that has been said about the natural right of noncombatants to immunity from direct attack is at one and the same time an analysis of the natural law of warfare itself. These people are not considered simply as they are in themselves, or before God, the bearers of rights, but specifically as "noncombatants," i.e., in their relation *of non-relation,* or remote relation, to the conduct of war. Therefore what is said concerning civilian rights is not an attempt to bring upon an alien affair which in itself has no intrinsic limits a sentimental or extrinsic criterion. What is said concerning them constitutes the very law of conflict between peoples, the intrinsic, natural law for the conduct of war, so long as this human action remains, by the skin of its teeth, a rational activity at all. Statements about the immunity of civilians are at one and the same time statements about the only kind of warfare that can have any minimal rational or human meaning at all. It is not a question of defining the humane and the inhumane in general, but of defining the natural limits of a barely minimal rationality inherent to this human activity itself. From this point of view, a rather inhumane means used to put combatants out of a war may not violate the natural law as much or as clearly as repressing noncombatants in some possibly humane manner. Thus Fr. Ford, whose declaration on the immorality of indiscriminate bombing we have examined, nevertheless writes concerning the use of poison gas against enemy soldiers that "it is not so clear, though, that such methods of putting the enemy soldiers out of the fight would be against the natural law."[2]

This means that the just war must be a limited war; and war that mounts destructive power to match the increased power of attack, so long as this can be limited directly to the objective of defeating this attack, is just war. This theory states, simply and explicitly, that warfare as an extention of *nothing but* specific national policy cannot in itself and of itself become the intentional, direct, and mutual destruction of *res publica*, without self-contradiction and an absolutely irrational contradiction of the very nature of warfare as a still just barely human enterprise. The love or agreement that constitutes a people, and informs their justice and the laws of their peace, may justly be defended; but for intrinsic reasons this may not be done in such a manner and for such ends that the whole people and its entire welfare are ventured and at stake on the outcome. Wars for the end of unconditional surrender, war in utmost devotion to some idea or abstract ideal, even war for the "seven pillars of a just and durable peace," all transgress this limit, as does also the unleashing of devastation upon a civil population. Nations that renounce the use of warfare as an instrument of anything but specific national policy, and renounce absolute ends, will find themselves even more closely bound as to means. Acting not from panic or from fear or even from an unlimited identification of the ultimate worth of the life of a soldier with that of a civilian, simply by doing what comes naturally (rationally) in war that is still at all purposefully governed, nations in conflict, if this remains justifiable at all, are bound not to conduct the war so that civil life itself becomes a legitimate military target. The maintenance of this relation of non-relation between a civil

[2] "The Morality of Obliteration Bombing," *Theological Studies*, V, 3 (Sept., 1944), 270.

society and its fighters, and of their non-relation in relation, is of the very essence of just war, of limited war, of war that may under any circumstances be chosen by men who have not wholly lost their reason. This is not to say that war has an "essence" or "nature," but that man has; and that political society has a nature to which military means must be kept subordinate.

Something of this I take to be the meaning of John Courtney Murray's statement that "the whole Catholic doctrine of war is hardly more than a *Grenzmoral,* an effort to establish on a minimal basis of reason a form of human activity, the making of war, that remains always fundamentally irrational."[3] Hardly more than this *Grenzmoral* is to be looked for. As for those who say that the *Grenze* has itself been destroyed by the weapons now available, who say that the limitation of nuclear war, or any war, is today impossible, "in face of this position, the traditional doctrine of war simply asserts again, 'The problem today is limited war.' " This is a moral imperative, not a mere counter-description of the facts, but a moral imperative to subdue the facts of our weapons technology by "a work of intelligence, and the development of manifold action." "Since nuclear war may be a necessity, it must be made a possibility. Its possibility must be created."[4]

Perhaps more might be gained from a concerted effort of human intelligence to make war possible, in this sense of its control by the *Grenzmoral* of war itself, linking force again with some minimal national purpose, than from attempting to "prevent" war without altering the shape which it now has taken in reality and, first of all, in the minds of men. The moralist, of course, cannot tell the leaders of government or of the military establishment precisely what

[3] "Remarks on the Moral Problem of War," *Theological Studies,* XX, 1 (March, 1959), 52.
[4] *Ibid.,* p. 58.

they should do, any more than he can blueprint how a doctor should apply the principles of Christian morality to
dilemmas in his practice. There are questions of fact in
diplomacy and in weaponry, just as there are in medicine,
in law, in economics, or in the treatment of the human
mind which the moralist as such knows nothing about. He
can at most say only that *if* the weapon facts are these and
the use proposed for them is this, then he cannot see how
such action can be squared with the tradition of civilized
warfare, or have any real purpose in a nation's policy; and
then make clear his reasons for saying so. Still, it seems to
the present writer that the views of a Linus Pauling, who
has belatedly discovered that Jesus Christ was a realist just
like him, or of a C. Wright Mills, who, having forgotten
more about religion than Jesus Christ ever knew, believes
himself competent to lecture the clergy on what it ought to
mean to be a Christian, are far less impressive than those
of Thomas E. Murray for the work of intelligence needed
at this hour. Mr. Murray takes his stand against pacifism
(the notion that war is always immoral) and even more
strongly against barbarism (the notion that the use of armed
force is not subject to any moral restraints). "Our appeal
must be to the high principles of justice that lie at the heart
of the Western tradition of civilized warfare," he writes,
and in the light of this he states his belief that "a nuclear
war can still be a limited war."[5] This is a moral imperative,
not first of all a fact; it is an indication of a work of intelligence still to be done. Men must control their arms,
not arms the man. Weapons technology and weapons stockpiled need not be allowed to dictate policy. The equation
now forged between the immoral use of nuclear force and
the destruction of all human security "should serve to jog
our memories of an old equation that we have forgotten,"

[5] "Morality and the Bomb," *America*, Dec. 1, 1956, pp. 259, 260.

the equation between real security and the moral use of force. In Murray's opinion, it is the rupture of the tradition of civilized warfare, and not the discovery of atomic energy, that "lies at the root of the terror experienced by the world at the thought of war."[6]

It is in this context that Mr. Murray's support of the continuation of nuclear tests, for the purpose of developing smaller nuclear weapons, is to be understood. By contrast, American public opinion, he believes, is "neither rational nor Christian." Dominated by fear, we think only of the Big War, "the War of Survival that no one will survive." Hence "Cape Canaveral is regarded as a symbol of security. On the other hand, the Nevada nuclear test site is regarded as a symbol of menace." The opposite ought to be the case. "The Nevada test site need not be considered a symbol of menace. . . . The fact is that our security vitally depends on continued progress in perfecting the technology of small weapons; and this progress cannot be assured without tests." Because of the link between security and morality in Mr. Murray's views, we may conclude that he also means to say that the test site should be regarded as a symbol of that work of moral intelligence and of manifold action to make the war that may be necessary morally possible. On the other hand, Cape Canaveral should be regarded as at one and the same time a symbol of menace and the symbol, indeed of actuality, of the work of intelligence devoted to preparing for the immoral action of carrying devastation to the heart of any nation on earth.[7] (Doubtless, the symbols Murray uses imply too clear a separation of elements in our government's military preparations.)

The books on limited war by Robert Osgood and Henry A. Kissinger are, therefore, of signal importance. While

[6] *Ibid.,* pp. 261-262.
[7] "Public Opinion, Public Policy, and the Problem of War," Address to the Catholic University of America Alumni Association, Nov. 15, 1958.

they may be contested at points on technical grounds, nevertheless they carry forward the needed work of intelligence; and they certainly make a "convincing argument that a vacuum of doctrine, military as well as moral, lies at the heart of the whole vast defense establishment of the U. S."[8] It is not the business of the moralist or of spokesmen for the churches to impede this movement; but from their side to do what they can to fill the vacuum in moral doctrine. The statement, made by another prominent Roman Catholic layman, that the efforts of the proponents of limited war "to restore the *status quo ante* as a product of decision rather than of scientific fact" sound to him "like social workers running up and down the corridors of a mental hospital demanding order,"[9] has its genesis in the fact that the just war may have become for him the equivalent of the idea-war,[10] which is precisely what it is not. Cogley's statement is one leading exception to the truth of Fr. Murray's assertion that "the Catholic mind, schooled in the traditional doctrine of war and peace, rejects the dangerous fallacy involved in [the] casting up of desperate alternatives."[11]

[8] John Courtney Murray, *op. cit.*, p. 58, n. 39.
[9] John Cogley: "A World without War," *Worldview*, June, 1959, p. 8.
[10] *Ibid.*, p. 7, where the idea-war, or "armed idealogues meeting rival idealogues," appears to be the only alternative to the aggressor-and-defender type of war—which latter distinction is no longer valid in Cogley's opinion. Gerald Draper, Lecturer in Law at King's College, in a talk on "The Idea of a Just War," *The Listener*, Aug. 14, 1958, reported in *Worldview*, Sept., 1958, p. 3, also surprisingly equates just war with an idea war (presumably because of its intention of justice and peace) and, ignoring all the limits on means, said, "in a just war everything was lawful."
[11] "Remarks on the Moral Problem of War," *loc. cit.*, p. 54. Mr. Cogley regains his equanimity by rejecting the positions both of those "who want to delay mankind's decision about renouncing war" and of those who "want to rush it." "Rushing it may be the more precarious," he writes, "for if the decision is prematurely recognized and acted on before it truly is the decision of mankind evil consequences of unimagined scope may result.... The day will come when mankind will realize that it has found [a substitute for war]." We may applaud his statement that "we must get used to living in the age of terror that we find ourselves in; at the same time we must learn to live in it as if the terror did not exist";

So far, in restating and interpreting the case for the moral immunity of noncombatants from direct attack, I have again cited mainly Roman Catholic authors. The aim of this chapter, however, is to demonstrate that this same conclusion is crucial for recent Protestant statements on morality and war, while at the same time pointing out that it is still a conclusion to be reached. On this matter of the limitation of war in principle by the immunity of noncombatants from direct attack, Protestants are in substantial agreement with the traditional Catholic theory of just war. The case is simply not argued as formally and as rigorously; and this may mean some loss in substantive understanding. Nevertheless, it is significant that Fr. Ford's article on obliteration bombing ranged on his side the views of Vera Brittain;[12] and that the statement issued during the last war by a group of leading Protestant theologians partly in protest against area bombing rests upon the same analysis and the same principles.[13] The latter, while not an official pronouncement of the Federal or National Council of Churches, comes, if anything, closer to being an expression of top-level ecclesiastical opinion in the churches, if that matters, than was the place accorded by the Roman church to expressions of opinion like Ford's during wartime. Moreover, even the later Dun report contained this single, saving declaration: "the destruction of life clearly incidental to the destruction of decisive military objectives, for example, is radically different from mass destruction, which is aimed primarily at the lives of civilians, their morale, or the sources

---

but without agreeing that either the limitation of war or its renunciation will come to pass without purposing it or that either will one day just be there to be "recognized."

[12] "Massacre by Bombing," *Fellowship*, X (March, 1944), 50; "Not Made in Germany" (a reply to statement issued by President Franklin Roosevelt), *Fellowship*, X (June, 1944), 106.

[13] The Calhoun Commission, *Atomic Warfare and the Christian Faith* (Federal Council of Churches, March, 1946), pp. 8-9.

of their livelihood."[14] On all sides, the fact was that, as Fr. Murray says—he is speaking of how "unconditional surrender" violated the norm of "right intention," but the charge applies equally well to silence on the matter of the unjust conduct of war—". . . no sustained criticism was made of the policy by Catholic spokesmen. Nor was any substantial effort made to clarify by moral judgment the thickening mood of savage violence that made possible the atrocities of Hiroshima and Nagasaki. I think it is true to say that the traditional doctrine was irrelevant during World War II. This is no argument against the traditional doctrine. . . . But there is place for an indictment of all of us who failed to make the tradition relevant."[15]

It must be said, however, that the Dun report is very confused and confusing throughout. The Commission called attention to the "overwhelming break-through in the weak moral defenses erected to keep war in some bounds," and it said: "At no point is this break-through more evident than in the widespread acceptance of the bombing of cities as an inescapable part of modern war." But then it asserted that "the only real escape from these evils of war is the prevention of war";[16] and it is not farfetched to suggest that this was related to its own degree of acceptance of unlimited war, if and when war comes, and a certain lack of urgency

---

[14] *The Christian Conscience and Weapons of Mass Destruction* (the Dun Commission), Report of a Special Commission appointed by the Federal Council of the Churches of Christ in America, Dept. of International Justice and Goodwill, Dec., 1950, p. 14.

[15] "Remarks on the Moral Problem of War," *loc. cit.,* p. 54.

[16] *Op. cit.,* pp. 6, 7. Cf. the statement made by the Calhoun Commission's report, *Atomic Warfare and the Christian Faith,* pp. 13-14: "The only mode of control that holds much promise is control directed to the prevention of war. We recognize the probable futility, in practice, of measures to outlaw atomic weapons while war itself continues. . . . War itself must go." The question here is not whether this may not be the somber truth; but whether whoever makes statements such as this can then with any consistency go on to bemoan the fact that the moral limits upon warfare are not now as strong as they should be; and whether the oft-repeated statement that war, which has no limits, "must go," does not itself help to weaken the limits there are and prevent the strengthening of these limits.

and clarity about the work of strengthening the moral boundaries of warfare. In one sense, the fact that war must now be "total" was taken to be obvious; and this to the direct contrary of the traditional limits still preserved in Catholic theory. "In a conflict between highly industrialized nations all human and material resources are mobilized for war purposes," the report states. "The traditional distinction between combatants and noncombatants is far less clear. Only small children and the helpless sick and aged stand outside the war effort. It is practically impossible to distinguish between guilty and innocent. Certainly men who are drafted into uniform may be among the least guilty. Total war, in this sense of the involvement of the whole nation in it, cannot be avoided if we have a major war at all."[17]

To this, it must be replied that, if Protestants must use terms imprecisely, they should really not use them to discredit the quite precise notions in the moral doctrine of war, such as the meaning of "noncombatant" immunity. Consider in succession the mistakes in the meaning of the concepts employed in the just-war theory made by the Dun report in so largely conceding the totality of modern war, and in *using* the terms of the just-war theory to reject in such large measure the traditional analysis of the morality of warfare. "All human and material resources are mobilized"; and only children, the sick and the aged "stand outside the war effort." Whoever defined a "noncombatant" in such a fashion, as one who "stands outside" of any relation to his nation's action? Who ever meant by a noncombatant a person who, to be one, would have to be utterly helpless, and capable of no activity at all with results important to the commonwealth? Evident here is no conception of the significance of degrees of remoteness or close-

[17] *Op. cit.*, pp. 10-11.

ness of co-operation in the war effort, essential in any definition of noncombatancy in the past. The traditional distinction today, it is asserted, is "far less clear." Evident here is no conception of the fact that, in the moral choice between direct and indirect killing of civilians, or between counter-forces and indiscriminate counter-retaliatory warfare, the distinction does not need to be clear. We do not need to know *who* and *where* the noncombatants are in order to know that indiscriminate bombing exceeds the moral limits of warfare that can ever barely be justified. We have only to know that there *are* noncombatants—even only the children, the sick, and the aged—in order to know the basic moral difference between limited and total war. Finally, we are told that it is now "practically impossible to distinguish between guilty and innocent." Whoever clothed noncombatants with moral immunity from direct attack by assessing their personal innocence? In the past, "guilt" has meant close relation to or direct participation in the conduct of war (or with the force which should be repelled); and "innocence," the relation of non-relation to this.[18]

[18] Fr. Franziskus Stratmann also seems to me mistaken on this point (in *Morals and Missiles,* pp. 25-28); and it is interesting that he, like many Protestants who reject the concept of noncombatant status, makes much of their innocence in the fully personal sense, and of guilt in the same sense as alone justifying killing an aggressor. "This Augustinian-Thomistic ethics of war was abandoned by the Catholic moralists themselves in the 16th century," he writes. "They now taught that it was permissible to declare war if your right outweighed the other side's (hence the other party also might be in the right to a certain extent). Indeed, a merely material wrong was enough (e.g., the illegal occupation of a section of land, even if the accused occupied it in good faith). Thus there was no more talk of serious moral guilt, and the concept of war as a punitive expedition against a criminal worthy of death was dropped." There is some truth to this, but Stratmann goes too far in the lesson he draws from it: "Isn't the theory of the old war ethic—that only grave moral guilt deserves death—perfectly correct?" and in his judgment that, in our age, conscript armies of men who do not wish to kill are made up of men who *therefore* give no one the right to kill them. The fact was that the "old war ethic," with its notion of corporate guilt for an armed attack, did not dwell upon guilt in the fully personal sense, nor seek to discover exactly who was personally responsible for the dastardly deed. The enemy soldier's "guilt" was identical with his direct participation in the military offensive that had to be re-

This demonstrates, it seems to me, that in rejecting as invalid the quite discriminating concepts of the just-war theory, all too many people have first employed insufficiently articulated terms, or blockbuster concepts, to get rid of the moral wisdom deposited in the traditional view. No wonder, then, we are morally ready to use blockbusters and metropolisbusters in fact! War first became total in the minds of men. I can only explain, in part, why this happened among religious people, who should have remembered more than they did out of their traditions and who should have cultivated conceptual clarity in moral analysis, by reference to the effort to persuade the pacifists, as World War II approached, that anyway they could not avoid "contributing to the war effort." Pacifists may have been wrong in the religious and political judgments they made in refusing direct participation in war; but they were certainly not wrong in discerning a significant distinction between civilian and combatant status. At stake in this discrimination is not only total war, but totalitarianism as well. In stating so blandly that practically no one "stands outside" the war effort and no one is "innocent," has not the Dun report included practically everyone, to the whole extent of their beings, within the direction of the common life toward political goals?

This left the Commission with a very imprecise sense in which to reject "total" war. "Christians and Christian Churches can never consent to total war in the second sense." What does this mean? Answer: "war in which all moral restraints are thrown aside and all the purposes of

---

pelled; the "innocence" of noncombatants, their non-relation, non-cooperation, or remote co-operation in the prosecution of the war. Moreover, we have seen that, for a long time in the context of the "old war ethic," no amount or kind of guilt in the fully personal sense gave any man the intrinsic right to kill another. This arose only because of the objective role such a man played in action believed to be against the public order which Christians were obliged to preserve, and from the intervention of public authority.

the community are fully controlled by sheer military expedience,"[19] and this in turn means in the main, it seems, wanton killing or a savagery that kills without reckoning. Some methods of fighting "cause more pain and maiming without commensurate military decisiveness. Some are more indiscriminate. . . . We cannot, therefore, be released from the responsibility for doing no more hurt than must be."[20] In other words, the main consideration effective in this report is the principle of proportionality, or the prudential balancing of effects, of greater against lesser evils. When this stands so nearly alone, as the limit upon justified warfare, it is not surprising that for long stretches of the way, with the signal exception of the one saving sentence quoted above, condemning destruction "aimed primarily at the lives of civilians," and a few other passages, this report sounds rather like standards for the Housing, Care, and Surgical Handling of Laboratory Animals. After all, in the latter case no one countenances wanton cruelty, and the S.P.C.A. is quite ready to rule that it is immoral to use methods that cause laboratory rats more pain and maiming without commensurate medical or scientific decisiveness.[21]

[19] *Op. cit.*, p. 11.
[20] *Ibid.*, p. 12.
[21] For this reason we should not, without pressing for further analysis, agree with the statement of Reinhold Niebuhr: "Surely the fact that it is necessary for Christian nations to preserve their defenses against nuclear attack by the power of nuclear retaliation, hoping that in this way a nuclear war may be avoided, is merely the old problem of the difference between individual and collective morality in a new dimension." "The Church in the World: Nuclear War and the Christian Dilemma,"*Theology Today*, XV, No. 4 (Jan., 1959), p. 543. It is true that the present dilemma is for Niebuhr only a new form of his own distinction between individual and collective morality, with the latter conceived almost entirely in terms of prudent calculation or a teleology of greater or lesser evils expected as a consequence of action. But the question is whether the problem of war today does not reveal that such an understanding of political and military morality was all along defective and that such a view, unless it regains more of the substance of what we may call a deontological analysis of the morality of action and of means, drives on toward a reduction of human collectivity to the nature of any other collectivity from

Robert L. Calhoun, therefore, was quite correct when in his minority statement he wrote concerning the majority viewpoint: "The norm of practically effective inhibitions turns out to be, after all, military decisiveness; and beyond ruling out wanton destructiveness, Christian conscience in wartime seems to have chiefly the effect (certainly important but scarcely decisive) of making Christians do reluctantly what military necessity requires."[22] The majority were right only so far, in pointing out that "the real moral line between what may be done and what may not be done by the Christian lies not in the realm of the distinction between weapons but in the realm of the motives for using and the consequences of using all kinds of weapons,"[23] and "we have found no moral distinction between these instruments of warfare, apart from the ends they serve and the consequences of their use."[24] But not only the motive behind their use, and not only a teleological or prudential consideration of consequences, or justifying war in terms of the lesser evil, cuts across weapons as such. The morality of means referred to in the just-war theory meant more than the inert weapon as such; this meant the *action* as a whole and its nature, which had a morality or an immorality not wholly swallowed up in consequences or in motive to ends believed to justify any action that may be thought to have military decisiveness.

Far less ambiguous about fundamental principles is the "background paper" prepared by John Bennett for the Fifth

which ends and consequences are to be wrested after having been rationally projected for the determination of present action. We must find out, and quickly, whether the sharp distinction between individual and collective morality really means a conception of the "group" as a whole consisting of subordinate parts, or a whole consisting of wholes (persons) who may not justly be reduced to mere means of attaining urgent social or historical ends.

[22] *Op. cit.*, p. 23.
[23] *Ibid.*, p. 13.
[24] *Ibid.*, p. 13.

World Order Study Conference of the National Council of Churches in Cleveland, 1958, entitled "Theological and Moral Considerations in International Affairs." It is true Professor Bennett affirms: "It has become increasingly difficult to distinguish in detail between combatants and noncombatants and sometimes the teaching about the just war has been legalistic at this point, if we grant that the use of military force is ever justified at all." That unexamined statement is not worth having. And upon examining the statement, it should at once come clear that to prohibit the *direct* killing (while allowing the *indirect* killing) of noncombatants it is not at all necessary to distinguish them "in detail." But Bennett also says with no equivocation that "the use of weapons to slaughter civilian populations, recklessness in regard to future generations, and the destruction of the fabric of national community and of civilized life are opposed to all that the churches have taught in the past."[25] And concerning massive deterrence, he asks: "Should deterrent power be thought of as directed against the opponent's power to strike or against the whole population in the hope of deterring the will to strike? If the latter is the objective, we are again in the realm of unlimited terror and unlimited striking power and an unlimited arms race. If the former is the objective there may be a better chance to avoid the errors that result from panic. Also the former objective raises a less acute moral conflict than the latter. Do we know what the present presuppositions of the U. S. government are on this matter?"[26]

A comment should be made concerning Bennett's summary of the moral limits upon warfare in terms of prohibiting "the destruction of the fabric of national community

[25] P. 10.
[26] *Ibid.*, p. 7.

and of civilized life" in the enemy nation. He repeated this summation, in an unpublished paper before the American Theological Society in 1960, as the "intrinsic evil" of military action "when it takes as its target of attack, whether intentionally or not, the recuperative powers of the enemy" and the "fabric of national community" in a nation at war. Such formulations of the criteria for the just conduct of war are of considerable worth. Certainly Christians and any just man should have a regard for the uniqueness of the various peoples of the world, in their traditions, ways of life, and distinct contributions to the enrichment of mankind. The nations also are creatures of God. Yet it seems clear that such statements of the principles that should limit warfare are *reducible* to the more fundamental principle surrounding life with moral immunity from direct repression. It is to be feared that, unless this reduction is carried out with conceptual clarity in the analysis of morality and warfare, we have not yet elaborated the firmest possible moral guard against total war. Moreover, it seems to me that an in-principled Christian love does not first of all fashion itself in terms of regard for the fabric of community life, nor does Christian faith, going into political action, take effect primarily in fidelity to the recuperative powers of an enemy nation. The neighbors and companions God has given us are primarily persons within the separate national traditions he has provided for them and for us. Bennett's way of articulating the point at which the conduct of a war becomes unjust seems clearly derivative and secondary. Logically and Christianly, it is predicated upon the claims pointed out in the tradition doctrine.

Surely it must be confessed that when that outstanding Baptist layman, President Harry S. Truman, said, "I regarded the bomb as a military weapon and *never had any doubt that it should be used,"*[27] he voiced the opinion of the American people. He who is of a contrary opinion should sit down first with Harry S. Truman, Commander-in-Chief, and count the cost, in a people's self-discipline and otherwise, of a policy that might have contributed to keep war limited and just. The proposal made by many highly placed scientists that the bomb *first* be dropped as a warning demonstration on some unpopulated area and not first on open cities was by no means an adequate limitation in our intention and action, for still the implied threat to use violent repression directly against civilians as a means of forcing a decision to surrender on the part of the Japanese military command would, if exerted, itself have been grossly immoral. The retrospective applause of this proposal betrays a willingness to resolve moral issues in quantitative terms, or upon the basis of the avoidance of devastation, alone. Nor would it be right to support the belief the bombs should not have been dropped by reference to the fact that the Japanese were ready to surrender anyway, and thus attempt to deny the assertion that in total number more lives were saved by dropping the bombs than would have had to be expended in defeating the military forces of the enemy by invasion. For the question is whether we refuse to count one for one a civilian directly attacked and a fighter directly attacked or sacrificed. The test of this will be, if such in fact was not the case at the time of Hiroshima, what we would judge to be licit in a case *supposed* in which to renounce direct attack upon the civil centers of the enemy nation and to attack only military targets would actually require a totally greater sacrifice of life on the part of both combatants. In the mirror of such a supposition it will be revealed whether in the secrets of many hearts the moral underpinning of the just-war theory still remains intact, and

[27] *New York Times,* Oct. 19, 1955, p. 35 (italics added).

whether there exist today any real moral limits upon the waging of war.

Perhaps because of the Calvinism gone to seed in the atmosphere, and the lack of any doctrine of the Two Realms in which a human destiny is played out, the American people are ill prepared for the self-discipline necessary for the limitation of warfare. One has only to recall the frustration over the limited goals of the Korean war. We tend to suppose that the sacrifice of even one life, itself of infinite worth, can be justified only in terms of infinite goals and achievements made to appear ultimate and permanent. The Two Realms are confused; and in getting rid of the one of these in which infinite passion is fitting, some measure of this same passion and its great expectations is transferred over to the flat realm of historical, political action. Therefore the idea does not go down easily with us that, while a man lives finally in relation to the infinite goodness of God, he also lives in the realm of the State where men must be content with small gains and exceedingly limited aims sought by self-discipline and at apparently great, in fact quite incommensurate, cost. In all this, ends and means commingle, unlimited ends justifying any means; while political goals, distended into some approximate resemblance to *the* Good we in its realm no longer believe in, or in its realm and only in its realm no longer believe in, call for extreme actions on their behalf. The test is whether we are willing to limit ends and means in warfare and yet sustain the burden of this evil necessity, whether we as a people are willing, if war comes, to accept defeat when our fighters cannot win the hoped-for victory rather than venture more and exact more than the nature of just endurable warfare requires, whether we can mount the resources for action with at most small effect and plan surrender when none is possible.[28] The test is also, I think, whether we judge it more important for man's obedient life on earth that the child of a Bantu in the bush or an unborn descendant of one of the readers or of the writer of this book die of leukemia as an indirect result of tests by means of which men are striving to develop a variety of controllable nuclear weapons (I do not here settle the question whether this was in fact the purpose of the tests, or the reason they are now suspended) than for that same child to die as (it is true also, only) the indirect result of that collossal scientific experiment upon the universe and upon the whole human race, Project Argus, by which a belt of man-made radiation was thrown around the earth, from which doubtless there was obtained a lot of interesting and not unimportant "pure" scientific knowledge.[29]

The test, finally, is whether we regard our flight as an entire people to the paramount importance of consumer goods, the dismantling of our defenses, the failure to maintain sufficient military power in all kinds of weapons clearly related to any national resolve on our part to preserve the peace and order and justice of our own and of many other peoples whose destiny has been and may yet be inextricably bound in with ours as *equally questionable morally* as the building and stockpiling of the bomb, which was our excuse for playing as if we are not a nation. Here Kissinger's re-

---

[28] Cf. John Courtney Murray's earnest but ironic description of our national mentality on the matter of war: "When 'Washington' thinks of 'surrender' [our own, or of the enemy], it apparently can think only of 'unconditional' surrender.... Thus patriotism, once the last refuge of the scoundrel, now has become the first refuge of the fool. It is folly not to foresee that the United States may be laid in ruins by a nuclear attack; the folly is compounded by a decision not to spend any money planning what to do after that not impossible event.... For the Soviet Union survival is not an issue in war; for us it is the only issue. In Soviet thought military action is subordinate to political aims; with us military action creates its own aims, and there is only one, 'victory,' scil., unconditional surrender." *Op. cit.*, p. 55 n. 35. This is the morality of "Western" movies: the good against the bad with all-out determination.

[29] Christophilos was the name of the chief originator of this otherwise superb plan.

mark is pertinent: "President Eisenhower is reported to have expressed puzzlement that our repeated warnings that we would fight for Berlin have apparently failed to impress Mr. Khrushchev greatly. The reason is not hard to find: our threat to resort to our only strategy has lost its credibility, not because our leaders are irresolute but because the threat of all-out war has become inherently implausible."[30] War must be made morally possible, not only because it is not improbable at some distant time, but because, even now, a nation's purpose has no embodiment and no effect until a substitute has been found, not for war, but for the deterrent that deters no one so much as ourselves. Until that day—which Christians know, or ought to know, is an eschatological vision and not an event in time—on which men beat their swords into plows and their spears into pruning hooks, the nations will need some "alternative to peace." They will need to know and to do what is just in arming themselves and in the use planned for their weapons.

b. *What Shall be Said of the Weapons Now Ready or In Preparation?*

We have also examined the thought of a number of men who, from differing points of view and at diverse places in their analysis, find their Christian consciences buckling under the weight of the problem of existing weapons and the probable conduct of war by such means. Responsibility for directing defense to justifiable ends and choosing justi-

[30] Henry A. Kissinger: "The Khrushchev Visit—Dangers and Hopes," *New York Times Magazine,* Sept. 6, 1959, p. 44. Kissinger also notes, at the Foreign Minister's Conference in Geneva, "the lack of conviction with which the Western plan for German unification was presented and the haste with which it was pigeonholed at the first sign of opposition. After the first week in Geneva, the foreign ministers dealt with only one problem: the transformation of our position in Berlin, for which the *quid pro quo* was to be the withdrawal of a Soviet threat. We were asked to give up our rights while the Soviets would give up a menace" (pp. 5, 44).

fiable means, held together in the traditional theory, break apart in the face of the nature of warfare today and in the future. This leads to what has been misnamed "nuclear pacifism" or "relative Christian pacifism."[31] This is not the name for it, since the correct conclusion on this matter can be arrived at only from an earnest attempt to apply the principles of the just war. That always entailed that some war, and some of the use of means, should be declared unjustifiable; and Christian support and participation be withheld at that point. Some today think about this problem largely in terms of the amount of devastation involved in modern war, and they deliver their verdict against specific weapons as such. There can be "no greater evil" than war with A-bombs, but war with conventional weapons may still be a lesser evil than the evil resisted; or war with smaller A-bombs but not the largest may still be justified; or war with A-bombs but not with H-bombs; or, finally, some specified and limited use of megaton weapons may still be licit, but not "all out" nuclear warfare. It is better, it should be said, to begin with some principle that runs right through the various weapons that might be used, determining licit and illicit actions in the military use of all weapons, even if finally this in effect compels the conclusion that some weapon in and of itself is immoral. It is better, in short, to begin with the traditional immunity from direct killing surrounding noncombatants in the just-war theory, than with only the limitation of proportionate grave reason or lesser evil. The verdict about a single weapon may be the same from these two approaches; but the Christian in his conscience will know better where he is and why he is there in coming to a decision not willingly to engage in such a war, or such

[31] John Courtney Murray, *op. cit.*, p. 40. Cf. also Christopher Hollis, "The Two Pacifisms: The Old Case and the New," in *Morals and Missiles,* pp. 47-50.

use of a weapon in a war where, in his view, just means are also used.

The second approach will also make clear that the Christian still operates from the sound premise that all moral means may be mounted against an attack, no matter how greatly increased the force may have to be. This position is radically different from what deserves the name of "nuclear pacifism" today—a pacifism which, so to speak, is again on the offensive in response to the nuclear crisis, and which secretly may hope to win some theological battles at the same time, against recent theological "realism"[32] and on behalf of a, now proved, coincidence of a "pure" Gospel ethic of non-violent resistance with political prudence. "There is now no conflict," writes A. J. Muste, "between ethical sensitivity or Gospel obedience, on the one hand, and prudence on the other."[33] This statement is supported by citing "a prominent American theologian" who now agrees that unilateral scrapping of nuclear weapons would be "better policy *in terms of prudence*"; and this is said to "wipe out" the distinction between pacifists and non-pacifist Christians who feel they must be "politically responsible." The present writer cannot take responsibility for the fact that the theologian in question may have stated his position only in terms of "prudence," i.e., "lesser evil" or the balancing of evil and good effects, and not also in terms of the other clear and more primary principles of the just-war theory. Perhaps pacifism and prudential nonpacifism are now forced to say much the same thing upon the particular matter in question, but the spirit and the rationale behind each are greatly different. That theologian should, and probably did,

[32] Is there not too great a degree of theological animus in the recent article by Stewart Meacham, "Arms and Theological Responsibility," *The Christian Century*, Aug. 5, 1959, pp. 896-899?

[33] "Now Is the Appointed Time," *Fellowship*, July 1, 1959, p. 9 (in reply to the Provisional Study Document of the W. C. C.).

have in mind an analysis of the just war which, when he concludes from this that the main weapon today should be abandoned and never used, at one and the same time upholds the probable necessity of other warfare and therefore the *positive* moral obligation to make it morally possible.

Unfortunately, it may be true that apologists for the just-war doctrine today, especially in Protestant circles, have formulated their position too exclusively in terms of prudence. This is all that stands or falls by the argument advanced in a book that is still one of the best of Christian responses to the atomic crisis.[34] Professor Long distinguishes between a secular ethic, which is "calculative morality" or a "problem-solving ethic," and a religious-vocational ethic, which is an ethic of "obedience." He grants that in the past, and in principle whenever the situation permits this, a religious ethic of obedience contains an element of calculation; but there is this difference in *how* it is contained. "In a secular ethic calculation is *a reliance;* it is a means of 'saving the situation.' In a religious ethic calculation is *a service;* it is used to find the best means of implementing the demands of faith" and of obedience.[35] "The Christian finds that he must again balance claims; and calculation is now affirmed, not as a reliance, but as a means of service," when he faces the task of relating the ultimate demand of *agape* to the concrete needs of everyday experience.[36]

What has happened since the atom bomb burst upon the world is that "a religious ethic must rediscover obedience in a situation in which calculation becomes less and less possible."[37] Neither pacifism nor bellicism can afford any longer to be concerned primarily with historical success; neither can derive its choices backward from prudential consideration of

[34] Edward Leroy Long, Jr.: *The Christian Response to the Atomic Crisis.* Copyright, 1950, by W. L. Jenkins, The Westminster Press. Used by permission.
[35] *Ibid.,* pp. 62-63.   [36] *Ibid.,* p. 79.
[37] *Ibid.,* p. 64.

what will work or save the situation. "Neither pacifism nor nonpacifism, if either is suggested as a workable technique, is adequate to handle the situation created by weapons of great power." The real import of the bomb is not that pacifism is proved to be workable, nor even that nonpacifism is proved unworkable, but that any "horizontal and calculative approach to the problem of force" is now wholly inadequate.[38] "An ethic that would rely solely upon analysis of the given factors of a situation in deciding its course of action, and depend solely upon historical accomplishment for its vindication, does not make sense in an atomic age."[39]

What does this position demonstrate, on the assumption (which we are not concerned to question here) that its analysis is correct? It demonstrates that perhaps a largely prudential nonpacifism is today inadequate. It shows that the case for choosing war as the lesser evil has become exceedingly difficult to make. But actually the just-war theory never attempted that alone, not until the final point when proportionate grave reason in the several effects of military action were weighed as in a balance. Such counting of the cost was never very certain, nor was a nation believed to be in the position of guaranteeing the actual outcome simply by making these calculations, without which, of course, it could not proceed. Prudence might declare a war to be unjustified; but by itself it was never supposed to be able to justify it. Calculations that come up with no measure of good over evil results predicted cannot, of course, lead to "a service"; but this should control our deliberations only after we know what has to be served, and how morally this service may be undertaken (on the assumption for the moment that it may be effective).

At bottom, in the just-war theory there was demanded "an ethical choice that is based finally upon the intrinsic

[38] *Ibid.*, p. 67.
[39] *Ibid.*, p. 72.

nature of the act as judged by an ultimate frame of reference, rather than upon the overt effect of the act upon the immediate situation."[40] These, significantly, are the words with which Professor Long describes his own non-prudential pacifism to which he judges Christian prudential non-pacifists will be driven in the atomic era.[41] If instead they are driven to a restoration of the just-war theory, this will be so not because of miscalculation but precisely because of an ethic of obedience, in which calculation is only, but is required as, a service. The just-war theory will be restored because Christian love shapes itself for enactment in terms of certain principles of right or proper conduct, before ever calculating the consequences to see whether one effect justifies another. And if in doing this men are driven also to draw the line at the use of certain weapons, or at certain uses of all weapons, the reason will not be simply that the prudential ground on which they formerly depended has now been cut from under them by the force of modern weapons. Their views will in no sense be a "nuclear pacifism" or nuclear disarmament; but rather "rational nuclear armament," or at least "rational armament."

Professor Long, of course, is not alone accountable for how he opposes the doctrine of war he opposes. The fact is that in Protestant circles in recent years this is all we have clearly known and effectively said on the question. Since in one lump "killing" and the number killed was believed to be the thing to reconcile with Christian conscience and with the love-commandment, in case a total economic

---

[40] *Ibid.*, p. 73.

[41] "When two nations, both of which are atomically armed, are pitted against each other, a decision for or against the use of the bomb cannot be made on calculative grounds, since none of the historical alternatives is to be preferred over the other. When all considerations except those of ultimate religious obedience are eliminated, it seems that the ultimate principle of love would demand the pacifist position. This would be a pacifism rooted solely in a vocational reference, and seeking to justify itself neither as a workable scheme nor as a way to avoid the tragic ambiguities of life." *Ibid.*, pp. 81-82.

blockade of a nation was believed to be most effective, when in short this proposed action passed the test of prudence as a lesser evil, that was asserted to be the way to bring an enemy to heel and keep him there. Hit him in the belly, i.e., the civilian population as a whole, and shorten the war, i.e., the killing of combatants! Herbert Hoover was not enough to atone for that immorality. In other words, lacking any very firm moral distinction between killing "unjust aggressors" or the fighters and killing non-fighters, lacking the impulse to determine and control the means we intend to use for any end, and being fittingly modest about claiming justice to be wholly (or even, on balance, more) on one side, we have justified warfare largely in terms of assertedly "nice" but precarious predictions of good and evil consequences. What we are witnessing now is not, it is to be hoped, the substitution of one prudential judgment (pacifism) for another (nonpacifism), or the isolation or elevation of obedient action from any consideration of the service to be done, but a return to a proper location of the work of prudence, i.e., after a determination of the right military action, or if not *after*, then clearly *along with* judgment as to the intrinsic nature of the act proposed and its conformity or non-conformity with the nature of limited or justified warfare. This surely is the highest limit to be placed on war, not first in terms of weaponry but by keeping war subordinate to the ends-means of civil life. A symptom of what we have to recover from is the widespread opinion that rules for the immunity of noncombatants is only a detail added incidentally to the theory in the Middle Ages, a dispensable relic of the age of chivalry or of the pageantry wars of the eighteenth century; and that prudence will be sufficient to guide us in the conduct of war or the limitation of war. (To this, pacifists now seem to add that prudence added to obedience would be sufficient to eliminate war altogether, were it not for those people who want to make war morally possible again just when it has become impossible).[42]

That this is the active frontier in contemporary Christian thinking about war, in filling the vacuum in the moral doctrine of war, has been shown by many of the points of view we have examined. George Kennan is only the most distinguished in this line, most distinguished because most practiced in responsible statesmanship. In his book *Russia, the Atom, and the West,* published in 1957, Mr. Kennan

---

[42] This is to say, the Protestant nonpacifism which replaced Protestant pacifism, at least in the non-peace churches, as World War II approached, and which still prevails today, dwelt too exclusively on only one of the classical teachings, on the requirements of morality in war: the *modus debitus,* or the due proportion between the good to be defended and the evil permitted.

This is the place to indicate that the same looseness, pointed out above in Protestant statements, is beginning to appear also in the writings of Roman Catholics on the morality of war. In the recent Roman Catholic symposium, *Morality and Modern Warfare,* ed. Wm. J. Nagle, Baltimore: Helicon Press, 1960, Wm. V. O'Brien, in his chapter entitled "Nuclear Warfare and the Law of Nations" (pp. 126-149), misunderstands the terms prescribing the just conduct of war very much as does the Dun Report. He focuses on the details (pp. 134-138) without seeing that noncombatant immunity meant, and means, that *counter-forces* warfare alone is just. He gives *primacy* to the principle proportioning means to ends. This same centrality of prudence in determining proportionality is making possible today, exactly as in our present Protestant ethos, a prudential or "no greater evil" pacifism among Catholics instead of just-war conscientious objection. Still this significant difference should be noted: Catholic ethics is committed to some kind of *ethics of means* along with its morality proportioned to ends to a greater extent than is Protestantism. Thus, O'Brien knows very well that the *first* use of a weapon for mass destruction has nothing to do with the morality of the same conduct on the part of a nation in reprisal (p. 140). And the constructive statement of his own position includes the importance of examining with some independence the morality of the means proposed to be used. He justifies "the use of all means of war which bear a reasonable proportionality to a legitimate end"; he wants *legitimate* military necessity to be determined as well as the legitimate *goals* of any act of war (pp. 141-143). He is wrong, however, in believing that the *essence* of "legitimate military necessity" is proportionality—else it would be morally permissible for nations to inflict a *barely-intolerable* damage without distinction between counter-forces and counter-*people* warfare. In defining legitimate necessity in the use of military means, O'Brien will have to move again in the direction of criteria for the just conduct of war, or else he is bound, with the Dun Report, to move in the direction of endorsing any conduct that has "military decisiveness" in gaining the end of victory.

said that *if* all the future had to offer was that we must "resign ourselves entirely to the negative dynamics of the weapons race," he would be *tempted to* join those who say "let us divest ourselves of this weapon altogether, let us stake our safety on God's good grace and our own good consciences and on that measure of common sense and humanity which even our adversaries possess; but then let us at least walk like men, with our heads up, so long as we are permitted to walk at all." This characteristically eloquent statement is perhaps susceptible of being interpreted in terms of a prudential calculus of the relative values at stake. But in his address last year at Princeton Theological Seminary,[43] Kennan removed the hypothesis from before this conclusion, and at the same time he stated more clearly the real ground in morality for taking such a position. He affirmed unequivocally that the bombing of Hiroshima and Nagasaki, and the area bombing of World War II as well, went "farther than anything the Christian can accept." These military actions should never have been performed; and he adds, "I think it should be our aim to do nothing of the sort in any future military encounter." Why? "If we must defend our homes" we should do so "as well as we can in the direct sense"; but we ought never to take part in making "millions of women, children and non-combatants hostages for the behavior of their own governments." Then, only in the last place, does he reply to the crucial question whether this will "work."

It will be said to me: This means defeat. To this I can only reply: I am skeptical of the meaning of 'victory' and 'defeat' in their relation to modern [all-out] war between great countries. To my mind the defeat is [such unlimited] war itself. In any case it seems to me that there are times when we have no choice

[43] "Foreign Policy and Christian Conscience," *Atlantic Monthly*, CCIII, No. 5 (May, 1959), pp. 44-49.

but to follow the dictates of our conscience, to throw ourselves on God's mercy, and not ask too many questions.

If we may make the above bracketed insertions,[44] then it seems to me that Kennan's statements, taken together, are a concise summary of the principles of justified warfare, with the explicit inference drawn as to the warfare that would be entirely without justification, in no wise to be distinguished from the viewpoint, for example, of Fr. Ford.

It seems clear to me that this must be our conclusion as moralists, our finding as to the moral law, the moral limits, of warfare. The moralist, however, should take care how he advises, if he presumes to advise, statesmen and military leaders upon questions of application that involve matters of fact which, as moralist, he has no expert knowledge of nor responsibility for determining. After all, diplomats and commanders do not preach our sermons on Sunday morning; nor do we have charge of the defense of this nation over any weekend. Therefore, I say simply that any weapon whose every use must be for the purpose of directly killing noncombatants as a means of attaining some supposed good and incidentally hitting some military target is a weapon whose every use would be wholly immoral. I will also add that the manufacture and possession of a weapon whose every use is that just described, and the political employment of it for the sake of deterrence, is likewise immoral.

[44] The insertions are correct, unless by defending our homes in the "direct" sense Kennan meant only by hand-to-hand combat, and by never holding noncombatants hostage for their government's action he meant to hold them immune from being killed even as an indirect result of tactical bombing, or in the unlikely event that Kennan now believes that any war today or any war between great powers must be all-out nuclear war. In this article he expressly states that he is "unable to accept the view which condemns coercion in the international sphere but tolerates it within national borders." A personal letter from Mr. Kennan to the author confirms the foregoing interpretation. It is puzzling to me how an editorial in *Worldview*, June, 1959, p. 2, could couple Kennan, and a report of his address, with the remark "it is more and more agreed that the concept of 'just war' is an anachronism."

Seriously threatening to kill an innocent man for some good end, say, in order to compel him to take a Salk vaccination or to negotiate is, as means, the same as threatening to kill him for some evil end, say, to get him to hand over his pocketbook. At this point, the reader should be reminded of what was said earlier in this book about politics as an arena of "deferred repentance," along with the need for the clear enunciation of principles, such as those just stated. This, the moralist can only say, is the moral context of policy decision.

Findings of fact, however, may not be so clear. This difficulty was taken into account by the distinction, made by the Provisional Study Document of the W. C. C., between "all out" nuclear warfare and a possible use of such weapons in a more limited fashion (subject to the further limitation that even this should not be initiated first). I confess I find it difficult to imagine a limited use of hydrogen weapons, especially if smaller, even fractional kiloton atomic weapons would be just as destructive of legitimate military targets and less indirectly destructive of civil life. I think, therefore, that we have to say that megaton weapons would always destroy military objectives only incidental to the destruction of a whole area; and that in the very weapon itself, its use, its possession, or the threat to use it, warfare has passed beyond all reasonable or justifiable limits. But this is a question of weapon facts and of the military attack that has been mounted, or may be concentrated in a certain place. There may be politically prudent reasons for the unilateral or negotiated abandonment of this weapon anyway; but the *Grenzmorality* of its merely military possession and use depends on whether in fact, now or in the future, there are any conceivable circumstances in which it would have importance against military targets against which less powerful weapons would not serve as well. In the fluidity of historical events and changes in the concentration of political and military power perhaps this cannot be entirely ruled out as a possibility.

The Provisional Study Document does not rule it out, in its statement about a discipline that is able to possess yet not use nuclear power. This has been misunderstood by A. J. Muste as clinging to the belief that it is moral to possess weapons for their deterrent value, which, however it would be immoral ever to use.[45] Instead, the use that should unequivocally be renounced, in the opinion of this Commission, is "all out" use. If it had not held open the question whether there might not be a legitimate use (though not *first* use) of these weapons, in limited fashion, I do not see how their possession as such could be justified. I agree with Muste that there is intolerable contradiction between prohibiting any use and allowing possession (for deterrence or any other reason), but not between prohibiting all-out use or first use and allowing possession. "To have but not to use" was not the dilemma of the Christians on this Commission, as Muste supposes; but "to have and not to use all out." The latter is only an enormously difficult policy, that of limited war, even "for the time being"; while the former, if every use of the weapon is bound to be immoral, would be morally repulsive. The commission did not say this. What it said was that, allowing that not every possible use of megaton weapons would be necessarily immoral, a nation or group of nations need not announce in advance the precise point at which it will understand all-out use to begin and to be prohibited to itself. In other words, the Commission counts on a deterrent effect *in addition* to the use of force that may be intended or justifiable, i.e., from a quantity of force resolutely not intended to be used, or intended to be not used, or from uncertainty as to where

[45] "Now Is the Appointed Time," *Fellowship*, July 1, 1959, pp. 5, 6.

the point is beyond which a disciplined nation will not go. It seems to me that this may be questioned, on grounds both of morality and security; and it was so questioned, as we have seen, by members of the Commission itself.

But what this means is that it is difficult if not impossible to determine the exact nature of the force that is intended to be used and that intended to be not used; for a nation itself to know this, and not just for it to decide whether to announce the point or not. Not to announce would be deceit; and worse, for it is surely immoral even to leave standing an assumption that one may use immoral means. But not to know in advance is another matter. There is therefore everything to be gained from repeated announcement that it is the power of the military attack that we intend to destroy or force to withdraw, by every legitimate means and with the limitation, running through the use of all weapons we possess, that a whole people are not the object to be indiscriminately and violently repressed. If this means in fact that it is *certain* that specific weapons have to be expressly renounced, or particular uses unilaterally proscribed, then, it seems to me, a clear statement of this is also desirable. From an immoral, wholly irrational deterrent no deterrence worth having can come, for the simple reason that the "just" are more deterred from using such weapons, or from making such use of them, than the "unjust" are deterred from employing lesser, but still powerful, means to gain their ends by the practically non-existent danger that "we" will use them. What is the use of now devoting our energy to changing the balance of terror, or of defense against this open-ended terror and violence, in our favor, when we were rightly unwilling to use the monopoly we once had in atomic weapons—not only unwilling to use these weapons in actual fact but *therefore* unable to translate the sole possession of them into usable political power to attain limited goals in the cold war? Is it not the case that once the monumental bluff of the massive deterrent is called, the West, if it lacks sufficient conventional and small atomic weapons, would have no sane alternative but to accept a settlement on the enemy's terms? The Great Deterrent leaves us without a link between force and purpose. We needed then and need now some substitute for the kind of warfare that can in no sense be an extension of national policy; and this can only mean the creation of the possibility of limited applications of power. The more this is understood, the better. If this requires the designation of open cities, by agreement or unilaterally, and publication of specific policies as to the limited use of weapons, or the means we are willing to use in certain areas of the world to preserve stated interests, that is well; for an enemy cannot know what he really has to fear unless he also knows what he has not to fear, and (what is more important) we cannot translate power into policy without letting him know. He will probe anyway, and find out. In politics, there is perhaps some usefulness in bluffing about the weapons we may or may not possess, but very little usefulness in bluffing about what we intend or are willing to do with the weapons we are known to have. The risks involved in this are the risks of walking the earth as men who do not deny that they know the difference between murder and war, or between warfare that is justified and that which exceeds all limits. The risks are the risks of seeing to it that war, if it comes, will have some minimal national purpose connected with it. Nevertheless, the moralist as such cannot decide the whole question that must rest with the leaders of government, as to whether in fact it may sometimes be necessary to use a given weapon in circumstances which the moralist may not envision and which might then be brought under the tradition of civilized warfare of which the moralist has the duty to speak. Perhaps, then, the Commission of the World Council of Churches was wise in leaving rather open the conclusions they were able to reach. (I say this against my own "better judgment" in the matter of megaton weapons as such, or for that matter the upper ranges of kiloton weapons.)

There is one final question. Against a nation known to possess the H-bomb, and believed to be willing to use it all-out, would we be justified in mounting every reasonable and moral defense by limited means? By discrediting the all-out use of the ultimate weapons available today, have we not destroyed the moral basis for a nation's making any defense at all? While limited war may have been justifiable in the past, against an enemy who, whatever his intentions, had only limited means, has not the possession by even one side and his potential threat to make all-out use of megaton weapons rendered all defense immoral, on the grounds that it would be utterly useless? Since the preservation of desirable peace and order is the only justifying reason for the use of violence, would not self-defense by means of lesser weapons be *morally unjustifiable because impracticable?*[46] Does it not follow that the only right thing to do in these circumstances is to sue for peace on the enemy's terms?

It seems to me that an answer to this question is to be found in the fact that megaton weapons are no longer weapons *of war,* and that their all-out use would not be *war.* We have to find out whether the enemy wants to make *war* or not. We have to determine, upon a breakdown of negotiation and of attempts to compromise a conflict in which two nations both find themselves too vitally challenged to give in, and when there is to be resort to a trial of strength, whether this is to be the arbitrament of *arms* or not, in the course of which the will of one nation upon the issue in

[46] See above, p. 77.

question may be broken or both be compelled to accede to
a settlement they were unwilling to accept before making
trial for a better advantage. We have to find out whether
the appeal is to be to the *ultima ratio* of war or the *ultima
irratio* of immoral mutual devastation. In the past, it was,
of course, immoral for a nation to mount a defense which
it itself knew in advance to be useless. That meant, in advance, to know that the national purpose had to be altered
and a settlement sought. When it is complete devastation,
however, that is threatened, and not war, a nation still has
the right and the duty to make it clear that it is ready for
war, and mighty powerful war, if that is the weapon the
enemy chooses. In its quest for a connection between force
and national purpose, a nation need not face an imagined
state of affairs when it will have no national purpose as the
reason for now giving up every embodiment of national
purpose. In fact, no nation *can* do this. It is right that the
enemy be made to realize that he will have to exceed the
limits of warfare to gain his ends, that he will have to destroy utterly where he thought to conquer and to bend.
Then only will he be deterred from using a weapon that is
not a weapon of war. The enemy's political power depends
mainly on his possession and use of weapons *of war,* not on
his possession of weapons that exceed the purposes of war;
and clearly, our possession of the same non-military weapons
of destruction deters mainly ourselves from positive action.
To renounce this, and at the same time to mount the greatest force that may morally be used, would require the enemy
to ask himself the searching question whether there is any
point in gaining what can only be gained by power greater
than war.[47] To our surprise this may be a world in which

[47] I agree, therefore, in general with the conclusions Franziskus Stratmann reaches in the end, in his essay in *Morals and Missiles*, pp. 35-36. He
affirms that "atomic armament no longer consists of 'weapons' in the proper
sense of the word," and that "if the opponent should nevertheless start a

security and the power of making a moral defense are joined together by a cord not lightly broken; and one in which there is such a reality as the natural law of warfare which nations cannot fall below *or* exceed in the power they mount without ceasing to be nations with purpose.

The fact of the matter is that, eschewing pre-emptive war and conceding the first strike, the supposed deterrent effect of our great weapons lies in our second-strike capability alone, or in such capability as will remain after the first strike. Since this is known well enough to any potential enemy, and since our capability to deliver unacceptable damage to him after receiving the first strike is dubious indeed, wherein now lies the deterrence? Such deterrence may not actually be feasible, or rather it may work only because he too may deter mainly himself from the use of his own morally unshootable, because politically purposeless, weapons.[48] In any case, nothing in the present world situation can provide sufficient reason for altering radically the very meaning of *ratio* even in a nation's appeal to *ultima ratio* of war, least of all for Christians who have come to an understanding of what is reasonable and just in the conduct of war only from a love-transformed justice and a faith illuminated reason. To this they would tempt us whose moral premises are so thin as to lead logically to the verdict which justifies most of all that act of war which will be the most immoral, because the most stupid and politically purposeless, in the whole history of warfare, namely, the unleashing of counter-nuclear retaliation by means of push-buttons. This—the end result of

war, in my opinion uncontrollable atomic weapons may even then not be used in defense, because this means is bad in itself" and also because "the damage, including the moral damage, will be greater if atomic weapons are stock-piled and employed by *both* sides" than by one only. But then he affirms that "all means of legitimate defense must be employed."

[48] We will return to this question of deterrence, and the military analysis of weapons systems and their political consequences, in the two final chapters of this volume.

replacing the just war by the aggressor-defender war—is certainly a *dictamen irrationis* now passed off as military necessity. To press the button in counter-retaliation will also be the most unloving deed in the history of mankind, only exceeded by those who, for the sake of some concern of theirs, cause the little ones to stumble and fall into hell. I had rather be a pagan suckled in a creed outworn, terrified at the sight of hands made impure by any shedding of blood, than a skilful artisan of technical reason devising plans to carry out such a deed. I also doubt if any man not wholly dispossessed of humanity can actually purpose and will to do any such thing. Here is exposed to view the natural connection between power and purpose in political action which is at all human. Technology and reflex action may, however, "do" it anyway (if that can still be called "doing").

Chapter Eight

A THOUGHT-EXPERIMENT: CANNOT THE USE OF UNLIMITED MEANS OF WAR SOMETIMES BE JUSTIFIED?

This chapter is an experiment in thought, with finally a negative answer to the question it poses. First, I shall suggest, and argue for, a fundamental change in the use made of the rule of double effect, of the principle that one may never do "wrong" that good may come of it, and of fixed natural-law means as these principles have come to be understood in Roman Catholic moral theology; and then ask whether this affords us any escape from the limitation that prohibits direct killing of noncombatants in war.

To lay the ground for this exploratory question, it is necessary to take up again the use of double effect in the conflict between rights to life in the case of two individual human beings, in such issues of medical practice as pregnancy in which the life of both mother and child are in peril. In case of a conflict of one life with another life as yet unborn[1] the problem cannot be solved by treating the child as no more than a part of the woman's body, to be excised on the principle of the whole, or the principle that a

---

[1] I grant for the sake of the argument that a fetus from the time it is animate and before it is viable should be regarded as a human being and should properly be referred to as "he" even if it is not yet possible to address "him" as a "Thou." It should also be stated that the question whether the fetus is a living soul from the moment of conception and before animation may still be debated among Roman Catholics.

part may be sacrificed for the sake of the health and welfare of the whole body. Instead, these cases are "solved" by Roman Catholic moral theologians in terms of "indirect" killing, which is permitted according to the rule of double effect. In the case of a pregnant *cancerous* uterus, for example, the diseased organ may be excised, for the sake of the whole, even though it is certainly known that this operation will unavoidably cause the death of the child as a secondary effect.

The case of ectopic or tubal pregnancy is more difficult, but this, too, has been solved according to widely accepted opinion. The difficulty lies in the fact that, even if it may be said that there was some prior minor abnormality in the tube itself, this would not be a pathological condition of the organ grave enough to require its removal if the woman had not become pregnant in this way. The danger to her life comes from the pregnancy itself, it would seem, and not from disease in her own body. Nevertheless, Bouscaren is able to show that even though the fetus lodged in the tube originally caused the impairment of the tube, the present and proximate cause of the danger to the mother's life is in the condition of the tube itself. The pathology of the tube is now *"entitatively distinct"* from the present and future growth of the child.[2] Because of the intervention of the (now) impaired organ between mother and child, the conflict between their rights to life, which are equal, is not so direct as to make it impossible to act to save the life of the only one who can be saved in such a case as this. In intention and in fact an ectopic operation *"stops hemorrhage."*[3] These operations can, therefore, be brought under the rule of double effect, which permits an action done directly and intended directly to save the mother, but which

[2] *Ethics of Ectopic Operations* (Milwaukee: Bruce Publishing Co.; 2nd ed., 1944), p. 14, *et passim*.
[3] *Ibid.*, p. 151.

also is foreknown to be certain to cause the death of the child as a secondary effect.

In determining the proportionately grave reason still required to make even indirect killing licit, it should be remembered that one right to life is not to be measured against the right of another (which, even so, would leave the decision in balance); but instead one ought to weigh "the actual probability of saving one life against the actual probability of saving the other."

In view of the fact that the chances of the fetus to survive to viability if the operation is deferred are extremely meager in *early unruptured cases* of ectopic pregnancy, it would seem that a *notably greater probability of saving the mother's life by the present excision of the tube* constitutes a proportionately grave reason for the operation.[4]

Here in the end there comes in the prudent calculation which Protestant ethics generally regards as the dominant or only consideration in cases such as these.

This brings us to cases of the conflict of life with life in which present-day Roman Catholic moral theology finds it impossible to apply the rule of double effect so as to make merciful action morally possible. One such instance is the case of secondary abdominal pregnancy after the rupture of the tube in tubal pregnancy. This is a very rare termination of ectopic gestation, itself comparatively infrequent, in which after rupture the fetus passes from the tube out into the abdominal cavity where it continues to grow, seriously endangering the life of the mother before reaching viability and with little or no chance of itself surviving until it is viable. Here we have a clear case of life against

---

[4] *Ibid.*, p. 159. To this may be added another motive in favor of the operation: "the greater chances of conferring valid baptism on the child," although the fetus may *not* be extracted *in order to* baptize him, since that would be direct in intention, and one may not do wrong even for the sake of supernatural good. See pp. 157-158.

life, each with rights granted to be equal to the other. Can a choice be made, and a "modest defense" be undertaken of one at the cost of the other?

In this instance Bouscaren is compelled to take in effect the "severe view" he rejected in cases of tubal pregnancy where a disintegrated organ, belonging to the mother, and subject to direct action, intervened between the two lives that are at stake and in conflict with each other. "Where, in this case, is the dangerous organ, which must be the *direct object of the operation?*" There is no organ, no designatable part of the body of the mother, to which the placenta has attached itself and which as a danger is "entitatively distinct" from the pregnancy itself, i.e., the fetus himself. An operation may not be performed which in effect detaches the placenta (which belongs to the child) simply in order to avoid danger to the mother when and if the placenta is detached and hemorrhage occurs.

If the operation is performed before viability, it is difficult to escape the conclusion that its purpose and object is to detach the placenta now in order to have a better opportunity to take care of the hemorrhage. But to detach the placenta directly is direct abortion.... We do not see how we could justify the excision of a secondary abdominal pregnancy, except in the very crisis of the detachment of the placenta, where intervention is necessary to stop present hemorrhage.... We must wait until the child is viable (at least with the aid of the most modern incubator methods) or until the crisis of dangerous hemorrhage makes intervention necessary, in which case the removal of the fetus is incidental and indirect.[5]

This very unusual case may stand for the many, more usual cases of normal uterine pregnancy in which medical opinion may be that there is no chance of saving either mother or child without an operation that directly kills the

---

[5] *Ibid.*, p. 165. This is a severer view (1944) than that taken in the first edition (1933) or in the original dissertation (1928).

child. I do not say there is absolutely *no* possibility of saving both in secondary abdominal pregnancy in general (in exceedingly rare instances, these have been brought successfully to term), nor that there is *no* possibility of saving both lives in a specific *type* of circumstance that may develop in normal pregnancy. I do not say, e.g., that a woman with a certain heart condition may never bear a child until he is viable. Nor certainly do I mean to suggest that every effort should not be made to save both. Nor, finally, do I mean to suggest that there is not something of immense moral significance in the distinction between direct and indirect killing, or that the application of this principle should cease to be used to the utmost possibility of its application to cases. I suggest only that there are *individual* cases that go beyond it; not, I repeat, that there are *types* of cases where statistical certainty of death to both can be proved; but that in a given instance the choice may have to be made between saving one by direct action upon the other or allowing both to die. Even if there were demonstrably no instances of this sort, we would have to suppose one in order to see, in a thought-experiment, the ingredient that is lacking in Roman Catholic moral theology. The case supposed assumes only that in some circumstances a physician, taking into account the woman's condition in its entirety and in every detail, may judge it to be quite impossible for him, *in this given instance,* to save both lives, that action must be taken before the fetus becomes viable, that the action which can be taken can find no intervening organ of the mother's to remove, that it is the mother's whole life, and not this by way of the disintegration of a specific organ, which is under attack by the fetus simply by its trying to be born and that in this he cannot succeed, that prompt direct action must be taken else both will die, or finally that even after the time of viability there is believed to be a forced choice between one or none and the mother can be saved only by means of the death of the child who is going to die anyway.

This has only to be reasonable and conscientously *believed* to be the choice for us to have our problem of determining the subjectively responsible action to be taken. Catholic moralists say that ever to take direct action against the fetus, even when it cannot possibly be saved (or is believed to be impossible to save), would be wrong, and never justified by the good of saving the life of the mother. It would be better for both to die than for an intrinsically wrong means, murder in fact, to be used. While it may be agreed that, so long as there is a possibility of saving the child, this limits what may be done for the mother, I suggest that it would be *wrong*, and not only exceedingly regrettable and a suffering to be referred to the providence of God, for a physician to stand by and, by failing to take indirect or, if need be, direct action, for him to allow both to die.

What is the chief issue here? It is too weak for Protestants to say only that prudence or a more flexible practical wisdom should be allowed to govern and to override the conclusions of a static ethics of natural law. What we have to say is that Catholic moral theology, especially in its consideration of cases, fails to allow divine charity any vital role in the matter of morality. As Bouscaren observes: "... what the Natural Law commands in God's name is not merely the attainment of certain ends, but the *observance of the order of nature as a means to their attainment.*"[6] The determination of these natural-law means, which are always the only intrinsically right means ever to be used, becomes then the consideration overriding in its importance in implementing the principle that it is never right to do wrong for any end whatsoever. One way to attack this viewpoint

[6] *Ibid.,* p. 30.

is to make frontal objection to the natural law as such, and this is the way usually taken by Protestants, who succeed thereby in arriving at no other result than that they simply become less rigorous in thinking out the implications of the ingredients of the natural law that insist on remaining in force in their own thinking. Prudence and contextualism become excuses for lack of disciplined analysis. The other way is to join to the full in the enterprise of searching for the meaning of the natural law, but without making the error of supposing that, even if this may be finally and certainly known, and correctly applied in a given case, it constitutes the only or the main source of moral judgments in Christian ethics. Thus will theoretical reflection about right and wrong in concrete cases be kept open to the impact and guidance of Christian love, rather than smothering the requirements of love under what "nature itself teaches."

The Word of God is not bound, neither is charity a cripple, or an exile from the domain of fundamental ethical decision. In the doctrine of Christian virtue, Roman Catholic moral theology knows this well enough, whether this be expressed in Augustinian terms as the total substantive transformation, conversion, redirection, and renewal of the formal, natural virtues of moral character, or in Thomistic terms as the perfection and elevation of the natural virtues by infused charity, which in turn infuses moral virtues bending the natural ones more in a Christian direction, to the end that, in the gifts, fruits, and beatitudes, the whole character of man shall be devoted only to his supernatural end. It is regrettable that nothing comparable to this is allowed to take place in the treatment of cases and analysis of actions to be done in Roman Catholic moral theology, and indeed that this is programatically excluded by the subordination of the ends of charity to natural-law means.

For fear that the sway of love of God and one's neighbor in God will introduce unruliness and antinomianism, the determination of permitted and prohibited actions is given over entirely to the natural or rational moral law, which seems completely closed off from the impact of charity upon its decisions.[7]

Instead, we must say that as there is a prudence or practical wisdom in making application of the principles of natural justice so also there is a prudence or practical wisdom which applies charity to every case of action deserving of the name Christian. At the point of decision in a concrete case there takes place a convergence of judgments guided in these ways, a convergence in which sometimes love does what justice requires and assumes its rules as norms, sometimes love does more than justice requires but never less, and sometimes love acts in a quite different way from what justice alone can enable us to discern to be right. When one's own interests alone are at stake, the Christian governs himself by love and resists not one who is evil. When his neighbor's need and the just order of society are at stake, the Christian still governs himself by love and suffers no injustice to be done nor the order necessary to earthly life to be injured. He governs himself by love and develops the theory of justified war as a reflection of the action which he judges is demanded of him. In this, and in private cases of conflict of life with life, he governs himself by love and develops the rule of double effect, and the distinction between direct and indirect killing, as logical and necessary limits of action that is permitted and sometimes required

----

[7] In this sense, and so far, one must welcome the statement of Fr. Franziskus Stratmann that "particularly in the moral teaching on war—the Gospel notions of love, of suffering wrong, of brotherly concord with all people and all nations, these largely retired before the single principle of natural law: the right is to be defended and wrong punished" (*Morals and Missiles*, p. 20, cf. p. 30).

by a love-informed justice. In all this he goes into action in ways which he would not be so free to adopt, or so strictly bound to adopt, if he were ruled only by a purely natural justice. In all these ways he yet finds in love's guidance, it is true, powerful support for rational and limiting rules of conduct. But it follows from the motive from which he has proceeded to do all this, and the light in which he has walked amid these dire necessities, that, still governing himself by love and never believing himself to have been finally justified by the moral reason he nevertheless exercised, he can do differently and indeed contrary to the behavior that alone seems licit in terms of a system of natural justice when such an action seems unavoidably required of him to save life. One thing charity will never allow him to do: namely, to stand by idle while two of the companions God has given him inevitably die from "natural" causes or processes when one might have been saved had he been willing to soil his hands by performing an action which, according to his view of natural-law means, was defined as wrong. Perhaps we should not say that for the sake of the end supremely demanded by charity it is sometimes right to do wrong that good may come of it, nor even say that *this* end justifies (not in *every*, but) in *this* case (not *any*, but) *this* necessary means. For the fact is that, in the view here proposed, charity enters into a fresh determination of what is right in the given concrete context, and it is not wholly in bondage to natural-law determination of permitted or prohibited means. These rules are opened for review and radical revision in the instant *agape* controls; this was, indeed, what all along drove the Christian to the very act of devising them, and to employ them for centuries not as a reliance but as a service.

It is a fact of the greatest significance that, before the

Holy Office spoke[8] and foreclosed debate on the subject among Roman Catholics, many of their moralists were seeking, and by seeking finding, in nature itself sufficient ground for merciful action in the crucial cases we are now considering of incurable conflict between life and life and for which the rule of double effect provides no escape.

Avenzini argued,[9] for example, that since the child in the case supposed must die anyway, God has not placed in him an operative right to life, but only the right to choose in what manner he shall die. But no one should exercise such a choice to the detriment of another's life, especially not his mother's. Since the choice on the part of the fetus to wait and die within the womb, rather than to die by excision from the womb, would necessarily entail his mother's death, the child has no right to choose this. Therefore, contructively and impliedly he chooses aright, and the operation may be performed.

Before 1898 Lehmkuhl argued that (1) if the inherence of the fetus in the womb is regarded as a good *extrinsic* to him, though necessary, then he can renounce his right to it in favor of his mother's life, just as when two men shipwrecked are clinging to a plank one may slip off into the water soon to drown or a mountain climber dangling from a rope that holds him to a partner above may, to save his partner's life, cut himself loose; and especially if by renouncing his inherence in the womb (which does not increase one bit the certainty of his own death) his risk of

---

[8] May 4, 1898, and May 5, 1902, declaring that operations which attack the adherence of the fetus to the womb or separating the placenta are still direct attacks upon the fetus himself, the same as craniotomy; and that not even the ectopic fetus may be killed as a materially unjust aggressor (applying to this instance the ruling of May 28, 1884, that in no case may a uterine fetus be regarded as a materially unjust aggressor).

[9] The following summary, taken from T. Lincoln Bouscaren, *op. cit.*, pp. 6, 15-16, 13-20, 53-54, is his account of positions taken in the vigorous debate that was going on near the end of the nineteenth century, some of it in articles that appeared in *The Ecclesiastical Review* during 1893.

dying without valid baptism is lessened. On the other hand, (2) even if inherence in the womb belongs *intrinsically* to the fetus, it seems vital and to belong also with equal justice to the mother. Not their equal right to life but their equal right to this on which life depends becomes less certain, just as a man's right to the common air they breathe in a case where this is not sufficient both for him and for a guest. Therefore, abortion which attacks the fetus' inherence in the womb or separates the placenta was, he said, essentially different from a direct attack upon the fetus itself by craniotomy.

"The Holy Office, however, thought otherwise," in holding that an attack upon an element vital to the fetus is no less a direct killing of the child. Whereupon Lehmkuhl was led to see the speciousness of his former line of reasoning. "To tear asunder violently the membranes and tissues which connect the fetus to the womb of the mother, is nothing else than to inflict a fatal wound upon him," like—if this were possible—withdrawing or extracting from him the necessary air he has already breathed in order to place it at the disposal of another. Like cutting a rope that belongs essentially to another man's life, even though mine is inextricably bound in by this with his, this would be the same as bashing in his head.

Sabetti, who believed that all operations for the removal of an inviable fetus from a pregnant tube were directly death-dealing, yet held them licit when, in ectopic pregnancy, there was deadly danger to the mother, on the ground that the fetus might be regarded as an unjust aggressor, at least materially. Lehmkuhl denied this, but held that excising a pregnant tube was not directly death-dealing, and therefore permissible when a fatal rupture was imminent and could be averted by no other means. In dealing with

this case Lehmkuhl harked back to the opinions he had renounced concerning therapeutic uterine abortion. He
would, at this point in the church's teaching, not have said
this apart from the principle of double effect applicable in
the case of tubal pregnancy where an organ of the mother
(and not just an element belonging to the fetus) intervenes
between the two lives in conflict and in mutual peril; but
in addition to this he said: "It is lawful for the fetus to deprive himself of a vital element, or, since he is as yet incapable of actual volition, it is lawful for another acting for
him in accord with his interpretative volition, to deprive
the fetus of a vital element, in order that the mother may
be saved and that the child himself may have a chance of
baptism. I said it lawful for him to *deprive himself,* and
not *to be deprived....*"

Instead of rejecting all this because it foolishly assumes
an act of choice (even if only constructively) on the part of
an inviable fetus, it is better to see here the free operation
of a concept of nature transformed by grace, of reason perfected and directed by charity. The fetus is not only a man,
with a right to life, but something of a Christian man who
would not willingly exercise this right to the detriment
of another, at least not when this abstract right is of no
advantage to him. The natural man himself is presumed
not properly to be willing to do such an unmerciful thing
as to bring about the death both of himself and another
when there is a means, and in his own death the only means,
of avoiding this result. And all this to the end of establish-
ing that no responsible person should stand by and see this
result occur without taking the action necessary to save
life. Indeed, we should assume that *if* a fetus is capable
of bearing rights he is also capable of exercising them in a
charitable manner; and at the least this means that his own

right to life should not be held on to in vain, to the detriment of that of another.

Contemporary Roman Catholic teaching, however, has perfected the solution afforded by the rule of double effect in those cases to which it can be applied, and at the same time closed off the moral possibility of taking action in those cases of conflict of life with life, where both will die, to which it cannot be applied—a possibility which was significantly emerging in some of the opinions we have reviewed. In these, charity, which first produced the rule of double effect and should continue to learn as much as is merciful from its direction, was proving itself the master and not the slave of this rule. In contemporary moral theology, too often the rule by itself suffices to determine what is right or wrong action. This is a function not of the necessarily rigid and impervious character of an ethic of natural law, but of the "republication" of this for its supposed inculcation and preservation in positive ecclesiastical law.

Thus Bouscaren rejects appeal to the consent of the fetus as either entirely inefficacious or entirely unnecessary. If the unavoidable killing is indirect, his consent is unnecessary; while if it is direct, his charitable consent avails nothing, for "the child is certainly no more master of his life than is any other human individual; and no human being can make the direct killing of himself licit by consenting to it."[10] In reply to the argument: "Between two evils, one should choose the lesser. Now the death of one person is evidently a lesser evil than the death of two. Therefore it not only may but ought to be chosen," Bouscaren says that "the answer to this sophism is of course that the death of one person *intended and produced directly by violation of the moral law* is not a lesser evil than the death of two from natural causes without any dereliction of duty on the

[10] *Ibid.*, p. 54.

part of anyone."[11]   This is the fashion in which the prohibition of suicide or murder, the determination in general of natural-law means and the dominion of the rule of double effect have come to ascendancy in a closed system of ethics. These principles—so understood—supply the substantive or material understanding of the principle—not in itself formally incorrect—that one should never do wrong that good may come of it, not even that charity may serve her ends. This is evident, for example, not only from the foregoing, but also in the tardiness with which Catholic thought has moved from justifying "mutilation" only for the sake of the whole health of one's own body to permitting organic transplantations for the sake of a neighbor. The reason for this should be amply appreciated. Indeed, it is not so evident that as a matter of natural justice I, a parent, should make the decision to have a kidney transplanted from the body of one of my non-identical twins to the other, even after they are eight or ten years old and able in some slight measure to understand and make the sacrifice and the benefit their own. This, too, is to treat human nature as if

---

[11] *Ibid.*, p. 55. A remark should be appended here concerning Bouscaren's treatment of medical abortion *before the fetus is animate* and when there is question whether it is yet a "he." This author does not appeal to the remaining doubt or to the probabilities in order to reduce cases of this sort in practice to violations of the commandment "Thou shalt not kill"; but instead he regards such abortion as "gravely sinful" in violation of the commandment "Thou shalt not commit adultery," i.e., an unnatural interference with the process of conception and birth. In other words, abortion before animation should be classed with contraception, self-abuse, and onanism as unnatural acts in violation of the right order of the entire generative faculty. "Although that material [the fetus] is not yet a man, and can as yet have no rights, yet God has rights in it, just as He will later have rights over the human life which will be formed from it" (*ibid.*, pp. 38-41). Since God has not yet given the fetus in and of itself a right to life, there is not yet a parity with its mother's right to life; and, in the cases we are dealing with, even if it lives until animation, its right to life will be utterly useless. Then surely charity should be able to discern and to perform the action that will save life; and it would do this but for the fact that it is prevented from doing the work of love by the binding requirement that observance of the order of nature exhaustively determines the means to the attainment of any end.

it should prove merciful; and, on the assumption that the fetus is a man alive, to venture an even more extreme action on his behalf would, indeed, be a grave responsibility. This is why I think Roman Catholic moral theology is mainly correct in its principles and precautions there where it deals with problems of a conflict of life with life. Therefore, I have suggested a significant alteration only in cases where none of these love-produced rules can be made to apply and where charity plainly requires that something be done.

This is, however, a significant change, the freedom of *agape* and of prudence based on it, apt to make its presence felt throughout the scale and not alone in the cases we have considered. From this it certainly follows that, just as long ago in the tradition we have traced love gave up the attempt to justify the necessary killing of an unjust aggressor as "indirect" or unintended and simply resolved to do what love prudently applied requires in the defense of justice, it should likewise give up the attempt to justify self-sacrifice of life as "indirect" or unintended killing. It is just as difficult in taking one's own life to see to it that this is *done* indirectly as well as intended indirectly, as in the case of killing an unjust aggressor to do and intend that indirectly. When a general captured in war swallows the suicide pill with which he was provisioned in order to save his secrets from extraction by torture and to help his cause and save his comrades, it is better analysis simply to say that this is not the *prohibited* suicide, or even that it is not *suicide*. It is, therefore, worth repeating here that what I have suggested means a fresh determination of what is right in a given context in which the requirements of love prevail, and that right should not be determined by the natural law alone. It is better to save life than to allow to die, even on the Sabbath day or in the face of rules that in very many instances helped and do still help to show love what should be done. By this end, the absolutely supreme end of *agape,* not every means, not even every indispensible means, is justified, but surely every means to save life the only alternative to which is that death will even more abound. To make this choice, on behalf of life and against death and inaction, is not to do wrong but to do what we know to be right in order that good may come of it.

Now, in mortal combat between nations, when to repel injury it is judged necessary and highly important for the civilized life of mankind to have recourse to arms, it may be that life is pitted against life, one cause or nation against another, in such direct engagement and with so forced a decision between them that practical wisdom and the ends of justice may require that the traditional immunity of the enemy's civilian population from direct attack be ignored. Of course, if the destruction of military targets that are "entitatively distinct" from the total life of the nation, if the pathology itself—the enemy government, military concentrations, and munitions centers—may be directly the object of attack, and if we may intend and do directly *upon them* our successful resistance to aggression, this should by all means be the rule for the conduct of war, with the killing of however many noncombatants only permitted. But may not there be times when it is proper to exclaim: "Where, in this case, is the dangerous organ, which must be the direct object of the operation?" Do not the whole enemy people so effectively challenge the peace and order of the world, in their thousand-year Reich that is striving to be born, that nothing intervenes between their life and ours, between their justice and ours, by repressing which it would be possible to mount a modest and limited defense and yet one that is proportionate to the evil that would result from their victory?

In posing this question, I ask that two suppositions be granted: that as a matter of military fact it was impossible to defeat the Nazi power without area bombing (this first assumption may well not have been true, and I personally doubt it and therefore believe that the immorality of indiscriminate bombing was in no sense necessary to attain the desired and desirable end of victory), and that the successful prosecution of World War II was in the end just. On the second point we must at least say, in the words of John Cogley, that, while the pacifists may have been right then in their belief that the evil involved in crushing Nazism actually weighed more heavily on the moral scale than the evil an unchecked Nazism would have led to, "most of us are not convinced of this and believe that the world, for all its present woes, is still better off than it would be if Nazism were not crushed";[12] and this opinion, searchingly and conscientiously held, is all that was required subjectively to justify the act of taking up arms against them. On the first point, it is not possible to demonstrate beyond all doubt that the military facts were not such as to require for victory the policy of area bombing; and even if this were demonstrated for that time it still could not be taken to be a universal description of the fact-situation in every possible case of warfare, now and in the future. We must simply suppose a case in which indiscriminate bombing is in fact indispensable to victory over a great evil, and ask what, then, should be judged to be lawful.

Therefore, I ask whether the proposal made above, as to what may morally be done to save life beyond the point to which the rule of double effect can be extended and applied, may not be used to justify obliteration bombing. Cannot prudence, in implementing both charity and the principles of justice, and in the face of the enormously evil

[12] "A World Without War," *Worldview,* June, 1959, p. 7.

consequences of a Nazi victory, carry through a complete revision of the means that are permitted to be used in just war? Should we not weigh, not life against life, or right against right, but the actual probability of saving life against the right of those we would deprive of life, and act on the basis of a notably greater probability of saving for millions a decent order of life for years to come by means of area bombing now? May it not be justified to hold hundreds of thousands of men, women, and children who are not in any sense fighters hostage for the action of their government, and may not the decision to do so be derived backward from balancing prudentially one set of predicted consequences against another? I do not wish to fail in appreciation for the integrity of Christian conscience of those whose judgment has been that the church's doctrine of war must now simply consist in decision as to the greater or lesser evil. They have a strong case for the belief that the only relevant action the Christian can put forth in the world will be action which cleaves tumultuous waters with only this sort of knife. But a negative answer seems to me the correct one to give to this question, and for reasons that should be obvious. Charitable action should be free and sovereign over its own limiting self-direction prohibiting the direct killing of the innocent only when the innocent are soon going to die anyway and where this is certain to save life. Neither of these conditions holds true in warfare: those innocent ones are not necessarily and inexorably going to die simply by continuing to do what comes naturally as participants in their little private affairs and in the larger civil life of their nation, nor can the architects of a policy of indiscriminate bombing have the surgical control to know that they are going on balance to save life. Almost the reverse is now the case in modern war: *both* will die if the immunity of the innocent from direct, wholesale attack is ever breached again in a major war. Any other answer to this question amounts, in fact, to a reduction of people to the position of parts of a totalitarian whole in which they and their government and its military power are not allowed to be in any sense "entitatively distinct." This would be to treat the entire population of a nation as if they—men, women, children, the sick, the helpless, and the barbers—all live to the whole extent of their beings in one unelevated earthly city. Even if they so understand themselves, a Christian as such can never agree with them, or act as if he did. Here Bouscaren's words are the truth: the answer to this sophism is that the death of one person intended and produced directly in violation of love's requirement of the saving of life and in violation of the moral law is not a lesser evil than the death of two, or of many more, without any dereliction of duty in their defense. It was therefore not an emotional reaction alone, nor British atomic neutralism, but the heart and soul of the doctrine of limited war, expressed by Philip Toynbee when he wrote: "It would be wicked and pointless to launch a nuclear attack on Russia *before* we have ourselves been attacked. Wicked for obvious reasons; pointless because we would get back a great deal more than we were able to give. It would be wicked and pointless to launch a nuclear attack on Russia *after* we had ourselves been attacked. Wicked for obvious reasons; pointless because we would not longer have anything to gain by it. . . . There are therefore no circumstances in which we could use these weapons without behaving both wickedly and insanely."[13]

In this chapter we have posed in all seriousness the question: Is there any way of escape from the criterion that the just conduct of war requires that power be mounted against

[13] *The Fearful Choice* (Detroit: Wayne State University Press, 1959), p. 14.

the attacking force (wherever it may be found) and not directly against populations? There do seem to be instances of the conflict of life with life in which Christian love, in view of the future consequences (the greater good or lesser evil), *should* not be bound by the prohibition of the direct killing of the innocent. The case of international armed conflict, however, is by no means similar. Here, an ethic of Christian love has no alternative but to renew and recreate its own articulation in the rule or principle which surrounds noncombatants with immunity from direct killing. If there is any reader still with me who is seriously allergic to Roman Catholic moral theology, I ask him to notice especially the mode of moral reasoning employed in this chapter. Christian love, which often acts within the law and lays down rules or principles for the guidance of action, still continues to exert a free and sovereign pressure —since Jesus Christ is Lord—toward fresh determination of what should be done in situations not rightly covered by the law, by natural justice, or even by its own former articulation in principle. This should the more be noted, since the argument of this chapter reaches the conclusion that, in determining justifiable and unjustifiable warfare, the work of love will be to return ever again to the prohibition of the direct killing of any person not directly or closely co-operating in the force that should be repelled. The just-war theory, in both its aspects, requiring the use of force and limiting the use of force, is nothing more than an application of the supreme standard for Christian living as this is received in Protestant Christianity, namely, "Everything is quite lawful, *absolutely everything* is permitted which love permits, everything without a single exception. . . . *Absolutely everything* is commanded which love requires, absolutely everything without the slightest exception or

softening."[14]   Therefore, the Christian is permitted to use
force, nay, even positively obliged to do so; and he is at the
same time required to limit the use of it, nay, his faith permits him to limit it in situations where men are hard pressed
to do wrong, vainly imagining that in this, God's world,
some good may come of it.

[14] See my *Basic Christian Ethics* (New York: Chas. Scribner's sons, 1950),
p. 89 *et passim*.

Chapter Nine

THE POLITICS OF FEAR, OR THE END IS NOT YET

One of the unfortunate results of the reduction of Christian ethics to a teleological morality based on consequences (rather than a morality of right, present action) is that, when among the "ends" of action appears the possible destruction of human life on this planet, policy decisions come to be based on dread of this consequence alone. It is well to remember that thermonuclear destruction is not the *eschaton* toward which Christians live.

In his reply to Philip Toynbee's passionate plea that capitulation now would be better than mutual nuclear destruction, printed along with others in *The Fearful Choice*, the Archbishop of Canterbury stated that "for all I know it is within the providence of God that the human race should destroy itself in this manner. There is no evidence that the human race is to last for ever and plenty of Scripture to the contrary effect."[1] This apparently unfeeling statement produced such a minor uproar that the Archbishop attempted an explanation.[2] Apart from invoking a dubious and characteristic Anglican distinction between the foreknowledge of God and his predetermination of such an event, the Most Reverend Geoffrey Fisher wrote, ". . . as Mr. Toynbee

---

[1] Philip Toynbee: *The Fearful Choice* (Detroit: Wayne State University Press, 1959), p. 43.
[2] "Not by Dread Alone," *Frontier*, Oct., 1958, reprinted in part, *Worldview*, Nov. 1958, p. 8.

brought the human race in more than once, I thought it well to suggest in a sentence or two that fear for the human race was no ground on which to base policy." This was to say in effect: "You need not trouble yourself as to whether or when or how the human race will come to an end. There is no evidence that it will last forever. There is reason for thinking that it will come to an end. Neither you nor I can tell whether in the providence of God it will end by the effect of nuclear war or by some other means or not at all. So don't base your policies on fears about the extinction of the human race."

In one way, Fisher's reply was to the point. If the "end of the world," or of human history as we know it, twenty-four hours from now has the power to render meaningless all human action up to that point, so does the end that will come two billion years from now by the world's energy petering out or by some cosmic collision. The possibility of total nuclear destruction, by shortening the time during which this planet may still be inhabited or fit for human habitation, has only strengthened or excited the imagination and made it possible, indeed necessary, to conceive of an ending of the whole human story. But it has not made it a bit more certain. This was of itself conceivable before, indeed known to be bound to happen. People who before were not able to draw correct inferences from this fact should not now be advised to do so simply by the heightened power their imaginations have received. If there was no point in cherishing a friendship or reading Plato or the Bible while roasting the last potato over the last dying ember of a universe run-down, and therefore no point in all the efforts and experiences that went before, there is of course no point now in any of the things we do or feel or know that is not fundamentally threatened by nuclear destruction, and all policy has despairingly to be determined in sole

reference to dread of the end. But we should have had sufficient intellectual powers to know this all along, since philos-
ophers of enlightened one-world views of human destiny
began systematically to darken the human horizon of all
reference to transcendence. What, for example, are we to
make of Hannah Arendt's statement that with the appear-
ance of atomic weapons all appeals for the limitation of warfare and all appeals to courage have become totally meaningless, when we observe that the situation which places "in
jeopardy the very value of courage itself" is just that there
may be no more people to come after us? "Man can be
courageous only so long as he knows he is survived by those
who are like him, that he fulfills a role in something more
permanent than himself. . . . Or, to put it another way,
while there certainly are conditions under which individual
life is not worth having, the same cannot be true for mankind. The moment war can even conceivably threaten the
continued existence of mankind on earth, the alternative
between liberty and death has lost its old plausibility."[3] To
find a man's *telos* in mankind, and mankind's *telos* in the
continual existence of mankind, was all along to find his
telos seriously threatened by his certain *finis*. How long
away in time the end may be makes no essential difference.
If my courage and devotion find their justification only in
reference to those who survive who are like me, and this is
the meaning of my role in relation to something more permanent than myself, then I must ask how permanent are
they, and so on through the generations until we come to
the last man with that last potato, only to discover that the
last link in the chain on which the whole meaning of my
existence depended is grounded in nothing. What has happened today is that absentmindedness about this has now
been shocked into taking thought. The answer to this is

[3] Quoted in *Worldview* editorial, Sept., 1958, p. 1.

to say that no such view was ever true or was ever the meaning of Christian eschatology.[4]

Yet the Archbishop's reply was not sufficiently to the point; for the new issue raised by modern weaponry is not simply the vivid presentation to our imaginations, heightened by foreshortening the time, of the fact that an end will come, but instead the possibility that this may take place *by human action*. This is an issue of policy, and it is a problem for morality. In considering this question, we must make certain further distinctions, between the great *evil* of all-out war and the *risk* of such a war, and between the *evil* of destroying mankind by human action and the *danger* that this may happen. These distinctions have not often been clearly made by those who simply affirm that there can be "no greater evil" than nuclear warfare or that there can be "no greater evil" than man's destruction of mankind. This may be true, yet there may still be greater evils than *risking* war or than risking enormously large-scale destruction; and in any case decisions have today to be made in the light of these enduring dangers without as such *choosing* all-out war or such destruction as a lesser evil to any other alternative.

Among the opening sections of the Provisional Study Document of the World Council of Churches is this statement, "It is part of our Christian hope that all men may experience God's victory as mercy as well as judgment, and we may *therefore* never consent to the prospect of terminating human history by human act" (#18, italics added). This conclusion is clearly a *non sequitur* where it stands; or else in the premise of the statement God's mercy and judgment have been reduced wholly to the plane of future

---

[4] C. Wright Mills writes of nuclear war as "sudden hell," thereby proving the truth of one statement of his: "I am religiously illiterate and unfeeling." "A Pagan Sermon," in *The Causes of World War Three* (New York: Simon and Schuster, 1958), pp. 145 ff.

human history on this planet. That was never the Christian hope, nor Christian eschatology.[5]

The curious expression, "never consent to the *prospect* of terminating human history by human act" also needs to be clarified. In one sense, this is a "prospect" no one asks us to "consent" to, but to accept as among the possibilities intrinsic to man's knowledge of the created world. An extraordinary article by William G. Pollard stresses this point:

> .... The natural hydrogen bomb is by far the most common thing in all creation. God has made hydrogen bombs in profuse abundance and scattered them throughout his creation. Whenever one is tempted to denounce the hydrogen bomb as an inherently evil, man-made contraption dependent for its very existence on an esoteric form of scientific necromancy, one would do well to look out at the sky on a clear night and reflect on the extent to which hydrogen bombs are an essential and abundant part of the world which God provided for us to live in.
>
> .... Our earth is one of the very few spots in all creation where the ingredients for an ordinary fire can be found. From the standpoint of a being capable of freely ranging throughout space, the observation of fires here on earth would be an extraordinary curiosity, quite bizarre and unnatural. Such a being, on the other hand, would ... look upon hydrogen bombs as the most common and ordinary kind of thing in existence and so as natural a process as could be imagined. He would also know, as some of us do not realize, that a universe from which hydrogen bombs had been banned would be a dead universe with no life or warmth in it.
>
> [Fission, which unlike fusion does not *occur* in nature, is still a possibility inherent in the sort of world God has provided us, on which many actualities in nature depend.] All that we know of God as He has revealed Himself to us suggests that it

---

[5] One of the points in the critique submitted by the C. C. I. A. Executive Committee (#2 which opens with the words "In what sense is this a theological discussion?") states in particular that "the tremendous dilemma of the relative claims of the preservation of earthly life and the sustaining of justice and order require exploration in terms of the Christian revelation."

must be an occasion of rejoicing on the part of our Creator that His creature man has now come to share with Him this vision of the wonderful scope and fitness of His handiwork. When seen in this broader perspective, we realize that it is not only fruitless but really irreverent to rebel against the existence of atomic and hydrogen bombs, and to wish for a world in which we would not have to contend with such vast power. When in our littleness and finiteness we come forth with proposals to ban atomic or hydrogen bombs forever from our scheme of things, we would do well to reflect on the consequences of the application of such a ban by God to creation as a whole.

. . . . The real question is not whether scientists should or should not engage in work which leads to atomic energy developments. The real question is how can man, finite, perverse, and sinful creature that he is, find the power and the wisdom to inhabit a world in which such fearful vessels of destruction exist.[6]

To consent or not to consent to this prospect is not a matter of human choice; nor could this consistently have been the meaning of the statement in a document which also recognizes that, because the bomb is now an indestructible possession of mankind, the prospect of its use will always be present. "Never consent to the prospect" can only mean "never consent to the adoption of a policy or a military action whose consequence would probably or likely terminate human history by human action."

This statement in turn is greatly in need of clarification, for a whole range of meanings and possible actions are contained within the—as yet unspecified—degree of possibility, probability, or likelihood of this consequence of a particular human action. Without saying more, one cannot tell what actions are prohibited on this principle. By failing to distinguish between the evil of all-out nuclear destruction and the evil of *risking* such destruction which the policies of

[6] "The Christian Man and the Nature of Atomic Energy," *The St. Luke's Journal*, II, 3 (Whitsuntide, 1959), pp. 6, 7, 10-11.

nations may have to endure or consent to, or rather by allowing the gravity of the evil of nuclear destruction to become confused with the gravity of the evil even in the slightest risk of it, many people today are inclined to say that to consent to policies that involve any risk whatsoever of nuclear destruction is the same as to consent to the termination of the human race by human action. They say, with Hannah Arendt, that "the moment war can even *conceivably* threaten the continued existence of mankind on earth," all justification for warfare vanishes, and all justification for action that might lead to nuclear war vanishes, because the alternative between choosing liberty or choosing death has vanished. But has it? To choose liberty by means that could conceivably threaten the existence of mankind, to choose liberty by means that *might* lead to destruction, is not yet the same as *choosing* death. What we have to compare is the evil of capitulation with the evil involved in risking war, or the evil to be repelled by war with the risk of nuclear war, or the evil sought to be repelled in warfare by means of conventional weapons with the risk that more powerful weapons will be used, or the concentrated power of evil that would have to be repelled by the use of limited atomic weapons with the risk that strategic weapons will be used. In no case would we be choosing war; or, by choosing war, choosing nuclear war or choosing megaton weapons, or choosing to terminate the human race by human action. If the causal connection between these steps, or the necessary connection between risking war and war itself, is so great as to abolish the distinction between the whatever degree of *danger* there is of so great an evil and the *evil itself*, this has to be shown. It cannot simply be asserted. It may be that there is now "no greater evil" than modern war. At the same time, it may be that there are still many greater evils than the rather permanent danger of war which is the destiny of men to endure in any age, or greater evils than the present danger we face in the degree of likelihood that our actions will lead to, rather than prevent, the destructiveness of modern warfare.

I am not now asking whether there can be any greater evil than our all-out *use* of megaton weapons, or any greater evil than an *act* of indiscriminate bombing. To my satisfaction that question has already been answered and the moral limit to warfare fixed. We should in that connection be resolved to make the affirmation of Socrates in the *Gorgias* that it is better to suffer evil than to do it. The question now is whether, in mounting a defense proportionate to an attack, i.e., against the attack itself and not directly against a people as a whole, there is sufficient prudential reason for attempting to disengage ourselves from all use of armed force, or any form of warfare, to be found in the fact that there is danger of starting nuclear destructiveness and even of terminating the human race by human action. Of course, it may be pointed out that if war is limited or just, if even only one side disciplines itself to restrain the use it is willing to make of the weapons mankind now possesses, that in itself will limit the destructiveness of any future war and forestall the prospect of universal nuclear doom. But the question now posed is *whether,* independent of the limitation of killing to the indirect, even if vast, effect of tactical bombing, *and in what sense,* dread of destroying the human race by human action *should* provide the ground, in a prudent calculation of the consequences alone, for the conclusion that all modern war is morally prohibited, because there can be no greater evil than this, and certainly no commensurate good to justify it.

There is much to be commended in the exactness with which Catholic moral theologians address themselves to this issue. When they say that under no circumstances would it ever be right to "permit" the termination of the human race by human action, because there could not possibly be any proportionate grave reason to justify such a thing, they know exactly what they mean. Of course, in prudential calculation, in balancing the good directly intended and done against the evil unintended and indirectly done, no greater precision can be forthcoming than the subject allows. Yet it seems clear that there can be no good sufficiently great, or evil repelled sufficiently grave, to warrant the destruction of mankind by man's own action.

I mean, however, that the moral theologian knows what he means by "permit." He is not talking in the main about probabilities, risks and danger in general. He is talking about an action which just as efficaciously does an evil thing (and is known certainly and unavoidably to lead to this evil result) as it efficaciously does some good. He is talking about double *effects,* of which the specific action causes directly the one and indirectly the other, but *causes* both; of which one is deliberately willed or intended and the other not intended or not directly intended, but still both are *done,* while the evil effect is, with equal consciousness on the part of the agent, foreknown to be among the consequences. This is what, in a technical sense, to "only permit" an evil result means. It means to *do it* and to know one is doing it, but as only a secondary if certain effect of the good one primarily does and intends. Of course, grave guiltiness may be imputed to the military action of any nation, or to the action of any leader or leaders, which for any supposed good "permits," in *this* sense, the termination of the human race by human action. Certainly, in analyzing an action which truly faced such alternatives, "it is *never* possible that no world would be preferable to some worlds, and there are in truth *no* circumstances in which the destruction of human life presents itself as a reasonable alternative."[7]

Naturally, where one or the other of the effects of an action is uncertain, this has to be taken into account. Especially is this true when, because the good effect is remote and speculative while the evil is certain and grave, the action is prohibited. Presumably, if the reverse is the case and the good effect is more certain than the evil result that may be forthcoming, not only must the good and the evil be prudentially weighed and found proportionate, but also calculation of the probabilities and of the degree of certainty or uncertainty in the good or evil effect must be taken into account. There must not only be greater good than evil objectively in view, but also greater probability of actually doing more good than harm. If an evil which is certain and extensive and immediate may rarely be compensated for by a problematic, speculative, future good, by the same token not every present, certain, and immediate good (or lesser evil) that may have to be done will be outweighed by a problematic, speculative, and future evil. Nevertheless, according to the traditional theory, a man begins in the midst of action and he analyzes its nature and immediate consequences before or while putting it forth and causing these consequences. He does not expect to be able to trammel up all the future consequences of his action. Above all, he does not debate mere contingencies, and therefore, if these are possibly dreadful, find himself forced into inaction. He does what he can and may and must, without regarding himself as lord of the future or, on the other hand, as covered with guilt by accident or unforeseen consequences or by results he did not "permit" in the sense explained. By

[7] *Worldview* editorial, May, 1958, p. 1. However, the statement in this journal, June, 1959, p. 2, is by no means the same, to the effect that "there *are* things which the religious conscience must reject, and the possible [*sic!*] destruction of the human race is chief among them."

contrast, a good deal of nuclear pacifism begins with the contingencies and the probabilities, and not with the moral nature of the action to be done; and by deriving legitimate decision backward from whatever may *conceivably* or possibly or probably result, whether by anyone's doing or by accident, it finds itself driven to inaction, to non-political action in politics and non-military action in military affairs, and to the not very surprising discovery that there are now no distinctions on which the defense of justice can possibly be based.

Mr. Philip Toynbee writes, for example, that "in terms of probability it is surely *as likely as not* that mutual fear will lead to accidental war in the near future *if the present situation continues.* If it continues indefinitely it is *nearly a statistical certainty* that a mistake will be made and that the devastation will begin."[8]   Against such a termination of human life on earth by human action, he then proposes as an alternative that we "negotiate at once with the Russians and get the best terms which are available," that we deliberately "negotiate from comparative weakness."   He bravely attempts to face this alternative realistically, i.e., by considering the worst possible outcome, namely, the total domination of the world by Russia within a few years.   This would be by far the better choice, when "it is a question of *allowing* the human race to survive, possibly under the domination of a regime which most of us detest, or of *allowing* it to destroy itself in appalling and prolonged anguish."[9]   Nevertheless, the consequence of the policy pro-

[8] *Op. cit.*, p. 13 (first and final italics added). "Can World War III Start by Mistake," by Brigadier (Ret.) C. N. Barclay, *New York Times Magazine*, Aug. 23, 1959, pp. 11 ff., gives a far saner estimate of the chances, which, of course, are still awful to contemplate. In the above, I pass by the serious problem of calculating the chances and also omit discussion of the work of intelligence and manifold action to *reduce* the risks. I ask rather what bearing, if any, and how, future consequences have upon the determination of present action.

[9] Toynbee, *op. cit.*, p. 19. Notice, in the words I have italicized, a quite different meaning of "permit."

posed is everywhere subtly qualified: it is "a possible result, however improbable"; "the worst, and least probable" result; "if it didn't prevail *mankind* would still be given the opportunity of prevailing"; for "surely anything is better than a policy which allows for the *possibility* of nuclear war."[10] If we have not thought and made a decision entirely in these terms, then we need to submit ourselves to the following "simple test": "Have we decided how we are to kill the other members of our household in the event of our being less injured than they are?"[11] Thus, moral decision must be entirely deduced backward from the likely eventuality; it is no longer to be formulated in terms of the nature of present action itself, its intention, and proximate effect or the thing to be *done*.

Several of the replies to Mr. Toynbee, without conscious resort to the traditional terminology with regard to the permission of evil, succeed in restoring the actual context in which present moral and political decisions must be made, by distinguishing between choosing a great evil and choosing in danger of this evil. "It is worse for a nation to give in to evil . . . than to run the risk of annihilation."[12] "I am consciously prepared to run the continued risk of 'race suicide by accident' rather than accept the alternative certainty of race slavery by design. But I can only make this choice because I believe that the risk need not increase, but may be deliberately reduced" [by precautions against accidents or by limiting war?][13] "Quoting Mr. Kennan's phrase that anything would be better than a policy which led inevitably

---

[10] *Ibid.*, pp. 18, 19, 21.
[11] *Ibid.*, p. 10. "We should no longer talk of dying to the last man but of killing to the last child. I would say, of torturing to the last child" (p. 108). This last statement is an acceptable statement which calls for decision in face of the moral limits to just warfare; it is not only decision in face of a calculus of probabilities; i.e., it has to do with the nature of the action and not only speculation about remote consequences.
[12] *Ibid.*, p. 26 (Lord Portal of Hungerford).
[13] *Ibid.*, p. 32 (Richard Lowenthal of the *Observer*).

to nuclear war, he [Toynbee] says that anything is better than a policy which allows for the *possibility* of nuclear war."[14] "If asked to choose between a terrible probability and a more terrible possibility, most men will choose the latter."[15] "If ... Philip Toynbee is claiming that the choice lies between capitulation and the *risk* of nuclear war, I think he is right. I do not accept that the choice is between capitulation and the certainty of nuclear war."[16] Even Professor Arnold Toynbee, agreeing with his son, does so in these terms: "Compared to continuing to incur a constant *risk* of the destruction of the human race, all other evils are lesser evils. ... Let us therefore put first things first, and make sure of preserving the human race at whatever the temporary price may be."[17]

Mr. Philip Toynbee affirms at one point that *if* he shared the anticipations of Orwell in *Nineteen Eighty-Four*, *if* he believed Communism was not only evil but "also *irredeemably* evil," then he might "think it right to do anything rather than to take the risk of a communist world. Even a nuclear holocaust is a little less frightful to contemplate than a race of dehumanised humans occupying the earth until doomsday."[18] No political order or economic system is so clearly contrary to nature. But one does not have to affirm the existence of an evil order irredeemable in that sense, or a static order in which no changes will take place in time, to be able truthfully to affirm the following fact:

[14] *Ibid.*, p. 38 (Nigel Nicolson, M.P.).
[15] *Ibid.*, p. 40.
[16] *Ibid.*, p. 62 (Noble Frankland of The Royal Institute of International Affairs).
[17] *Ibid.*, p. 80. (italics added).
[18] *Ibid.* p. 103. Taken together, the replies from men in many sorts of professions, and even the statement just quoted from Philip Toynbee, seem to me to confirm the view of Fr. John C. Ford that the rule of double effect is intrinsic to human moral and political reason, not externally imposed upon it; and that the rule is simply "a practical formula which synthesizes an immense amount of moral experience" ("The Morality of Obliteration Bombing," *Theological Studies*, V, 3, Sept., 1944, p. 289).

there has never been *justitia* imprinted in social institutions and social relationships except in the context of some *pax-ordo* preserved by clothed or naked force. On their way to the Heavenly City the children of God make use of the *pax-ordo* of the earthly city and acknowledge their share in responsibility for its preservation. Not to repel injury and uphold and improve *pax-ordo* means not simply to accept the misshapen order and injustice that challenges it at the moment, but also to start down the steep slope along which justice can find no place whereon to stand. Toynbee seems to think that there is some other way to give justice social embodiment. "I would far rather die after a Russian oc-cupation of this country—by some deliberate act of refusal—than die uselessly by atomisation."[19] Would such an act of refusal be useful? He does not mean, in fact he addresses himself specifically to reject the proposition, that "if we took the risk of surrendering, a new generation in Britain would soon begin to amass its strength in secret in order to reverse the consequences of that surrender."[20] He wants to be "brutally frank and say that these rebellions *would* be hopeless—far, far more hopeless than was the Hungarian revolution of 1956." This is not a project for regaining the ground for limited war, by creating a monopoly in one power of the world's arsenal of unlimited weapons. It is a proposal that justice now be served by means other than those that have ever preconditioned the search for it, or preconditioned more positive means for attaining it, in the past. "It is no good recommending surrender rather than nuclear warfare with the proviso that surrender could be followed by the effective military resistance by occupied peoples. Hope for the future . . . would lie in the natural longing of the human race for freedom and the right to de-

[19] Toynbee, *op. cit.*, p. 103.
[20] *Ibid.*, p. 42 (Nigel Nicolson, M.P.) and p. 105.

velop."[21] This is to surrender in advance to whatever attack may yet be mounted, to the very last; it is to stride along the steep slope downward. The only contrary action, in the future as in the past, runs the *risk* of war; and, now and in the future unlike in the past, any attempt to repel injury and to preserve any particular civilized attainment of mankind or its provisional justice runs some risk of nuclear warfare and the danger that an effect of it will, by human action, render this planet less habitable by the human race. That is why it is so very important that ethical analysis keep clear the problem of decision as to "permitted" effects, and not draw back in fright from any conceivable contingency or suffer paralysis of action before possibilities or probabilities unrelated, or not directly morally related, to what we can and may and must do as long as human history endures.

Finally, just as no different issues are posed for thoughtful analysis by the foreshortening of time that may yet pass before the end of human life on this earth, but only stimulation and alarm to the imagination, the same thing must be said in connection with the question of what we may perhaps already be doing, *by human action,* to accelerate this end. We should not allow the image of an immanent end brought about indirectly by our own action in the continuing human struggle for a just endurable order of existence to blind us to the fact that in some measure accelerating the end of our lease may be one consequence among others of many other of mankind's thrusts toward we know not what future. This may all the while be taking place from manifold human actions we none of us would condemn or see a choiceworthy means of stopping.

Because of some such reason as this, William Pollard writes that "life at best is a hazardous and dangerous busi-

[21] *Ibid.,* p. 104-105.

ness with many of its hazards *directly attributable to our own technology,"* and therefore "the moral problems with which atomic energy confronts us are not so radically different from those which confront us in many other areas." He points out that "the present level and contemplated increase in the rate of combustion of long buried fossilized fuels may be producing a poisoning of the atmosphere much more grim for the status of human life on the earth than that attendant on the present level of nuclear testing"; and, as with technology so with humanitarian endeavors, there are ultimate consequences of obviously right action which are not in our hands. Some geneticists are cited as authorities for the fact that "the widespread application of modern scientific measures in public health and sanitation may in fact be retaining undesirable genes in the whole human species on a scale far greater than any which could conceivably be attributed to mutations from the excess radiation due to nuclear fallout."[22] This further prospect of an end to human history by human action may be mentioned: If our scientists learn to control fusion reaction they will present us with an indefinite source of power, and answer the question where the exploding population of the world is to obtain the power by which it must live; and this in turn, by giving us the power for monstrous irrigation projects, etc., will for a while help ward off the problem of where we are to find the food we must have to live. But there is no final solution to the problem of providing food for an ever-mounting world population. Therefore, it is not altogether farfetched to say that the man who on a pleasant night draws his wife to his bosom may be doing something which by human action permits results which will finally render this earth insufficient to contain and support human habitation (unless, of course, he intends to beget a geneticist

[22] *Op. cit.,* p. 18 (italics added).

or a population expert, and that is something no one can do directly). There is, I am told, an old Chinese proverb which says, "He that goeth to bed early to save candle light shall beget twins." That would seem to be laudable on both counts; yet no one can trammel up the consequences allowed to be set in motion by this simple occurrence. As with the life-acts of men, so with the life-acts of nations and civilizations. With the destroyer commander, "one must do what one must, and say one's prayers"; or rather, one may do what one must with confidence and gladness because one can and will and must say one's prayers.

Much to be commended is the concluding section of the Calhoun Commission report. The peril we face today is, indeed, "not the impersonal closing down of an Age of Ice but a possible man-made disaster that will come, if at all, because of specific human decisions." On the one hand, "man may be able to prolong the period during which the earth will sustain human life"; on the other hand, "it seems at least as likely that by misdirection of atomic energy, man can bring earthly history to a premature close." This new disclosure of man's dreadful freedom raises, however, no unique problem as to our understanding of the justice and mercy of God; only an old question in poignant, new form. To this recurring question of man's existence before God must be returned an indication of the Christian hope in both historical and trans-historical terms. This report did not think it sufficient to point out that "there is at least a fair chance that not all human life on earth would be destroyed," survivors from among "agricultural and nomadic people in out-of-the-way places"—who of themselves cannot, however, provide ground for meaning and hope because they are a " 'faithful remnant,' saved by reason of obedience to God," but whom hope that is placed in God may regard as chosen in their weakness and ignorance, and concerning whom *therefore* "there is no reason to doubt that God could make them also become great peoples, and bring to realization through them new stretches of history, perhaps new levels of spiritual community." That is the penultimate word that was said. The ultimate word of this report draws our attention to the fact that "God lives and holds in eternal presence the life of His children in time"; "His creating and redeeming work will not end if the earth be destroyed, and whatever men have done, whatever of human existence has been good, He will cherish forever."[23]

[23] "Atomic Warfare and the Christian Faith," *loc. cit.,* pp. 20-24.

Chapter Ten

NUCLEAR TESTING

The argument of this book (both against those neo-pacifists who base present decision on dread of conceivable consequences alone and against bellicists who also base present decision on an attempted calculation of the balance of good and evil consequences alone) has application also to the moral problem of nuclear testing, and in some measure against the position Professor John Bennett has taken on this problem. Of course it is exceedingly important that the view Bennett opposes be utterly rejected and given no quarter. "Often it is said that while fallout will produce a number of deformed children in the future, these will be only a small percentage of all future children and, in any case, we shall never know which these are because there will be many other children deformed for other reasons." It is senseless and immoral simply to take refuge in such generalities, or to say that the tests have only added a minor amount to the sea of radiation which already surrounds us, that there is now only one-thirtieth more, while a family that moves from New Orleans to Denver suffer a doubling of the dose from cosmic rays due to the increase in altitude, that the amount man has added only comes to the same increase a family would experience by moving three hundred or four hundred feet higher up the hill or by moving from a frame house to a stone or masonry house in some localities. The question has to do with increasing the sea of radiation surrounding the people who already live in Denver, or up the hill, or in stone houses. People who live in granite houses should not throw tests. The question concerns the death of anyone from man-made leukemia, or the slightest trace of genetic havoc that may be left in the wake of atomic experiments. Therefore, Professor Bennett is forever right in asserting that "this type of argument indicates an extraordinary reversal of moral assumptions. To become insensitive to the injurious effects of what we do to a large number of people because it is a *relatively* small number is a great departure from everything that Christians have believed in the past"; and in his finding "the real issue" to be "the tendency of the official scientists to speak in averages and percentages to disguise the human realities which are involved."[1]

Nevertheless, one cannot simply oppose averages and percentages by appeal to the significance of even one life that may be taken. That would be to oppose thinking in terms of large and relative numbers by reference to the number one, without sufficient analysis of the nature of the *action* which may imperil his life. It is not enough to have recourse to an undifferentiated "Thou shalt not kill." Kennan also makes this mistake in the *way* he deplores the scientists' assurances that "not many deaths" will occur: "I recall no quantitative stipulation in the Sixth Commandment. Whoever gave us the right, as Christians, to take even one innocent life? I fail to see how any of this can be reconciled with Christian conscience."[2] This manifests, of course, an opposite attitude from the nonchalance some of our official scientists may have expressed toward the facts in their calculations about nuclear testing. Nevertheless, it is the one grave mistake Kennan has made in the use of ethical *prin-*

[1] "Atomic Testing," *Christianity and Crisis*, XV, 11 (June 9, 1958).
[2] "Foreign Policy and Christian Conscience," *Atlantic Monthly*, May, 1959, p. 48.

ciples; and this mistake in principle has to be corrected before anyone launches upon another calculation of the facts in order morally to oppose the tests.

The basic error in theoretical analysis is that, in what they say about the *future* innocents who may die as a result of present tests, Kennan and Bennett treat the probable *effect* of our present actions as if it were a *means* at present employed to obtain the ends we desire. The time-sequence of the acts put forth by men or nations cannot be reversed in this way. All action thrusts toward the future, and many or most actions have double or multiple effects or consequences in the future; and this raises questions of a different order from the use of intrinsically wrong means in present action as such. Granted that the death of one child from man-made leukemia will be evil in itself, there is a significant distinction still to be made between whether this is an *effect* among many other good and evil effects that will result from our present course of action, or whether it is a *means* which, intentionally and in and of itself, objectively as well as subjectively, is ordered to the achieving of some choiceworthy goal. This is what is meant by saying that one effect may justify another, but never an intrinsically wrong means. Kennan's is a mistake *in principle,* in not distinguishing between taking human life as a means, and unavoidably taking human life as one of the indirect effects of action, to some good end. This good and that evil effect have to be calculated and weighed the one against the other; and any refusal to pay proper attention to such facts results from a failure to see that in principle a possibly evil effect that may follow along with good effects from any action is not to be understood as an immoral means causally conducive to one of these other effects as an end. No one should wince at these statements, *provided* it is clear that a society engaging in calculations as to the indirect effects of action would already have become uncivilized if it engages at all in a like calculation at another point, i.e., if it might under certain circumstances be persuaded that the life of one or the lives of ten or ten thousand may be directly repressed simply as a means that good may come of it.

It is not that this calculation attempting to justify indiscriminate nuclear war, like David, has already killed its ten thousands, while calculation in the case of nuclear testing, like Saul, has already killed only its thousands. At its heart, ethics counts not in quantities and, as Kant said, you cannot do morality a greater disservice than by deriving it from experience. It is rather that the death and devastation contemplated in the case of all-out nuclear war would be both *directly willed* and *directly done* as a means, while the death brought about by nuclear testing *as such* is only *indirectly willed* and *indirectly done* as one among several effects of the tests. The first is murder, the second tragic. In the one case, death to the innocent is the instrument used for defense or victory; in the other case, death to the innocent is a foreknown side-effect of action done in such a way as may be judged to be good, or at least neutral, in itself, and to be necessary to obtain great good results. The latter calculation concerning nuclear tests may be wrong; but in the former case it would be wrong to calculate and count on the good or less evil consequences that may come from a wrong done (acts of all-out nuclear war).

The recent utterances of George Kennan have all been, not calls to abandon calculation, but to abandon calculation in the wrong place, in the place of fundamental moral principle. He has tried to recall us to the only doctrine of civilized warfare the West has known, to a re-examination as a "straight issue of conscience" of the degree of acceptance of indiscriminate bombing by nuclear weapons that is present in our nuclear deterrence policy, and to call us back from our apparent willingness to rest our security (as he said recently to the Women's Democratic Club in Washington, D. C.) on weapons designed to "destroy innocent noncombatant human life, including the lives of children, on a vast scale," back from "an infinitely costly and hopeless exercise of reciprocal menace" by means which it would be vastly immoral ever to use. There can be no greater evil, I take Kennan to be saying, than the act of *using* unlimited weapons all out; and the one thing worse than to suffer such an evil would be to do it. Sophistry has always opposed the Gorgias who declares this to be the case. Kennan is quite right; no calculation taught him this, nor should calculation be allowed to deprive him or us of a forever valid moral judgment. Nevertheless, he is mistaken *in principle* in not using a proper calculation of the proportionality of the good and the evil expected to result from nuclear testing.

What Christians and men of the West have believed in the past, in their sensitivity to the injurious effects of what they may do, in careful discrimination as to permitted and prohibited killing, should be applied to the question of nuclear tests. I find this wanting when Bennett writes, in the article previously cited, "The Communists, whose ruthlessness is the excuse for our actions, sacrifice living persons to a future political goal. We sacrifice future persons to a present political goal." In a later article (provoked by an extreme and apparently calloused statement of calculative morality), Bennett extends even further the conclusions he would draw from an, in principle, mistaken analysis. He writes that "of the two types of ethical calculation, I think that the Communist calculation as a form of ethical calculation, is more defensible."[3] And he adds to the confusion by attempting to classify future generations as "non-combatants" ac-

---

[3] Letter in *Worldview*, Nov. 1959, p. 7.

cording to "the traditional distinction" which, however, he says, "does not fit the present realities." To this, the proper reply is: Let them be noncombatants. No moralist ever said before that it may not be tragically necessary to kill non-combatants *indirectly* as a result of action, for which there is sufficiently grave reason, ordered to another, good effect. Bennett also points out, in another case subsumable under a necessary balancing of the effects, that "the people who are killed in automobiles usually choose to ride in automobiles; whereas most of the victims of tests and of nuclear war would have no chance to make such a choice." I suppose that the author of that statement might have some difficulty accepting traditional theological reconciliation of divine predetermination with real human freedom in matters where men cannot do otherwise! We do not have to abandon responsibility for preserving our heritage for our as yet unborn children to many generations yet to come in order to say that Bennett ignores, as he should not, the time sequence in any life-action put forth by men or nations, confuses the distinction between means and effects, and, in these articles, fails to sense the wisdom summarized in the principle of double effect. By sacrificing living persons to a future political goal it is likely that Bennett understands the use of them as mere means, to "manure the soil for the future harmony," and not only tragic loss of the lives of persons now living as an unavoidable secondary effect of legitimate and necessary action. The sacrifice of future persons to a present political goal may not be the same thing at all.

Indeed, it is difficult to see how one would use an unborn person as a mere means if one tried to do so. No one can stand now upon that future effect, and then turn around and face backward in time toward the present action with its formal intention and immediate objective results regarded as an end toward which the future serves as mere means. Here, with regard to the future, we have to think entirely in terms of effects, and of effects done directly or only permitted. Otherwise, we will be forced to say that every civilizing thrust the human race has yet made, from the stirrup and that most dangerous weapon the family bathtub and the issuance of hunting licenses to the invention of any of our modern means of transportation, has sacrificed future persons to a present goal believed to be worthwhile. The real question is whether there is any proportionate reason for permitting the future death of some innocent ones—say, in the control of warfare by the skin of our teeth through the development of limited atomic weapons needed to be sufficient to an attack that may be mounted or in the conquest of power for the saving of many people alive or by releasing a "negligible" amount of additional man-made radiation in order to perfect the instruments for detecting underground tests.[4]

In the *form* of their argument, the official scientists have not been wrong. The calculation and balancing of effects which they propose is proper calculation, in the right place. Of course, their conclusion from this may be wrong, because of the weight given to the gravity of the evil to be avoided or the great good to be attained by one effect of the testing. This may too readily seem to justify the damage done in the other effect. But public debate in this country would be greatly clarified if this were always said in reply to these scientists, instead of sweeping condemnation of anyone who approves continuing nuclear tests—on the assumption that nothing at all could ever justify the tests to conscience, but only amoral power-political considerations. Nuclear testing *may* be justified: this should be our finding as to moral law. Our finding of fact, or prudential judgment as to the

[4] See the testimony of John A. McCone, Chairman of AEC, on the Geneva Test Ban Negotiations, given before a subcommittee of the Senate Foreign Relations Committee, June 24, 1959.

greater good or lesser evil, may be otherwise. In general, the life-acts of men or of nations put forth in the present and reaching toward the future have this character that from them all flow multiple effects. With the destroyer commander, "one must do what one must, and say one's prayers"; and that second "must" means "should," since even in the midst of actions that also have tragic consequences, it must be prudently believed that one effect justifies another, or else the action ought not to be done. A peaceful use of nuclear energy, e.g., the use of a nuclear bomb to dig a harbor in Alaska, may not have enough good in its effects for the peacetime economy to outweigh the other, and evil, consequence of increasing the contamination of the atmosphere. On the other hand, perhaps that result is so good and necessary and perhaps the evil effect can be controlled enough to justify such action. Nor may the reactor be safe enough to be worth building near Detroit (a case now going through the courts), despite our inveterate confidence that industrial progress is—progress. Exactly the same alternatives face us in the case of weapons testing. This is the form of the argument that would have to be sustained by anyone who approves the tests. We shall return to the *matter* of this argument in the course of our final chapter.

Chapter Eleven

TWO DEEP TRUTHS ABOUT MODERN WARFARE

a. *The Feasibility of Deterrence, and Just War*

In the preface to his book *The Question of National Defense*[1] Oskar Morgenstern draws upon the views of Niels Bohr concerning truth statements in physics to suggest that, in the analysis of modern warfare, there are " 'deep truths' whose opposites are also 'deep truths.' " Indeed, my colleague Morgenstern has discerned a "deep truth" which must be regarded (on Monday, Wednesday, and Friday) as a correct report of our contemporary political and military situation. He states the truth forthrightly in this cool-headed, cold-blooded, but ultimately compassionate book. At least, the book is as compassionate as an exercise of technical political reason and strategic gamesmanship can ever be, without moral *scientia* in force *in* its argument. If from another angle of vision there is to be seen (on Tuesday, Thursday and Saturday) another, and a divergent, "deep truth," this is contained in the ancient tradition of civilized warfare. Either the just-war theory provides the norm for what should be done and the context for particular policy decisions by any people or government that is not unprincipled, or else Morgenstern has stated what should be done. Query: Can the wisdom contained in each of these viewpoints both somehow be true?

[1] New York: Random House, 1959.

If national policies are not or cannot be governed by the principles of the just or limited war, then the most strenuous effort must be put forth to perfect the other sort of war for which we now are preparing, yet are indifferently or ill prepared. *"War has to become technologically impossible* in order to be stopped,"* writes Professor Morgenstern. "It will take too long for fresh moral values to develop which would make war impossible. It would take even longer for them to become effective enough to check the new destructive power."[2] We have only to face this other alternative squarely in order to be driven, not to the moral validity, but to the practical necessity of recovering the just-war doctrine as the context of policy-making. The problem first is to face without flinching the requirements which warfare in its present shape imposes on us; and Morgenstern more than almost any other recent writer helps us to do this. When it is clearly discerned that the task before us, on our present assumptions as a people, is to make the probability of retaliatory obliteration "equal to one," i.e., certain and automatic; and when we see how far from this we are technically at the present time, and what more would have to be done, then surely the word of the churches to the present generation will stand forth clearly as far more practical advice, and far more likely to conserve some human good, than

[2] *Ibid.*, pp. 295-296. Elsewhere (pp. 30, 35, 80, 129, 134-135, 153, 276) Morgenstern seems to me to acknowledge the *validity* (even if today the irrelevance) of the moral judgment underlying his own expressed revulsion to obliteration warfare *or to counter-obliteration*. The kind of attack that may be launched only makes necessary the absolute perfection of our power to retaliate with the same or greater obliteration. This author does not assume that such would make it right; and in this he displays a greater reticence and moral sensitivity than many a pragmatic religious writer on matters of military policy. Moreover, while he does not rely at all upon political morality to limit the means employed in warfare, and instead hopes by perfecting the deterrent to prevent uncivilized warfare, Morgenstern counts on political morality alone to limit the ends for which wars are fought. See the quotation from his book printed in chap. i, n. 2, p. 7 above. It is not self-evident that nations at war can limit their objectives in any such fashion, but are quite unable to choose only limited, politically purposive means.

what Morgenstern demonstrates with rigorous logic to be our only real way of making progress in the direction in which we now are only limping.

Morgenstern distinguishes clearly between a weapons strategy of *attack* and counter-*attack* (which may conform, we have seen, to the natural law of war, of war as a just barely human enterprise and therefore to perhaps justifiable war) and a weapons-strategy of *retaliation* and counter-*retaliation,* which has as its object people and not forces. But he finds the retaliatory strategy of the United States astonishingly ill conceived. These retaliatory forces must be made invulnerable. This requires an "oceanic system" of submarines, equipped with missiles with nuclear warheads, constantly moving at random over the entire watery globe, each with orders to go in case we are attacked to a designated point and fire upon the enemy nation no matter what has happened meantime to our own country.

Since it is now possible to increase firepower indefinitely beyond the defensive capacity to "harden" our missile bases, no bases should be located in the interior of the country, or even on its periphery, or upon the territory of any of our allies. Our present vulnerable retaliatory system is almost worse than none at all, since it invites the destruction we seek to deter by it. Nuclear-firing, nuclear-powered submarines and sea planes would, by contrast, constitute a truly invulnerable retaliatory power. Moreover, it would be a good thing if not only the United States but Russia as well could achieve an invulnerable retaliatory power. Then each nation, secure in its power to retaliate at will, could afford to wait to determine whether the enemy had actually launched a nuclear attack, or whether it was only a flock of geese or a shower of meteors on the radar screen, or the mistaken or insubordinate action of some junior officer that let go a minor part of the forces in being. Besides no nation will dare attack another whose capacity for instant or delayed retaliation cannot first be destroyed.

Then would ensue a period, extending over decades, in which every technological effort is bent upon discovering ways of getting at the hitherto invulnerable retaliatory power of the opponent. This will be a period of "deep peace." By the time a way has been discovered to break through the "oceanic system," further invulnerable systems of defense by *certain* retaliation will have been developed which will prolong the peace. Invulnerable retaliatory power may soon be located elsewhere than in the ocean. "Either side can put nuclear weapons into space and . . . eventually both may have them up there at the same time. Should a war occur then and should they represent the main threat, then *each side would be bound first of all to try to locate and then destroy the other's space capability.* If we are lucky, that war would then be mercifully fought away from the earth, and whoever loses would have to surrender an intact country."[3] In my own words, if the nations do as they should and resolve to keep in perfect invulnerability their retaliatory power, then the only war that will actually occur will be "just war," i.e., against the attacking or counter-attacking power itself; and the only war that can today be fought to the end—the unjust war—may not occur. Thus Morgenstern's proposal for a weapons strategy is oriented in the direction of keeping war just, i.e., in the direction of that other "deep truth."

The foregoing is the most important series of steps in strategic design to be taken. There is, however, a second series of actions now plainly necessary. Shelters against fire-power are, of course, worth nothing, but a wide system of fall-out shelters should immediately be constructed, and planned to face the fact that an enemy can deliberately in-

[3] *Ibid.,* p. 102 (italics added).

crease fall-out, delay or prolong or repeat "wilful radiation" at intervals. Moreover, a national decision has to be made to select that small part of the population to be saved (the countrymen and not the "citizens"), and these will have to be psychologically conditioned to endure in the knowledge that they are alive in the midst of the greatest catastrophe the human race has ever experienced and the greatest evil it has done. Moreover, a significant part of the economy must be selected and placed underground. The storage of large quantities of inert supplies will be of no use. Instead, there must be "active storage"; "a living thing," an active part of the economy, must be made to live underground. This "sub-economy" should be identified with two purposes in mind: to "secure the very barest *but continuing* existence" of that part of the population chosen to survive, and to be the means of reconstructing the economy after the devastation of everything above ground. Thus, it should include living machines not only for the continued production of necessary goods for consumption but also for the production of other machines that will be needed to enable men to emerge and live on the surafce again.

The sub-economy would probably contain machine-tool factories, nuclear power plants and installations capable of producing atomic power plants, pharmaceutical plants, hospitals, refineries, etc. These factories should be able to maintain themselves in functioning condition even if the economy above ground is essentially destroyed. In that case they would first of all take care of the people working and living underground, then supply the survivors of the attack with necessities, with organization, and information. They would then set out to piece together what could be salvaged above ground and provide power for expansion so that the whole economy could once more in some fashion arise from the shambles.

There would be no victor in the war, but the nation prepared to rebuild would be "the true survivor."

What will survival be like? What will be the result obtained by the colossal effort demonstrated, from one set of premises, to be necessary? Again, Morgenstern does not sweeten his reply: "From mere survival, in view of perhaps a hundred million people killed within a few days, to the construction of a society which adheres to the lofty ideals we cherish today is a long way. And the survivors may develop ideals so different from ours that we may not recognize the country—should we live to make the comparison, or, living, should we care to make it even if we could."[4]

This should be sufficient to expose the connection between the immoral conduct of war or preparations for unjust war, to the degree that they are logically and fully developed, and the loss of everything a nation may have hoped to save. It will be said, of course, that Morgenstern's conclusions are extreme and his reasoning abstract in not taking sufficiently into account the fluidity of historical events and the concrete nature of political affairs. If we limit policy within the range of actions any people is likely to adopt, some may still believe mankind will muddle through, as in the past, by accepting the necessity of unjust warfare yet not going so far in the direction of perfecting it. It is true that Morgenstern asserts that "in politics one sits down with murderers,"[5] and his analysis is informed by the belief that our present political enemies are wholly evil. Yet these extreme judgments are not necessary to his argument. All that is necessary to sustain his political and military analysis was stated earlier: "the mere possession of this overwhelming power constitutes a potential *supreme threat.*" Who the contestants are and whether they are open to negotiation will determine whether the political solution of conflicts is possible. Suppose settlements are possible on all sides. Still

[4] *Ibid.,* pp. 125-129.
[5] *Ibid.,* p. 272.

each nation must be prepared, now and in the future, to meet a potential threat, and not only the threats of men and nations known to be "evil." Therefore Morgenstern introduces his own estimate of our present enemy only by way of the statement that "while the mere possession of overwhelming power (now specifically thermonuclear power) *eo ipso* poses a threat, it will naturally be the greater, the more the basic interests of the parties differ."[6]

For example (to choose an illustration Morgenstern himself does not use), the mere possession, by any nation other than *de facto* or entirely reliable *de jure* allies, of the means of chemical or bacteriological warfare *eo ipso* poses a threat which military establishments are under the necessity of preparing to match. This need did not arise only during the height of Nazi or Stalinist animosity and brutality, nor will it disappear of itself as a result of some forthcoming "thaw." It is not a function of a nation's theological anthropology, or its general view of human nature and of sin. And so at Fort Detrick, near Frederick, Maryland, those who are responsible for the defense of this country quietly go forward with preparations for the mere possibility of chemical and bacteriological warfare.

Moreover, these may be forms of retaliation and counter-retaliation directed against whole populations which it is not possible to perfect (in the way Morgenstern urges for nuclear deterrence) to the point that such warfare will become technologically impossible, by each nation being forced to develop means of certainly getting at the enemy's germs before destroying his people—thus by adequacy of preparation for war by wholly unjustifiable means keeping actual war just and unjust war from actuality. Perhaps chemical and bacteriological warfare cannot be made automatically self-limiting. Since these plans and preparations

[6] *Ibid.,* p. 13.

may be a more or less static (at least a more secret) stance
of governments in an age when the norms of political and
military morality have eroded from the minds of men, and
since also Fort Detrick is currently in the religious news because of the year-long "Vigil" that many Christians are holding there to protest our government's action, these means
of making war may be chosen to illustrate the nature of that
other "deep truth" in dialogue with the truth Morgenstern
discerns also to be the case.

Initiated by the Fellowship of Reconciliation, under the
leadership of Lawrence Scott, so far nearly a thousand persons have participated in the discipline and the symbolic
direct action of the Vigil and Appeal at Fort Detrick. Included among these are conscientious opponents of unlimited warfare as well as nuclear pacifists and pacifists of the
traditional "peace churches." A letter went out over the
signatures of Professors Paul Deats (Boston University
School of Theology), Norman Gottwald (Andover-Newton
Theological School), J. O. Nelson (Yale Divinity School),
and Montgomery Shoyer (Wesley Theological School), addressed to seminary students and professors inviting men of
any and all of the usual opinions on the war-peace issue to
join together at the Vigil on March 25-28, 1960, by prayer
and communication to seek the truth to be done and to do
the truth they have already grasped.

What shall we say about this? About Christian action
vis-a-vis chemical and bacteriological warfare and our nation's preparation for this? Certainly every Christian should
be willing to lend visible support to Rep. Robert Kasten-
meier's House Concurrent Resolution #433 which would
reaffirm the Roosevelt policy of pledging the United States
government never to use these weapons *first,* and to agitate
for Senate endorsement of the Geneva Protocol outlawing
chemical and biological warfare, not yet approved by the

United States. But then the Vigil has not been properly placed; and instead Christians who find it possible to do so should stand from dawn to dusk (as a few did for one day in front of the White House) outside the Capitol Building in Washington every day the Congress is in session—at least they should be there *also*. As for the Vigil at Fort Detrick, it is difficult to see how to keep clear certain distinctions that should be made. This can be done in the course of the discussions that are also being held, but not so well or not at all in the witnessing action itself. These distinctions are two: between pacifism and just-war protest; and, within the latter, a distinction between objection to an inert weapon as such and to the intended, the probable, or the only possible *use* of a weapon. Only so will it become clear that objection to unlimited war or to the unjust conduct of war is not the same as pacifism reoccasioned by these modern weapons; only so can it be made plain that rational *armament* is the duty of the nation; and only so will the meaning of justifiable and unjustifiable warfare be clarified in the consciences of men and nations. This is that other "deep truth" which has to be made relevant in military affairs, or else Morgenstern is correct, and in general the entire problem of defense must simply be given over to technical reason.

Unless the *only possible use* of these weapons would require subjectively intended and objectively direct action against an enemy population as such, the Christian's action should not be, even symbolically, directed against *everything* the government may be doing in this matter. This seems clearly to be the case with regard to many of these means of warfare. Still, it is the *use* of weapons, and their planned use, not weapons themselves, which may be immoral. The question is whether the striking force or whole peoples are the objects of direct attack, by whatever physical means.

The sign used in the Vigil seems unambiguous enough: "An Appeal to stop Preparation for Germ Warfare." Still, many who go there should want it as positively stressed that they support necessary preparation for genuine warfare. Without allowing *wanton* cruelty ever to be justifiable, still it is the case that the force mounted in resistance not only must but *should* be proportionate to the attacking force, or the force it would be right to repel. Therefore, the question is not only the humaneness or inhumaneness of certain means of putting fighters out of the war, and those closely co-operating in the attacking force. The question is whether the "target" has been so far enlarged as to obliterate the distinction between peoples and their government, between peoples and their forces. One should therefore know whether the destruction or immobilization of civilian life as a whole is the sole aim and the sole use of these modern means of warfare before judging them to be intrinsically immoral. The tradition of civilized warfare is the thing that is most sorely lacking in influence today. The need is not for more pacifism, or more dread of weapons as such. And this, the church's doctrine of just and limited warfare, states that a nation would be justified in using even these modern means *against an enemy force* which has taken up the use of such means, *if* these means alone can succeed in repelling what they are attempting to do. It states this just as surely as it seeks to limit the conduct of war to means intended to repel military force, and to hold every nation back from calling wholesale murder "war" or from including among the laws of war the deliberately intended, direct killing of a million school children in order to get at their fathers.

There is this to be said for the Fort Detrick Vigil: that its stress is placed on our nation's military plans and on weapons development which (so far as the layman and the moralist know enough to judge) are going in the direction of making war more unlimited and preparing only for totally unlimited war. In contrast, opposition to nuclear testing, which may have the purpose of developing an arsenal of fractional kiloton weapons, seems to reject developments in technology that may be going in the direction of more limited applications of nuclear firepower. There is this only to be said against the Fort Detrick Vigil: that other forms of unlimited warfare should have been selected, *if* there are forms of chemical or biological warfare that can be limited to the direct repulsion of the force that may intend the use of the same deadly means and *if* there are other weapons now in being or preparation that cannot be so limited.[7]   Given these findings of fact, then, other weapons,

[7] The chief problem with regard to the weapons discussed above seems to be not their inappropriateness as a means (whether of unlimited *or of limited warfare*) but another consideration altogether: "It is hard to believe that Bacteriological and Chemical Warfare could compete on a cost-efficiency basis with nuclear weapons except possibly in specialized applications" (Herman Kahn: *On Thermonuclear War*, Princeton, N. J.: Princeton University Press, 1960, Lecture III, chap. x, p 485). I will now quote a paragraph from the author just cited which, along with their unlimited use, suggests the possibility of "specialized applications" of such weapons: "Off hand, it might not seem reasonable that bacteriological and chemical weapons might be acceptable when nuclear neutron weapons are not, but this might be true of specialized bacteriological and chemical weapons that could be used to enfeeble temporarily or otherwise impair the efficiency of the enemy's civilians or soldiers. The classical use of tear gas in civilian disturbances has exactly this character of being a much more acceptable weapon than ordinary bullets. In fact, it is conceivable that one might develop an effective capability of just having psychological effects on the enemy. For example, if one gave tranquilizers to the enemy soldiers in large amounts they might become unfit for military duty. It is not at all inconceivable that if the North Koreans invaded South Korea again in 1965 we would be able to keep all of North Korea continuously saturated with chemicals or organisms that reduced the efficiency of the exposed inhabitants markedly, but did not injure them permanently."

. . . .

"Certain types of bacteriological and chemical warfare might be developed, and used so subtly that the nation under attack will not know it is being attacked. The possibility of debilitating a nation over a period of years to reduce its competitive capabilities is not out of the question" (*ibid.*, Lect. III, chap. x, pp. 486, 500).

The horror we feel in face of such possibilities is not lessened by the fact that the destruction of lives is not aimed at. The distinction between actual killing or not killing, or the relative "humaneness" of such applica-

because of their sole or probably their sole intrinsic use, would be more certainly a political immorality than some of the use of the means being developed at Fort Detrick. This follows from the fact that conscientious objection should be directed against unlimited, unjustifiable warfare, and not against war as such. It should be said, forthrightly and in the same breath, that the church's ancient doctrine of *just* warfare means also just *warfare*. Only nuclear pacifism or germ pacifism finds occasion in modern weaponry for a renewal of the error of expecting peace and the solution of international problems to follow from disarmament, however important the achievement of some control of arms may be. In fact, lest language confuse us, it would be better not to speak of nuclear "disarmament," but of "arms control" and of controlled (or even unilateral) abandonment of weapons that are not weapons of war at all but of murder and devastation without limit and that have none of the purposes

---

tions of power, is not the issue; but rather obliteration of the distinction between counter-*forces* and counter-*people* warfare. Herein such proposals, or predictions, of weapons to be used overstep the laws of war, no matter if no one is killed; and to all such may be riposted the words of John Locke, deducing the right of liberty from the right of life: "He who attempts to get another man into his absolute power does thereby put himself into a state of war with him; it being understood as a declaration of a design upon his life. For I have reason to conclude that he who would get me into his power without my consent, would use me as he pleased when he had got me there, and destroy me too, when he had a fancy to it.... He that in the state of nature would take away the freedom that belongs to any one in that state, must necessarily be supposed to have a design to take away everything else, that freedom being the foundation of all the rest.... (*Second Treatise on Civil Government*, III, 17). It is *always already* totalitarianism to suppose, and to act on the supposition, that all the people of an enemy nation, without distinction, have put themselves into a state of war, or have sacrificed their right to life and liberty. Yet certainly the Christian knows that the just conduct of war should be limited to the use of all feasible, *and necessary,* means of destroying *or* getting the *forces* of the enemy into a defender's power. Perhaps it is relevant, finally, to point out that, in the first use of poison gas in World War I, at Ypres on April 22, 1915, the Germans acted in the main as if they were trying an experiment (which I suppose is not permissible even on soldiers) and not fighting a war: they were not ready to take any military advantage of the breakthrough they obtained by a "specialized application" of this weapon (cf. Herman Kahn, *op. cit.*, Lect. III, chap. viii, p. 353; and Fr. Ford's comment, in the text above at chap. vii, n. 2).

of war remaining in them; and to speak therefore of rational *rearmament,* and (so far as the moralist alone can know) this may include rational *nuclear* armament or rational biological and chemical armament.

In any case, the moral-political doctrine prohibiting indiscriminate obliteration warfare is "the certain trumpet" upon which the churches should be blowing, even as perhaps Morgenstern has sounded another very certain trumpet. The moral limits upon the right conduct of war provide the ultimate context in which policy decisions must be made and diplomatic negotiations carried out.   I say, this is the *context* for policy decision and the goal and ground of international agreements, not that the just conduct of war *is* a policy decision to be taken at once without consideration for other factors in the total context in which any political decision must be made.   The difference between justifiable and unjustifiable ways of making war is even the ground upon which Morgenstern's analysis proceeds, and the basic motive toward the conclusion he reaches.   Then when we face squarely those realistic military recommendations, the same impulse that drove the human mind to make them, and the ethical standards that would cause us at such cost to try to avoid the evil necessity of unjust war, may prove capable of driving mankind even in its wars again to self-control by restoring the ancient landmarks.   Let any reader of Morgenstern's book say whether it is worth trying to keep warfare just and limited—and trying to prevent unjust warfare—by the methods Morgenstern sees to be necessary and with the results for human life on this planet which he acknowledges to be highly probable!   He who sits down first to count the cost of survival into a country that will be unrecognizable, even if he lives to make the comparison, or, living, should he care to make it even if he could, may instead be driven to exclaim: "Alas, our only real hope seems to be a return to the fundamental principles of morality!" Thus is one "deep truth" productive of the other.

b. *The Infeasibility of Deterrence*

In yet another way the deep truth contained in the ancient tradition of just warfare emerges today as perhaps a viable option for the nations from an examination of the conclusions and proposals of military planners, as a whole, as they attempt rationally to subdue the problem of modern weapons. There are two main ways in which to disagree with Morgenstern's position. One is to assert that, without going to the trouble of perfecting the system, deterrence is already working well enough, all too well. There is even now a "balance of terror," it may be asserted; and the massive weapons both sides now possess have the power, and are known to have the power, to inflict far more than "acceptable damage" in retaliation against the side that makes the first strike. They can "over-kill," and can cause such "bonus damage" that it now is the case that either side is more than sufficiently deterred from starting a thermonuclear exchange. This is called the "minimum deterrence" theory. By means of gross retaliatory weapons directed at populations, by means of a "primitive" system, nuclear war has already been made entirely infeasible, indeed quite impossible as at all a rational action. Such deterrence has been, it would seem, our nation's policy in the not so distant past, under the rubric "more bang for a buck." By contrast, Morgenstern proposes "more exact, more limited and controlled bang for a buck" (a not wholly illegitimate goal). His view may be termed "finite deterrence" (plus, in addition, the admission that elaborate civil defense and defense of the recuperative power of the economy are still needed, and therefore the admission that even a perfected deterrent may fail). His is not a pure "finite deterrence" point of view, since a premise of this in its pure form is that deterrence is *so entirely feasible* that no other measures are necessary. "Minimum" deterrence, by means of gross, instantly reacting weapons systems, and "finite" deterrence, with dispersed, mobile forces (Polaris and Minute Man missiles) capable of delayed but still certain reaction—both affirm the feasibility of deterrence. Both propose a *retaliatory* strategy replacing, in the main, any emphasis upon *counter-forces* warfare.

Deterrence—it may be pointed out in passing—has an uglier face than we have yet quite uncovered in discussing Morgenstern's proposals (which, by perfecting the deterrent, aim at automatically transforming the retaliatory system for some time to come into a counter-forces system, drawing its fire away from peoples by insuring that the system can never be fired before the opposing forces are eliminated or neutralized). The true face of deterrence was more clearly evident in the Report of the Special Arms Project Committee on Security through Arms Control of the National Planning Association. That Report was directed *against* the policy of the United States in maintaining a counter-force strategy as well as a retaliatory policy, *against* planning to destroy Russian striking forces in addition to their cities. Such a policy, this report said, may have worked well enough in the fifties, but it is not sound for the missile age of the sixties. Now and in the foreseeable future: "A purely retaliatory strategy against key Russian industrial complexes can *by itself* soon provide adequate deterrence against a Russian attack against the U.S. as it can be based on essentially invulnerable retaliatory forces. . . ." This report calls for "a retaliatory policy, *devoid of counter-force ambitions.*" Among the advantages of this policy, we are told, is the fact that

The counter-force strategy is now the doctrinal source of the arms race, demanding big bombs to make up for bombing errors and to kill with certainty small and elusive targets. It also demands smaller packaging to permit more accurate and swift delivery systems. It requires virtually indefinite testing. However, a purely retaliatory strategy vis-a-vis Russia requires only "a sufficiency"—enough destruction to deter Russia from direct attack on the U.S. will be able to use deterrent forces (when necessary) and the credibility of the retaliatory deterrent can be maintained. The Polaris and Minute Man rocket weapons now being developed will provide the U.S. with an adequate and invulnerable retaliatory force for this purpose.[8]

It would seem that if there must be an "arms race," it were better a race in *arms,* i.e., *counter-forces* warfare, than in weapons *devoid* of any other purpose than the obliteration of people indiscriminately. The only thing that saves this system (morally or militarily) is the belief that the system will surely deter and the weapons themselves will never be used.[9] Of crucial importance, then, is the question: Is *this* deterrent credible? In fact, is *deterrence* feasible?

[8] *1970 without Arms Control.* (Washington: National Planning Association, 1958, italics added).

[9] It is notable that the *first* response of the U.S. government to the successful firing of a Polaris missile from a submarine underwater was to shift more budget funds to provide for swifter development of a larger number of Polaris submarines; and that these additional funds were secured by *cutting back* a projected development of *defense* by submarines against such an enemy system. Assuming that the *objective* of the Polaris system we are going to rely on in the sixties is an enemy's *population,* we are still relying exclusively upon deterrence, and an immoral deterrence; and for budgetary reasons—which makes the policy twice immoral. The acceptance by the American public of our government's policy of defense by counter-people deterrence rests in large measure upon the *quite mistaken* assumption that in the missile age there is no other defense. "...The usual remark, 'in the air and missile age the offense has an intrinsic advantage over the defense,' is only true, if at all, because our sensors are not reliable. It really is possible today to destroy an enemy object, destroy it reliably in a way that has not been possible in the past, if you know where this object is." Looking into the future: "the interceptor has an appreciable, if not 100 percent, kill probability against anything at which it gets a good chance to fire"; "this edge [on the side of *defense*] is as likely as not to be increased by further developments" (Herman Kahn: *On Thermonuclear War.* Princeton, N. J.: Princeton University Press, 1960, Lect. III, chap. x, pp. 495, 511; and chap. xi, p. 542). It seems far more possible to perfect a moral defense in this electronic age than to perfect an offensive defense by means of an immoral deterrent. Suppose both were equally possible: which war should be built into our sensors and computers? On which should this nation's effort be concentrated?

The second way, then to disagree with Morgenstern's central proposal is to question fundamentally the feasibility of deterrence as at all an adequate national policy in the face of modern weapons, or a way of subduing the problem these weapons have posed for the political life of mankind, in the short or in the long run. On the one hand, as we have seen, there are those who say that thermonuclear warfare today is not feasible and that therefore deterrence either is or can soon be made feasible. On the other hand, and countering that point of view, there are those who say that deterrence is not feasible and that therefore war, even thermonuclear warfare, is, or can and must be made, feasible. Herman Kahn's recently published book may be taken to represent the latter point of view.[10]

It is my contention that *neither* deterrence *nor* warfare with these immoral means is or can be made feasible. There needs now to be written a "Critique of Technical Reason" *à la Kant,* to show that the planners of military strategy (not because they are not good at this, but precisely because they are as good as they can possibly be) are now caught in a "Dialectic of Pure Military Reason." This dialectic means that, in attempting to include such weapons as we now have within the scope of a minimally purposive national policy, rational analysis has exceeded its own power. It falls into "transcendental illusion" by claiming that a feasible way to use these weapons, or a feasible way to use them by not using them, has been found or may be constructed. It only brings forth "Antinomies," composed of a Thesis and its direct Antithesis each of which it is equally reasonable to believe is true or propose can or *shall* be the case. Notice that I do not say that pure technical reason cannot grasp the *Ding an Sich* of how a nation can be made *secure* in

[10] *On Thermonuclear War* (Princeton, N. J.: Princeton University Press, 1960).

a world rendered permanently perilous by the irrevocable discovery of weapons too massive to be employed for any of the ends of policy. Nor can a national resolve to fight wars only justly any longer rest upon the confidence that thereby national security may be guaranteed. Security may now be beyond the grasp of both technical reason and moral *scientia*. I simply suggest that there is now some "critical reason" to believe that, for intrinsic reasons that have to do with the very nature of these weapons, they cannot be shown to have any active or passive use, in fighting a war or in deterring war. The two pairs of Antinomies are:

A. 1. *Deterrence is feasible.*
  2. *Deterrence is not feasible.*

B. 1. *Thermonuclear Warfare is not feasible.*
  2. *Thermonuclear Warfare is feasible.*

We have examined the view of some military planners who assert the Thesis in each of these pairs. In the writings of Herman Kahn, now to be examined, we have the truth affirmed of the Antithesis in each of these Antinomies. As every reader of Kant knows, the "solution" in the case of the "mathematical antinomies" is: *Neither is true.* Pure reason must be destroyed, or be shown to reveal its own limitation, in order to make room for moral *scientia*. Plan to use these weapons however we will, or plan to use them only passively by not using them—shoot them for the hell of it or not shoot them for the deterrence of the hell of it—but never imagine that reason in its "strategic employment" can demonstrate that intrinsically limitless weapons are usable, to fight a war or to deter war, there where the nations and national purposes conflict. A nation's purpose will not be deterred from finding a proper and feasible force by which to express itself. Reason in its "strategic use" can never show a connection, or make the connection, between inherently limitless force and inherently purposeful power.[11]

This, then, is my formal argument in this chapter. Its substance and demonstration is furnished, in large measure, by Herman Kahn's success in showing that the credibility of a "deter the war" policy depends on a nation's capability to "fight the war" (i.e., to fight precisely the kind of war it seeks to deter), and then by his *failure* to make it credible to believe in the feasibility of fighting a thermonuclear war (on which depends the ability to deter one, or to deter lesser wars or to conduct political affairs by any exertion of a nation's power under the shelter of such a deterrent).

Deterrence requires not only subjective or psychological capability, Kahn argues, but objective capability as well. Yet as force becomes more and more available, it becomes less and less usable; and as "we tend to consider weapons less and less usable," so "we emphasize more and more their role in deterring an enemy, rather than their objective capability to punish or defend. That is, *we emphasize the impact of our capabilities on the enemy's mind rather than on his body.* This introduces many subtleties and some wishful thinking into discussions of modern war."[12] Of course,

---

[11] My hesitation in advancing the above suggestion arises from two considerations: (*a*) my own reading of the military strategists has not been extensive and complete enough for me to undertake to finish the suggested "critique," and (*b*) I want to avoid the implication that moral and political principles can simply be deduced from the fact that the planning of military policy is exceedingly difficult, or that some simplicist ethical assertion could be said to gain strength and acceptability from the necessary complexity of strategic analysis.

[12] *Ibid.*, Lect. II, chap. iv, p.126. The fact is, if we are to believe the keynoter at the 1960 Republican convention, that since our present military policy is built on deterrence and since deterrence *consists* of what the enemy *thinks* we have and actually intend to use, the opposition party cannot criticize our present policy without weakening it to the core! He is correct: you cannot discuss an incredibility without making more evident to ourselves and to an enemy that it is incredible. Thus, the existence of megaton weapons and policy built around them makes impossible not only the sound conduct of international power-relations but also the conduct of domestic politics for the clarification of national policy. (This may be related to the fact that, as pointed out in

in war one is always seducing as well as coercing the enemy, "which automatically means we are working on his mind as well as his body."[13] However, against the current overemphasis upon the psychology of deterrence, it is important as a corrective to stress the need for an objective capability in order to maintain even for a very short run our capability to deter an enemy subjectively. By emphasizing psychological façade in this matter of deterrence and making the deterrent seem more and more horrendous, the first result is that we ourselves and our allies are deterred, and not only and perhaps not the enemy. "It is dangerous to use measures that work on the psychology of the enemy, because they work on our psychology also."[14] The proponents of Minimum or pure Finite Deterrence wrongly suppose that they have replaced political irresoluteness by certainty, even automation in the reply. They imagine that they can perfect the deterrent and remove the necessity for plans and for a real capability to fight the war through to a finish.

Unfortunately, this attempt to look like a force of nature that cannot be influenced or reasoned with, but can only be taken account of when calculations are being made, ignores the fact that the enemy also can threaten us, and he will simply refuse to believe that we will ignore his threats. If we believe the enemy is listening to our threats, then somehow we have to believe that he thinks we are listening to his threats. Even if we think we are sincere in our irrevocable commitments, the probability of a total response to a moderate provocation is still going to be close to zero, since the enemy can make such a response costly. When the time comes to act it just will not be worth it. The closest one can come to making the stand credible is to program it in a computer, to take a high moral position (saying, in effect, I would like to compromise but my integrity

---

chapter six, democracy means *justum bellum*.) Obviously, however, the Democrats did not intend to discuss our weapons policy to the depth Congressman Judd reached in that one moment.

[13] *Ibid.*, Lect. II, chap. iv, p. 164.
[14] *Ibid.*, Lect. II. chap. vi, p. 181.

will not let me) or to look slightly mad, intemperate or emotional. This technique was used by Hitler. It may also have been the technique used by Khrushchev in recent years.[15]

No merely declaratory policy will long stand under the pressures to which it will inevitably be subjected. A merely declaratory policy is one that can be tested without directly challenging and inviting the full force threatened.

While deterrence is a psychological phenomenon, it is not true that one has it for all practical purposes, just because the enemy and others believe that he does. Psychological non-objective capabilities are extremely unstable. They are subject to erosion by time and, equally important, to subtle tactics of the enemy or our own panic. The enemy can investigate and teach himself what capabilities we really have. He can also, by means of crises and other tactics, teach others what he has learned about our objective capabilities. One of the serious problems in psychological deterrence is that the learning is likely to be too convincing.[16]

If there is very little possibility of bluffing about what objective capabilities we have, there is even less for bluffing about what we intend to do with these capabilities. A mere declaration of our intentions and of our resolve can be tested without directly challenging or inviting the fulfilment of such announced policy, precisely because probing crises may very easily be kept ambiguous, and therefore no one of the decisions with which a nation can be confronted may ever seem to be "worth it." "A total reliance on being willing to commit [mutual] suicide cannot be even a moderately reliable deterrent against almost all 'ambiguous' and most 'non-ambiguous' challenges. . . ."[17] All this follows, it seems to me, from the fact that deterrence is not only a "system" but also a "calculation of the enemy's calculation" and a calculation of his calculation of our calculation and of

---

[15] *Ibid.*, Lect. II, chap. vi, p. 290.
[16] *Ibid.*, Lect. III, chap. ix, p. 446.
[17] *Ibid.*, Lect. III, chap. x, p. 470.

our intent, etc. As in the past—when wars were somewhat more reasonable—it is still the case today that the threat of war can be used to deter war only if by "war" something is meant that can be done, done politically as well as militarily. If the war we are talking about is feasible, or can somehow be made feasible as a matter of national policy, then and then only will deterrence be feasible; and deterrence is credible only if the war is credible. *Because* he is primarily interested in deterrence, Kahn's book (and the action he proposes that we should take as a nation) is directed to the end of making thermonuclear war feasible, and credible as well our nation's survival in a postattack environment.

Believers in Minimal or "primitive" Deterrence seem to believe that the deterrence of a rational enemy is "almost a simple philosophic consequence of the *existence* of thermonuclear bombs."[18] Believers in Finite or more sophisticated mobile systems of deterrence seem to believe that they have found a technical means to prevent war by accident. And (since deterrence now works very well except for mischance) they believe they have found a non-political means of preventing political acts of war. "Many of the more passionate devotees to Finite Deterrence believe consciously or unconsciously that they have abolished war."[19] We must ask, what does this amount to *politically?*

[18] *Ibid.*, Lect. I. Chap. i, p. 8; Cf. Lect. III, chap. xii, p. 556-564.

[19] *Ibid.*, Lect. III, chap. xi, p. 526. "Sober advocates of Finite Deterrence wish to have the various weapons systems so deployed and operated that they will have a guaranteed capability, even in a crisis in which the enemy has taken extraordinary measures to negate the capability. They want these forces dispersed, protected, and alert; the arrangements for command, control and communications must be able to withstand degradation by both peacetime and wartime tactics of the enemy. These sober believers in Finite Deterrence tend to insist on an objective capability as opposed to one that is only 'psychological.' And even those believers in Finite Deterrence who would be satisfied with a facade yearn for an impressive-looking facade. One might characterize the Finite Deterrence position as the expert version of the Minimum Deterrence position held by an expert who wants to look good to other experts.... The believer in Finite Deterrence is willing to concede that it takes some effort to guarantee Mutual Homicide, that it is not automatic" (*ibid.*, Lect. I, chap. i, pp. 14-15).

Under current programs the U.S. may in a few years find itself unwilling to accept a Soviet retaliatory blow, no matter what the provocation. To get into such a situation would be equivalent to disowning our alliance obligations by signing what would amount to a nonaggression treaty with the Soviets—a nonaggression treaty with almost 200 million American hostages to guarantee performance.[20]

This was in effect already ratified by Minimum Deterrence— "a reliable non-aggression treaty with their populations to insure adherence to this treaty"—and the perfection of the system has only removed "an accidental or unauthorized violation of this nonagression 'treaty.' "[21] This might be believed to be politically acceptable (even though it would mean renouncing any influence upon the world's affairs beyond the limits of Bastion America) if it could be made to work. We will see in a moment that the effectiveness of such deterrence as well as the advisability of renouncing war (and renouncing alliances) as a national policy, may both be questioned.

Another way Kahn expresses the *political* significance of deterrence, standing alone, is to say: "Many of the advocates of Finite Deterrence are advocating what amounts to a subtle form of unilateral disarmament."[22] This may be more difficult to see, since it implies that *two* nations may unilaterally disarm. Yet this all seems to me to follow from the determination to do the impossible, namely, to found a weapons system primarily on instruments that are *not armament* but instruments for the destruction of people that are comparable in power only to the gross forces in nature, such as hurricanes or earthquakes, if to these.

This would not be a feasible even if desirable policy. Kahn declares roundly that he has "yet to see a posture de-

[20] *Ibid.*, Lect. III, chap. xii, p. 559.
[21] *Ibid.*, Lect. I, chap. i, p. 12.
[22] *Ibid.*, Lect. III, chap. xi, p. 526.

scribed in which the Soviets could not degrade seriously the capability of our Type I Deterrent in peacetime by acts of violence which would not be deterred if we only had a Type I Deterrent."[23] Planners such as Morgenstern have not sufficiently analyzed the vulnerability of a Polaris submarine system, especially not in the power-political context. Kahn brings this against the feasibility of deterrence, as proposed.

Imagine, for example, that we had a pure Polaris system invulnerable to an all-out simultaneous enemy attack (invulnerable by assumption and not by analysis), and the enemy started to destroy our submarines one at a time at sea. Suppose an American President was told that if we started an all-out war in retaliation, the limitations on the Polaris system would make it unsuitable as a counterforce weapon and our active and passive defenses are so weak the Soviets could and probably would destroy every American. Now if the President has a chance to think about the problem, he simply cannot initiate this kind of war even with such provocation.[24]

When reading the opening part of this chapter, the reader may already have had serious doubt whether, before an enemy learned how to get at our dispersed retaliatory forces, another invulnerable force would be in readiness; and he may have wondered what would happen to keep war automatically deterred after that in turn was broken. There is here too easy an assumption that "fighting the war" has been technically abolished. An enemy may soon learn to pick off the submarines and sea planes one by one, while announcing either beguiling limited-war aims or wholesale blackmail. He may line the ocean with explosives to destroy gross parts of the system. More likely in this age of counter-electronic warfare, he may simply degrade any plans and devices for commanding all the units of such a dis-

[23] Ibid., Lect. II, chap. iv, p. 158.
[24] Ibid., Lect. II, chap. iv, p. 130.

persed, mobile system. Not only may an enemy interfere with our communications and command (which is an increased problem the more the system is dispersed and mobile), but also intrinsic to its successful operation is the problem of keeping the commands *credible* to those who receive them: "Many studies indicate that *unless a strategic force reacts in some appropriate way to false alarms, it runs a risk of not reacting at all when the real thing comes along.*"[25] If we do not want to start a war accidentally, we run the risk of complacency and the enemy may exploit the resulting requirement for officially verified command orders to degrade the performance of the system.[26] Not only deterrent *threats* but domestic military *commands* become incredible, unless these weapons are sometimes *used*.

More important than these technical difficulties is the political uselessness of this deterrent, standing alone:

A thermonuclear balance of terror is equivalent to signing a nonaggression treaty which states that neither the Soviets nor the Americans will initiate an all-out attack, no matter how provoking the other side may become. Sometimes people do not understand the full implications of this figurative nonaggression treaty. Let me illustrate what it can mean if we accept absolutely the notion that there is no provocation that would cause us to strike the Soviets other than an immediately impending or an actual Soviet attack on the United States . . . . Suppose, for example, that the Soviets have dropped bombs on London, Berlin, Rome, Paris, and Bonn *but have made no detectable preparations for attacking the United States and that our retaliatory force looks good enough to deter them from such an attack. . . .* Suppose also that there is a device which restrains the President of the United States from acting for about twenty four hours. . . . The President would presumably call together his advisors during this time. Most of the advisors would probably urge strongly that the U.S. fulfil its obligations by striking the Soviet

---

[25] *Ibid.,* Lect. II, chap. v, p. 205. For a humorous hypothetical case, cf. pp. 198-199.

[26] *Ibid.,* Lect. II, chap. vi, pp. 257-262, 269.

Union. Now let us further suppose that the President is also told by his advisors that even though we will kill almost every Russian *civilian,* we will not be able to destroy all of the Soviet strategic forces, and that these surviving Soviet forces will (by radiation or strontium-90 or something) kill every American in their retaliatory blow—all 180 million of us.

Is it not difficult to believe that under these hypothetical circumstances any President of the United States would initiate a thermonuclear war by all-out retaliation against the Soviets with the Strategic Air Command?[27]

Or what would be an "acceptable price" to pay in cold blood and with full knowledge, in order for the United States to have any power to stop a massive advance of Soviet power? Five million lives? Twenty million lives? Fifty million lives? We are already deterred from deterrence. It would not be difficult, by cold war tactics and ambiguous or even not so ambiguous challenges, to force an American President to think about these alternatives in a cool hour.[28] Suppose that without striking a blow the Soviets simply deliver the following ultimatum: "Unless the Europeans disarm themselves in thirty days the Soviets will proceed to

[27] *Ibid.,* Lect. I, chap. i, pp. 28-29.

[28] "It is just as difficult to imagine a President willing to risk the deaths of five million Americans as of fifty million" (London *Times,* Jan. 4, 1960). In an exchange of articles on "The Case for Neutralism—And the Case against It" in the *New York Times Magazine,* July 24, 1960, Bertrand Russell made use of Kahn's argument (citing his article "The Feasibility of War and Deterrence," *Stanford Research Institute Journal,* II, 2). To this Hugh Gaitskell (who presumably, since we exported our nuclear deterrence policy, would want his nation's policy aligned with ours in this regard) replied by admitting that "of course, the theory of deterrence does rest upon credibility—the belief and fear on the part of the aggressor that there will be retaliation against him if he attacks." But, wrote Gaitskell, "it is not necessary that the leaders of the Kremlin should be absolutely convinced that America will retaliate, but only that there is *considerable risk* that they would do so ... (italics added)." Since Gaitskell also correctly believes (unlike Kahn) that "the effects of a nuclear war will surely be so terrible that it is a waste of time to discuss how many people are likely to survive," how long will it be, we may ask, before the "considerable risk" that retaliation may come will evaporate *in the estimation* of the Russians (where alone—in their *estimation*—it has any power to deter)? Especially since *all* their challenges (Gaitskell practically admits) will be *less* terrible to contemplate than the one it is a waste of time to discuss.

disarm them (they have no other demands)," adding perhaps that all Europe, Asia, and Africa will hereafter be considered to be in the Soviet sphere of influence, promising to respect the Western Hemisphere, Australia, and perhaps the British Isles and Japan as within the American sphere. (Later, one or another of these remaining areas of American influence can be picked off by the same procedure.) Who would be justified in *using* the deterrent? Supposing its use to be reliably suicidal, who *would* use it? Without the ability and willingness to fight the war, we cannot stop the relentless advance of an enemy. What cannot be used, cannot deter. Then policy reveals itself as only declaratory.

c. *The Infeasibility of Thermonuclear War*

We move now from the more or less declaratory deterrent policies of the West during the fifties to the declaratory nuclear-war policies that may be adopted in the sixties, whoever may be the American President or the party in power. (Already, the Democrats and, under the prodding of Governor Rockfeller, the Republican party, without discriminating between shootable and unshootable weapons, have called for a far greater expenditure for military defense, and for a shelter program for the entire nation.) In this section I undertake to show that planning to fight the war and to prevail through the war cannot be seriously intended as a political action, if by war is meant a central use—even a supposedly limited, careful, or sanitary use—of unlimited means. We will continue to have under consideration the book by Herman Kahn *On Thermonuclear War*, but this time his signal *failure* to demonstrate how thermonuclear war can be made feasible (and therefore deterrence credible).

A "deter the war" capability depends on a "fight the war" capability for this crucial reason: Deterrence requires that we have a "credible first strike capability," or, if you prefer, a credible *answering* strike capability; and this in turn is clearly reducible to whether or not we have a credible *second* strike capability. The credibility of our striking at all depends on our ability and willingness to *accept* the other side's retaliatory blow, and then to be able and willing still to strike back. Credible *first* strike capability depends on credible second or answering strike capability and this means it depends on how much harm *he* can do us, not on how much harm *we* can do him. Kahn's whole book is an analysis of how we can obtain credible *answering* strike capability, for deterrence or for use.

The following paragraph indicates, in its italicized words, some of the purely military factors which will be re-required if war or deterrence are to be made feasible: The enemy

can strike *at a time and with tactics of their choosing.* We will strike back, no doubt, but with *a damaged and not fully coordinated force* which must conduct its operations in the *postattack environment.* The Soviets may use *blackmail threats to intimidate our postattack tactics.* Under these conditions, the Russian defense is likely to be *altered . . . augmented,* and their cities. . . *evacuated.*[29]

In deterrence, the really essential numbers are an enemy's calculation of our calculation of the damage our retaliatory forces can inflict after we have been hit and hit hard; and in war, the really essential estimates are estimates of the damage that retaliatory forces can inflict under these conditions.[30]

Consider only the difficulty of having an answering strike capability in the postattack environment. Even if nuclear weapons do not hit their targets, they may nevertheless

[29] *Op. cit.,* Lect. I, chap. i, p. 14.
[30] Cf. *Ibid.,* Lect. II, chap. iv, p. 128.

change the environment or damage critical equipment so as to cause important parts of the retaliating weapon system to be temporarily inoperable. The various effects of nuclear weapons include blast, heat, thermal and electromagnetic radiation, ground shock, debris, dust and ionizing radiation—any of which may affect people, equipment, propagation of electromagnetic signals, and so on. One might say that the problem of operating in a post-attack environment after training in a peacetime environment is similar to training at the equator and then moving a major but incomplete, *unpredictably incomplete,* part (that is, a damaged system) to the arctic and expecting this incomplete system to work efficiently the first time it is tried. This is particularly implausible if, as is often true, the intact system is barely operable at the equator (that is, in peacetime).[31]

There may be solution to these technical problems, as Kahn believes, once we succeed in putting our minds on how we are going to fight a thermonuclear war; and so there may be a solution to the problem of how we are going to get a credible answering strike capability for deterrence or for use, or for use in deterrence. So far as this is only a technical problem, it should be left to experts.

However, we edge closer to the point where practical political wisdom on the part of anyone may be competent to judge whether nuclear warfare and nuclear deterrence by means of megaton weapons can be made feasible, when we take up the question how we are going to get a credible answering strike capability in the face of postattack blackmail:

The enemy can then make some ferocious threats that may well cause us to be discriminating in our later counterattack. He could say, for example, "I have deliberately avoided your cities. I have treated them as open cities, and I wish you to treat my cities in the same way. In the confusion of the first attack you inadvertently or advertently may have tried to attack my cities. However, it is most unlikely that the handful of attacking planes

[31] *Ibid.*, Lect. II, chap. iv, p. 130.

got through, since I have such an adequate air defense. If they did, I will be more angry at my air defense commander than at you. However, from now on for every city of mine you destroy I will destroy five of yours." If he has been reasonably effective in his first strike, this is a credible threat. If he makes it dramatic enough, it might influence our action. For example, he could be specific and say, "If you destroy Moscow, I will destroy New York, Washington, Los Angeles, Philadelphia, and Chicago. If you destroy Leningrad, I will destroy Detroit, Pittsburgh, San Francisco, New Orleans, and Miami." He can finish his list with a remark to the general effect that "you know better than I do what kind of a country you want to have after this war is over. Pick which American cities you wish to have destroyed." This would be in any event a very credible threat....[32]

Is there any credible answer to it?

A large part of Kahn's answer to this question is to be found in the depths of an adequate civil defense program, and defense of the recuperative powers of the economy—first an inexpensive program in the early sixties, to be replaced by the very expensive one that will be made necessary by technological advance by the late sixties and early seventies. Relatively cheap radiation meters should be made available for quick distribution in the event of war—since in that event "if one man vomits, everybody vomits. It would not be surprising if almost everybody vomits. Almost everyone is likely to think he has received too much radiation"[33]— and the meters will tell a great many of them that this is not true, and not all will just lie down and die. Between 100,000 and 250,000 semi-military cadres should be created and trained for specialized purposes, e.g., decontamination (whose probability of success, however, is notably unanalyzed in this book). High quality shelter spaces should be constructed for about fifty million people in congested areas. Studies show that this can be done for Manhattan Island at

[32] *Ibid.*, Lect. II, chap. iv, p. 168.
[33] *Ibid.*, Lect. I, chap. ii, p. 86.

a cost of $700 per person, and that the shelters can be placed within five minutes walking time of everyone in the city. But it is admitted that these shelters, 1000 ft. deep and with 1000 psi doors at the surface, would withstand direct hits of only small bombs (i.e., less than 5 megatons) or "near" misses by larger bombs. For thirty billion dollars the nation could buy a couple of billion square feet of underground factory space, enough to stockpile between a fourth and a half of our current industrial capacity.[34] For ten billion dollars, 100 days supply of processed shelter rations at half a dollar per day per person; for another twelve billion dollars, 300 days semi-processed rations at twenty cents per day per person.

Kahn's proposals for civil defense and for defense of the economy, it seems very clear, and his proposals for alleviating the effects of thermonuclear war, are obviously little more than declaratory policy. He comes close to admitting this in a concluding chapter in answer to certain stated objections. To the objection that "the U.S. would never deliberately risk a war which might result in the calculated losses envisaged by this program," Kahn replies:

The best that any credible First Strike Capability can do is to make it rational (or not wildly irrational) for the U.S. to go to war as an alternative to tolerating extreme provocations. The word "rational" means that five or ten years after the war is over the country will not look back on the war as a mistake. (The Soviet Union, for example, undoubtedly feels that the cost of victory in World War II—20 to 30 million dead and one-third of its wealth destroyed—was preferable to domination by Nazi Germany. Similarly, it should be *credible,* that we will go to war if the President and the enemy both see plainly that going to War is rational. One can almost hear the President saying to his advisor, "How can I go to war—almost all American cities will be destroyed?" And the answer ought to be, in essence, "That's not entirely fatal, we've built some spares.") Under

[34] *Ibid.,* Lect. III, chap. x, p. 517.

these circumstances the enemy cannot *rely* on the U.S. not going to war when provoked beyond endurance. The object, of course, is to get most of what we want (including encouragement and support for our allies) by deterring the enemy from inordinately provocative tactics; we want to *avoid* actually going to war.[35]

And to the objection that an adequate shelter program will arouse more terror than it will allay, Kahn replies in part:

The major emphasis ought to be on its deterrence value and on the extra insurance if deterrence fails. *We do not really expect to have to use the system.* Still, it is vital the people realize that the system may possibly be used even though the existence of the program makes war or serious crisis less likely. Thus, the program will be realistic.[36]

Now, is it not obvious that, in these statements, Kahn stresses mainly (if not quite exclusively) the subjective deterrent value of effecting these proposals, in order to make them credible as a political decision now to be taken?[37] He comes close to repeating the words of "General Aphorism" he had criticized earlier: "If these buttons are ever pressed,

[35] *Ibid.*, Pt. II, Appendiv V, Ans. to Obj. 1, pp. 641-642.

[36] *Ibid.*, Pt. II, Appendix V, Ans. to Obj. 4, p. 644 (italics added). Or earlier: I find "Usually when I discuss expensive programs that involve elaborate shelters, that people are appalled at the idea of living underground for such lengthy periods as posed here. *It should be remembered that the program is not being set up in the expectation that it will be so used, even if we have a war; rather it is intended to limit the amount of damage actually done by a war, and to increase the capability of the U.S. to withstand blackmail tactics.* That is, even if the worst comes and a war actually comes, in all liklihood the war will be fought much more carefully than the preparations of the program indicate" (*ibid.*, Lect. III, chap. x, p. 518).

[37] At another point, however, in order to make palatable and credible a decision to "fight the war" with clear knowledge of the conditions of life in a postwar environment, Kahn had need to stress the "objective capability" of a national shelter program, and not simply its deterrent value, or its use if only we don't have to use it. He wrote: "If half of our residential space is destroyed, then, even if everyone survives, these survivors will be better housed than the average (very productive) Soviet citizen. (In 1970, when we might have a large underground shelter system that could be used for temporary housing, we could afford to lose perhaps three-quarters of our residential space and still be reasonably well-housed in terms of the economic efficiency of the inhabitants.)" (*Ibid.*, Lect. I, chap. ii, pp. 79-80.)

they have *completely failed* in their purpose! The equipment is useful only if it is not used."[38]   To the extent that this is true, then the country would be more interested in such measures *seeming* to be useful than in their actually being useful; more in seeming to be willing to do these things than in actually intending to do them; more in subjective capability to deter than in objective capability so to act; and the deterrent value itself would, as Kahn argued earlier, be weakened to the exact degree that the system of civil defense is intended to be not used.

This is even more clearly the case with regard to measures "at least 'to prevail' in some meaningful sense even if you cannot win" the war, for alleviating the danger, recuperating from it and living in the years to come in a post-attack environment. "The survivors will not dance in the streets or congratulate each other if there are 20 million men, women, and children killed; yet it would have been a worthwhile achievement to limit casualties to this number."[39] But our present problem is with the still living; and here Kahn asks the question: "Will the survivors envy the dead?" An answer to this question is important for his argument, because, unless it can be shown that, by proper planning,

[38] *Ibid.*, Lect. I, chap. i, p. 17.
[39] *Ibid.*, Lect. I, chap. i, pp. 24, 20. A shelter system is not so much for the protection of civilians as it is an instrument of war. "Even though civilians are not military targets they are hostages, and protecting them can negate some important enemy tactics. In this new and rather subtle sense, non-military defense can contribute to Type I Deterrence, even if civilians and their property no longer contribute to the war effort" (*ibid.*, Lect. II, chap. iv, pp. 173-174). For this reason some analysts today recommend that, in order to continue to make use of counter-people weapons in planning for war and to *stabilize* the deterrent, both sides tacitly agree *not* to try to protect their populations; others, that both sides go underground. Kahn seems to prefer the latter "fight the war" policy, even though he knows that, against the weapon of our shelters, an enemy "can emphasize ground shock by using weapons that penetrate the earth and explode underground," and that there will be no experimental way to prepare for this: "no matter how well the equipment is shock-mounted and tested, it is not likely that we will be able to work out realistic 'shakedown' tests" (*ibid.*, Lect. II, chap. vi, pp. 262-263. Cf. Lect. III, chap. ix, p. 431).

human life and the national economy after a thermonuclear war can be made choiceworthy, then no nation would be willing to adopt a "fight the war" policy; and, as we have seen, on this depends the success of a "deter the war" policy.

Kahn does not deny, of course, that "it is in some sense true that one may never recuperate from a thermonuclear war. The world will be permanently (i.e., for perhaps 10,000 years) more hostile to human life as a result of such a war."[40] But the question is *how much more* hostile will the post-war environment be, and how can human beings and a nation adjust to it? This question must be answered, and our plans carefully laid, because (for deterrence *or* for war) *we must believe* that there are programs that are likely to be successful under wartime and postwar conditions.

Kahn believes that "decision makers might define a post-war world as 'tolerable' if death rates increased by about one percent for tens of thousands of years, even though this might mean that at long length the war would be responsible for the deaths of more people than are now alive."[41] He believes this, because that would be to subject all survivors to the level of risk which industrial workers undergo now, which we seem to define as tolerable or even positively worthwhile. An increase of one chance in a hundred thousand of a fatal accident per year does mean that thirty thousand extra people a year would die as a consequence of the war, and over fifty years a million and a half would die prematurely. But, Kahn writes, "I think that any individual who survived the war should be willing to accept, almost with equanimity, somewhat larger risks than those to which we subject our industrial workers in peacetime."[42] After all, we now prefer to let automobiles kill forty thousand people a year (or about 25 per 100,000) and injure close to

[40] *Ibid.*, Lect. I, chap. i, p. 21.
[41] *Ibid.*, Lect. I, chap. ii, p. 41.
[42] *Ibid.*, Lect. I, chap. ii, p. 42.

a million (or about 600 per 100,000) rather than accept speed limits of twenty miles an hour! In short, the additional degree of risk of death brought about by the increased hostility of the postwar environment pertains now in fact to many of the activities people regard as necessary and desirable.

The number of children born seriously defective would increase because of the war to about 25 per cent above the current rate. In other words, 1 per cent of children who would have been born healthy would be defective. "More horrible still, we might have to continue to pay a similar though smaller price for 20 or 30 or 40 generations." Since that would still be a long way from annihilation, "it might well turn out, for example, that U.S. decision makers would be willing, among other things, to accept a high risk of an additional 1 percent of our children being born deformed *if that meant not giving up Europe to Soviet Russia!"*[43] Why does Kahn believe this? His reasons seem to be two: (1) We already demonstrate that we are able to live with a much higher actual incidence of deformity than this *increase* would amount to:

I can easily imagine that if we lived in a world in which no children had ever been born defective and we were told that as a result of some new contingencies 4 percent of the children would be born seriously defective we would consider such a world to be intolerable. We might not believe that people would be willing to bear and raise children if the risk is 1 in 25 that these children might have a serious congenital defect. However, *we live in that world now.*[44]

For another reason, (2) it may be possible to "alleviate" some of these congenital defects before they happen: "Research in genetics is less than a hundred years old, and it is quite possible that even the next ten or fifteen years will

---

[43] *Ibid.*, Lect. I, chap. ii, p. 46
[44] *Ibid.*, Lect. I, chap. ii, pp. 46-47 (italics added).

see spectacular improvements in our knowledge and capabilities. It is, in pure theory, conceivable that we will be to some extent designing our children rather than depending on the haphazard [!] methods of the past. There would be no long-term genetic problem."[45]

If we assume a three and one-half day decrease in life expectancy per roentgen of exposure to radiation, then ten years is about the greatest decrease in life expectancy that could be expected in survivors as a result of long-term chronic exposure. "Ten years happens to be the amount added to an American *adult's* life expectancy since 1900."[46] Presumably, then, in the postwar environment survivors will have, on this account, no more reason to envy the dead than did the people in the nineteenth century!

". . . 0,013 KT per square mile or a mere 13 megatons (MT) of fission products spread uniformly over the 1,000,000 square miles in which we grow food in this country would make the food unfit for human consumption"—at our present standards of what is fit for human consumption. That amount could be produced by one large bomb. This could (if equally spread about) "suspend agriculture in the United States for 50 years or so." By "relaxing peacetime standards to the point that the incidence of cancer begins to change average life expectancy by a significant amount, then we have a problem when there is between 2 and 20 kilotons of fission products per square mile. . . . The simplest decontamination measure or alleviation by natural process would make the land usable—always assuming we are willing to drop our standards."[47] Kahn seems to complain that nobody is even thinking of lowering the standard according to which we regard as unacceptable more than 67 strontium units in *new bone,* resulting from eating food grown on land with a

[45] *Ibid.,* Lect. III, chap. x, p. 499.
[46] *Ibid.,* Lect. I, chap. ii, p. 60.
[47] *Ibid.,* Lect. I, chap. ii, p. 66.

contamination from about 0.013 kiloton of fission products per square mile. Yet, since the suspension of agriculture in the United States for fifty years or more would be intolerable in practice, an attack would result at once in the dropping of standards, since "the survivors really have no choice."[48] Also, the housewife's lot, with members of her family of different ages to feed, will not be a happy one: everyone will have to eat different foods, regulating the different levels of acceptable contamination in diets according to age, condition of health, etc. A bird-lover may have special adjustments to make in order not to envy the dead, since, according to one piece of incidental information this book provides us, "radiation kills a much higher percentage of birds than of insects."[49]

The foregoing is, in my opinion, a fair summary of the intellectual effort Herman Kahn has made in order to show that it is feasible to limit the damage of a thermonuclear war and to plan to alleviate and recover from and forever thereafter live with the immediate and long-term results of such a war; and from this to show that a "fight the war" policy is feasible and therefore to show that deterrence can be made credible. Many of his arguments are astonishing, and his proposals grim. It is more significant, however, to point out how, in a *formal* sense, they miss the point; and that any such manner of reasoning cannot hope to establish the conclusion Kahn seeks to reach.

Simply by an analysis of the actions and attitudes it would be reasonable *in the future* to put forth in a post-attack environment, you cannot demonstrate the reasonableness or credibility of *now* choosing a policy and *now*

[48] *Ibid.*, Lect. I, chap. ii, p. 69.
[49] *Ibid.*, Lect. I, chap. ii, p. 91. "It is very unlikely that areas such as the Rocky Mountains would ever be decontaminated. Some people might be willing to visit and hunt or fish for a few weeks (the game would be edible) but, unless they had a very good reason to stay, it would be unwise to live there and even more unwise to raise a family there" (*ibid.*, pp. 58-59).

putting forth the actions that will lead as their effect to creating that environment. Neither the morality nor the credibility nor the feasibility of present action can be sufficiently analyzed by attempting to show the rightfulness or the credibility or the feasibility of the *next* action that may become necessary if the first be done. The question is not whether future "decision makers" should regard the postwar world as "tolerable." The question is whether decision-making in the present should ever regard the *choice* of that postwar world, rather than some alternative to it, as possibly a reasonable policy to be adopted. This has to be shown, if a "fight the war" policy is to be regarded as feasible, and if it is credible to believe a people can deliberately plan now to use these weapons, or for them to attempt to deter war by their planned use.

The question is *not* "What view should a reasonable (nonhypochondriac) individual hold toward his own future?"[50] under the circumstances brought about by thermonuclear war. Instead, the question is what view should a reasonable, nonhypochondriac individual or statesman hold toward actions that are foreknown to have the effect of bringing about these conditions and the necessity for such later actions. Let it be acknowledged that many such future attitudes and actions will or should be credible. Indeed, Kahn might have helped himself toward this conclusion by availing himself of our Western religious tradition which declares that, if for the living to envy the dead is not actually a grave sin, it would indicate a state of soul close to being in mortal sin. This is only to say that the acts and attitudes of living men should be acts of life and not of death. Certainly, survivors should not despair if the nests have no birds of the air to dwell in them. They should and will likely adjust to the vastly more hostile environment by radi-

[50] *Ibid.*, Lect. I, chap. ii, p. 41.

cally lowering their standards of life expectancy, etc. They should and will accept a higher incidence of cancer and diseases which result from chronic radiation exposure. They may be willing to bear and raise children when the increased risk of their being born deformed is far, far higher than one in twenty five. They will and should spend themselves to alleviate, if possible, these conditions. They will be content to live ten years less and still call life worthwhile, as it was before the twentieth century. Man is either hopeful or wretched enough to adjust to an environment in which the dangers that surround him everywhere are as many and as great as those at a blind highway intersection or in industries with inadequate protection for their workers. He may even be willing to join Kahn in making tentative plans to be *able* to do these things at some time in the future. But all this falls short of *justifying* the choice that will render all these things later on necessary to be done, or of showing that such a present political policy is a *feasible* one for any nation of human beings to resolve actually to perform.

There is only one way to construe Kahn's argument so as to be able to regard it as even possibly productive of the conclusion he draws from it. This construction is in great measure a reconstruction, and even then it will not yield the conclusion that thermonuclear war is feasible. This would be to interpret him to mean to analyze present policy decision and present action in terms of the rule of double effect. Of course, as a military planner he is not concerned to address himself to the definition of intrinsically wrong actions. Yet as a planner he should be concerned to balance two effects, or situations consequent to action, to see whether one effect (however hostile) may not be justified by the greater evil of the effect that may be avoided by choosing the first. Kahn may, then, be applying the principle of proportionality, i.e., he may be weighing the "feasibility" of nuclear war against some greater evil, as a way of rendering credible a "fight the war" policy.

If this is the case, his would be proper calculation; but it is clearly mistaken. As a matter of fact, Kahn does not attempt to complete the comparison of the evils between which choice has to be made. He tries only to show that the evil of *one* effect (the consequences of fighting a nuclear war) can be lessened, and to tell us how a nation may adjust to the new environment. He does not attempt to demonstrate, but only *asserts* or simply *assumes,* that this so great evil (when alleviated in the ways he suggests) *may* be regarded as more choiceworthy than the other political effect (the consequences of *not* fighting a nuclear war). A President has not only to be persuaded that living in a postattack environment will be worthwhile, but *more* worthwhile than living in another environment that avoids this attack. He has to *balance* alternatives, and not only to be persuaded that we *could* live in one of them. Kahn simply *asserts* that it is quite conceivable that decision makers may be willing to envisage deliberately accepting the destruction of fifty to one hundred metropolitan centers rather than accepting an even more unpalatable alternative.[51] Certainly this is

---

[51] *Ibid.,* Lect. II, chap. iv, pp. 169-170, 177-178, 184-185. Kahn imagines that a decision-maker might *initiate* military action on the understanding that "if necessary, we are willing to lose these 50 cities, but we are in no sense anxious to lose them" (p. 177). He asks that war-making and war-deterring policy now be based with sun-clarity on a *certain* destruction of lives and property as great as or greater than the Russians (it later turned out) accepted in declaring war on Nazi Germany. Concerning this case, frequently cited, Kahn can only say: "It is true, they *did not make a deliberate and conscious choice between the two alternatives* of acquiescing or accepting the kind of damage they suffered." Yet the military policy of any nation must now hold *consciously* before it the *certainty* of such destruction, and perhaps *choose this.* This possibility is supported only by Kahn's *opinion* concerning the devastation of Russia if that had been consciously and certainly in view as one alternative: "It is quite probable that they would have preferred accepting that damage (hoping to conquer the Germans) to not accepting it—that is accepting immediate defeat instead" (*ibid.,* pp. 142-143, italics added). The words in parentheses state

theoretically conceivable. Moreover, the decision makers *should* do so, provided they really are ever face to face with an even more unpalatable alternative, and one that is equally immediate and certain to result. But concretely what is a more unpalatable alternative? And one the predicted evil of which is more certain? It is hard to believe that any actual option would be worse; or that it would *appear* to be worse (remembering that a political challenge may be kept ambiguous and beguiling on the side of one alternative, while, on the other, the threatened destruction of all of a nation's largest cities will seem to be certain and will seem certainly evil). It seems clear to me that no one who reads Kahn's description of the state of affairs that must be envisioned to result from fighting a nuclear war could reasonably choose that course of action, in cold blood and with full knowledge, as promising more remote, lesser and less certain evils than the consequences of political accommodation. He cannot imagine that men can now believe they can adjust to the aftermath of war so as to make good come of it in the course of time more than they can

---

an expectation of victory in some meaningful sense, which is now certainly impossible in the decision to accept devastation which Kahn wants the nation perhaps to make in the future, and in its present "fight the war" policy. Is it not clear that, without this expectation, the Russians would have decided otherwise if that had been a deliberate and conscious choice, or else that the power to make any such clear choice would depend on a tyrannical government unresponsive to the people's assessment of their own and their children's welfare? Kahn as much as admits that nations cannot reasonably make the decision he asks them to prepare in advance, insofar as the center and final reliance of his "central war (see below) is concerned: "The Rationality of Irrationality war corresponds to a situation in which neither side really believes the issue is big enough to go to war but both sides are willing to use some partial or total committal strategy to force the other side to back down; as a result they may end up in a war that they would not have gone into if either side had realized ahead of time that the other side would not back down even under pressure" (*ibid.*, p. 293). It is impossible to avoid the conclusion that Kahn's proposal also is "deterrence-by-exaggeration" (*ibid.*, Lect. III, chap. xii, p 562)—which must be made mutual by committal, and automatically reliable. This is the only way to plan for war or for deterrence with immoral, trans-military, apolitical weapons.

now anticipate learning to live in the increasingly hostile environment of tyranny, with still the hope that, short and brutish as such life may be, even so the living should not envy the dead.

Not only is it the case that Kahn has failed to show the feasibility of thermonuclear war as a present choice to be made, or that massive deterrence can be made credible. Also it becomes increasingly clear that the mere possession of these unlimited weapons in increasing numbers is infeasible in actual fact and incredible to believe as a political decision to which the world can long adhere, in cold blood and with full knowledge. Consider the situation Kahn predicts in only ten years, especially the last sentence:

Give or take a factor of 5, there are quite likely to be about 50,000 ready missiles in the world in 1973, each with its own button. Whether the missiles are kept alert or not is hard to conjecture. It is very possible that unless a nation is prepared to fire rapidly it may, even possessing 20,000 missiles, be unacceptably vulnerable to surprise attack. On the other hand, the thought of having 50,000 alert missiles is a bit frightening. This is true particularly since many of them may be in the hands of "less responsible" powers than we. It is difficult to believe that under these circumstances an occasional button will not get pressed. However, as we have already pointed out, one button being pressed does not necessarily lead to immediate all-out war, although it increases the risk. *We may just be going to live in a world in which every now and then a city or town is destroyed or damaged as a result of blackmail, unauthorized behavior, or an accident.*[52]

Can any alternative be more unpalatable than this, except the escalating use of such weapons? I suggest soberly that our nation's present policies can endure, in prudent political judgment, only because we ride into the future facing backward upon the ass of notions about war and weapons that

[52] *Ibid*, Lect. III, chap. x, pp. 514-515 (italics added).

are no longer valid. These notions are that, since once war could be fought by all or most of the means available and since it was then feasible to deter the war by the means a nation actually planned to use if war came, we can still by thinking make it so, that it is feasible to fight a war with weapons that are not the arms of any national purpose, and that it is feasible to deter a war by the same means.

It seems clear, also, that Kahn secretly knows that prudent men cannot choose to fight such a war; and that, because he knows this, the policies he recommends, all along declaratory, now become plainly hortatory. We are exhorted to prepare for and to become willing to fight nuclear wars because only if this is the case will deterrence have objective capability behind its subjective capability to deter. Yet it is as much as admitted that we can decide to make ourselves objectively capable of fighting a nuclear war, and firmly resolved to do so, only by dint of a large measure of belief that deterrence will work and that we will never have to do any such thing.

It is true that Herman Kahn expects the next war to be limited. He avoids the words "Limited War," but only because "it is part of the argument of these lectures that in the future the Central War may have important limitations and the 'Limited War' may involve strategic capabilities, e.g., destruction of Polaris submarines at sea."[53] Even in a world of fifty thousand buttons and Doomsday machines, "we must at least make preparations *to fight wars carefully.*"[54] Kahn expects that tacit agreements will come into existence between the most hostile enemies, and even that explicit arrangements will be made for constant and reliable contact between their high command posts, so that it will be possible for one side to find out the intentions (if any)

---

[53] *Ibid.*, Lect. III, chap. x, p. 514 (italics deleted).
[54] *Ibid.*, Lect. III, chap. xii, p. 561 (italics added).

of the enemy in destroying one of our cities.[55]   There will
be time to evaluate the attack.

Moreover, Kahn recommends a very limited reply to
most forms of attack.   (1) If the enemy succeeds in destroying only 40 to 80 per cent of our forces, then, while that
which remains is capable of doing considerable damage, it
should nevertheless be limited in use to a "counterforce mission."   (2) If the enemy only succeeds in destroying 10 to 40
per cent of our forces, we should have "a rather peculiar
war."   The counter-force mission should be very carefully
executed.   The reply should not be directed against the
enemy's missile bases near large cities, and we should institute negotiations toward a cessation of hostilities while
proceeding to blunt his attacking forces.   (3) If the enemy
succeeds, in his first strike, in getting less than 10 per cent
of our forces, we should "temporize" by putting our military establishment on the alert and perhaps by destroying
some especially threatening SUSAC base near U.S. territory,
e.g., at Kamachatka, Siberia.   Such a limited reaction, Kahn
believes, would be more realistic than "initiating a city exchange," since "there is a reasonable possibility that the
enemy did not intend to start one.   I repeat, there is clearly
something incredibly wrong in the attacker's initiating a
war and doing it so badly."   Under these circumstances,
the counterattack should be conducted only "in the most
sanitary way possible," meantime getting in touch with the
enemy and sending him an explanation.[56]   This is sufficient
to suggest what Kahn means by some considerable limitation
in the "central war" that may be fought in the future.

[55] *Ibid.*, Lect. II, chap. v, pp. 238-239.
[56] *Ibid.*, Lect. II, chap. iv, pp. 186-187. Except in describing these ideal
"wars," Kahn uses the word "counterforces" to cover "anything which might
counter the use or effectiveness of the enemy's force." This includes
counter-people warfare, or what Kahn calls "malevolent (i.e. countervalve)
objectives," since "the best counter against the enemy destroying our cities
may be the use of retaliatory threats" and blows. *Ibid.*, Lect I, chap. i,
p. 16, n. 6; and Lect. II, chap. iv, pp. 184-185.

It is also true that at very significant points in his analysis Herman Kahn ventures to introduce a moral judgment into what he says about war and instruments of war. A criticism of pure deterrence theories, which rest upon the threat of mutual suicide, is that these are "uninspiring" concepts which lead to eventual loss of morale and efficiency in our military forces, to their not caring how the war comes out, or even to their not caring, once the war starts, whether the buttons are actually pushed or not. "This position is not very far from the one of not worrying if the buttons are not connected so long as they appear as if they are." In the midst of this criticism of mutual deterrence by threat of massive retaliation, Kahn asserts that if this "happened to involve explicitly the annihilation of all humanity it would also be *totally immoral;* one doubts if it could long remain an important part of United States policy."[57] Thus does a secular analysis invoke in behalf of humanity in general the moral immunity from unjust destruction which Christian morality lavishes upon any single individual whom it would be totally immoral to intend to annihilate unless he is a part of the force or forces it is just to repel. His own death, brought about in such a way, is every man's Doomsday Machine, which Kahn rightly regards as totally heinous when applied to mankind.

More importantly, Kahn directs the following moral argument against the notion of "bonus damage" and the "overkilling" of cities and civilians:

The notion of "bonus" damage is wrong in another sense. It is a basically immoral idea. It became reputable and could be justified in World War I and World War II, only because of military necessity. In those wars civilian morale played an essential role in furnishing men and materials to the fighting fronts. This is no longer true, and therefore civilians and their property are no longer military targets. The idea of bonus non-

[57] *Ibid.*, Lect. I, chap. iii, pp. 96-97 (italics added).

military damage is now not only immoral, it is senseless. It is hard to conceive of a Premier of Russia or a President of the United States who would prefer to go to war—other things being equal—with a plan that would exterminate the enemy's civilian population, rather than one which would simply force the enemy to acquiesce on certain points. Even if military advantages were not to be had by deliberately limiting one's attack to counter-force targets, I suspect that most governments would still prefer to observe such limits. Almost nobody wants to go down in history as the first man to kill 100,000,000 people.[58]

The reader will observe that this view is very much in line with the thesis of this book. Despite the powerful example of the wars of the immediate past, despite the hold over men's minds of the idea that in war as many casualties as possible must be inflicted, despite the evidence of Communist desire to overturn and destroy utterly and their statements to this effect, Kahn still believes that the Soviets would understand the force of the above "argument," because "after all, the Soviets, more than any other group in the world, are used to thinking of rational and profitable connections between force and coercion, between power and policy."[59]

The foregoing position on the moral dimension in military policy is somewhat inconsistent with Kahn's acceptance of blackmail and counter-blackmail tactics against cities and civilians carried out before, during, and after the first strike and while the "central war" is sought to be kept limited. It is also glaringly inconsistent with Kahn's recommendation for the kind of reply which should be made to an attack which succeeds in destroying far more of our forces than in the cases we have so far considered.

If the enemy is lucky enough to destroy 80 percent or more of our strategic force, we should devote the remaining force to

[58] *Ibid.*, Lect. II, chap. iv, p. 171.
[59] *Ibid.*, Lect. II, chap. iv, p. 172.

malevolent (i.e. countervalue) objectives—to punish the enemy in that way which was most hurtful to him. We might plan to do this even though he maximizes his blackmail threat, which would now be a very credible threat. In a way, I am saying that under these circumstances we should risk annihilation rather than attempt to alleviate the war. This notion may seem to contradict some other views that I have expressed. I stated earlier, for example, that no nation such as the United States should or would deliberately choose to commit suicide yet it is clear that if we lost 80 per cent or more of our force and attempt to use the rest malevolently in the face of an overwhelming enemy superiority, he may, in his anger, literally destroy the United States. The reason I think this contingency plan is reasonable is partly that *every effort should be made to insure that the enemy could not possibly destroy 80 per cent or more of our force on his first strike.* If we are successful in this attempt, then, the 80 per cent destruction case cannot occur and we do not care if the corresponding plan is reasonable or not.... [Yet] in this uncertain world of rapid technological change ... it is just possible that the enemy, in spite of our best thought and preparation, may (either because he is clever, or because he or we have made a miscalculation) develop a technique which *he believes* will destroy more than 80 percent of our strategic force on the first blow. We wish to assure him that *even if he thinks he can be this successful, he is still in serious trouble.* To the extent that he could rely on our using our small remaining force "sensibly," this might not be true.[60]

That is an exceedingly interesting paragraph which should be carefully examined. It now becomes clear that all effort to formulate deterrence policy, and all plans to make sanitary or limited use of strategic forces in an actual thermonuclear war, come to rest ultimately upon a nation's willingness to fight such a war unlimitedly. It is true, Kahn calls the proposed action "malevolent." His moral judgment has not been altogether suspended. It is true also that there is ambiguity in his present use of the words "rational" and

[60] *Ibid.,* Lect. II, chap. iv, pp. 184-185.

"irrational," "sensible" and "insensible." The proposed
policy is said to be both irrational and sensible. It clearly
has at most a "rationality of irrationality" in the use of
force. He wants it understood that our actions would be
"irrationally malevolent."

More important for our present purposes than pointing
out an inconsistency between this and the few but significant
references to a moral dimension in Kahn's analysis, all this
is plainly inconsistent with his understanding of what is
"feasible" and what is "infeasible" in war and in deterrence.
Here he is hoisted on his own petard. A *part* of the reason
he believes "this contingency plan is reasonable" is that, if
we have it for its subjective capability to deter, we may
never have to use it and "we do not care if the corresponding plan is reasonable or not." That is like not caring
whether the buttons are connected or not, if only they
seem to be!

When it is a question of *choosing* suicide in order malevolently to punish an enemy, it is, of course, important that
we be subjectively capable of using our objective capability
in this way, in order that a decision to do so may be regarded by the enemy as credible on our part—else there
would be no deterrent effect on his mind. Therefore Kahn
perseveres in the direction he is now going:

Sometimes people argue that it is all right to assure the enemy
before the war that if he attacks we will be irrationally malevolent, at the same time knowing that in the event itself it
would be silly to carry out the threat—particularly at a moment
when the enemy is far ahead. I believe this is substantially true
[*sic!*]. But I do not believe that the idea of using our small remaining SAC against his society, rather than against his strategic
force, is credible *unless we really intend to do it.* If we are
only *pretending* that we would do it, the credibility and therefore the deterrent value of our force is almost certain to be
lessened by the automatic and inevitable leaks. While we can

probably keep the details of our war plans secret, it is most unlikely that we can keep the philosophy behind them secret.[61]

But never before in this book has the credibility of a decision meant only whether there is an actual subjective intention to do something, and certainly not when this intention is stimulated only by hortatory appeals that we *must* be resolved so to do or else the deterrence will not work. Credibility has meant what it would be reasonable and purposive, at least minimally, for a nation and its leaders to do. This is now so far lacking that Kahn has to take this decision wholly out of the political arena at the time that it is to be made. He has to depend upon machines to do what no human being can be relied on to do, or be confidently credited with the irrationality of believing to be good policy.

If there were some politically acceptable accident-proof way to make this kind of retaliation completely automatic, it would be sensible to put it into immediate effect.[62]

Here "sensible" means such "irrational malevolence" and such "rationality of irrationality" that only the reply of some automatic weapons system can be believed to be characterized by any such sensibility of insensibility. This runs counter to all that Kahn has written in rejecting automatic response and the room he has made for deliberate decision, sometimes even by accepting higher risks. This also runs counter to all he said about the immorality of building or using Doomsday Machines. (Surely it is a lame and a mistaken excuse just to say of such irrational malevolence that, since in the supposed case only 20 per cent of the defender's forces remain, the destruction, and the threat of it, would be "relatively humanitarian," because this could not an-

---

[61] *Ibid.,* Lect. II, chap. iv, p. 185.
[62] *Ibid.,* Lect. II, chap. iv, p. 185.

nihilate whole continents.[63]) Elsewhere, when urging that our declaratory policies (what we *say* we will do) and our action policies (what in fact we will *do*) be made congruent (and while admitting there may be some circumstances in which there are some grounds for a difference between them, in order to keep our response ambiguous), Kahn warns against "the temptation to get off cheaply by overusing or otherwise abusing Rationality of Irrationality strategies."[64] This now is revealed as central in any "central war" with all the available modern weapons. As such, it must be done non-humanly and non-politically, i.e., by some automatic set-up. If we attempt to do this by anything short of an electronic mechanism, i.e., if we attempt simply to resolve firmly to be willing, and to appear to be willing, to join a mutual suicide pact, why then it will soon prove to be the case, in the arena where political powers actually meet and conflict (unlike a realm of ideal calculation) that "no matter what our *declared policy* might be, our *actual policy* could be probed."[65]

It may be excusable for an officer, who has the responsibility for training the troops to make use of thermonuclear instruments without blubbering, to teach them that these are "just another weapon" in the long history of warfare. But the time has come for military planners who are responsible for the defense of the nation to tell the people frankly that men in the military profession have now been saddled with a problem different in kind from any that has hitherto existed in the history of the world. Mankind can

[63] *Ibid.*, Lect. II, chap. iv, p. 185, n. 7.
[64] *Ibid.*, Lect. II, chap. vi, p. 306.
[65] *Ibid.*, Lect. I, chap. i, p. 34. Cf.: "...Today all-out war is so unthinkable that many officials not only do not know how to threaten credibly, but have suppressed the knowledge that they do not know" (*ibid.*, Lect. II, chap. v, p. 211, n. 8). This is the reason "malevolent (i.e. countervalve) objectives" or counter-people warfare, in actuality or as a deterrent, would have to be built into a computer.

no longer reasonably believe that it is possible to integrate these weapons into the fighting of a war that is an extension of national purpose, or to use them to deter the war a nation cannot make itself willing to fight. It is not that the bombs will penetrate the umbrella of deterrence under which, in a totally new environment, international politics is attempted to be carried on without an authentic "substitute for peace." It is also that any prudent opponent can see through the umbrella. Under these circumstances, statesmen (being unable to use relentless but measured applications of power) can only become more and more brutal in their threats. Military planners today are constantly running their heads up against what we have called the "natural law" of warfare, which determines, willy nilly, the nature of armaments that have any political usefulness. It exceeds the capacity of technical, strategic reason to formulate a plan for fighting a thermonuclear war or for deterring such a war by means of the very force it would never be politically purposive to employ.

Of course, all wars of the past have in their measure been conducted unjustly, some more than others. But what has been brought about by modern weapons is that the unjust conduct of war has now become the central war, and by no means can ever again be made peripheral, unless a radically different solution is sought for a radically different problem. Even ignorant tribes have in the past known that there are some things they cannot do in war:

In the Tourag society, which has learned to cope with the problem of living in the Sahara Desert where there are only a small number of oases, an enemy can commit all types of atrocities, such as torturing and murdering one's son, violating one's wife, selling one's daughter into slavery, and yet the injured party will not poison the wells of his attacker. He has simply learned that nothing that anybody does justifies poisoning wells. The Tourags had to learn this, otherwise they would not have lived very long.[66]

This is a parable of the plight of pure reason today in attempting to devise military plans which integrate the most powerful weapons to a people's purposes. We are trying to plan to fight the war *primarily* by poisoning wells, or trying to deter such a war by aiming at making it credible that we are going to poison wells. We shall soon all live in a great desert, whose wells are all poisoned, unless the people of the world are plainly told by their leaders that no political or human good can come from doing anything so essentially wrong (because so stupid) or anything so essentially irrational (because so immoral). Warfare is not feasible, deterrence is not feasible, and what is more, politics is no longer feasible, unless this central war, with intrinsically unjust means, is abolished.

Thus, the deep truth to be found in an analysis of modern weapons, and the lineaments of a hardheaded analysis that must be believed at least on Monday, Wednesday, and Friday of every week, thrusts the mind *in the direction of* that other deep truth which has been the theme of this volume, the just-war theory, which is the only credible viewpoint at least on Tuesday, Thursday, and Saturday. But this is not the main reason a Christian and a just man should have his mind formed by this teaching about the morality of war. He believes this, as of old, because there is also another day of the week. Because of what he celebrates on Sunday, the Lord's Day, a Christian knows that irrational malevolence should never be the nature of the human will or action, or of public policy, which is only an agreement of wills. This can only be a corruption of the will, and of *res publica*. Because of the truth proclaimed and re-enacted on the Sabbath Day, because of the shedding

---

[66] *Ibid.*, Lect. II, chap. v, pp. 239-240.

abroad of God's love and justice among men, a Christian need no longer halt between the two opinions presented to him as the recommendations of natural justice and of realistic military analysis. He can only affirm the deeper truth of the principles of justice surrounding justifiable killing with quite rigorous and precise theoretical limits. He can only totally reject counter-people warfare. He cannot have complicity in poisoning the wells, just because his enemy may do this. He can only say that he is required to save the life, and never directly or intentionally bring about the death of any man not engaged or closely co-operating in the hostile force that he must and in justice should repel. He cannot admit that all the enemy people live in only one unelevated earthly city, or that he himself lives in only one city; nor that total, counter-society warfare, simply by becoming a possibility and almost a reality, has today *ipso facto* become justifiable. If judgments such as these have no more relevance to public policy, if war and international politics must assume that totalitarianism is right in order to defeat it in its more overt forms, then Christianity, so long as it continues to exist in such a world, can only be a sect that declares that no Christian can have anything to do with political and military actions that, at the highest level through and through, are intrinsically irrational, evil, and malevolent.

We have seen that thermonuclear war and deterrence by the mightiest means cannot provide a feasible umbrella under which international relations can be conducted and force be used, when necessary, in limited, purposive measure through proper arms and just warfare. This conclusion leaves standing the possibility that international relations can be as readily and as feasibly conducted under the umbrella of a firm national resolve never to engage in counter-people warfare, nor to prepare or keep instruments that can

have only such a non-political, and at the same time immoral, purpose.   There is no policy *more* feasible than dismantling the era of immoral terror, while resolving not to
yield to blackmail in the conviction that it is better to suffer
than to do injustice.   We require only the fiber as a people
to conduct our affairs and to mount a powerful, reasonable
defense while not giving way before blackmail threats; and
the strength to do this cannot be found in massive "deter
the war" or "fight the war" policies (unless the people are
deceived by self-deceived political leaders or strategists). The
question about this, in turn, is only the question *where* are
the principles—not *what,* but *where* in the fabric of the national life is the ethos, where the mind and heart of a community that is willing to do what can be readily known to
be the right?   The Protestant churches between World Wars
I and II spent their thought and energy expelling a utopian
pacifism from their bosom.   That was a proper work, but
in doing this, and in creating a religiously motivated political realism in its stead, we have neglected to keep alive
the teachings that should be constantly addressed to the
churches, to political realists, and to the nations.   Before
policy-making becomes such that in relation thereto Christian teaching can only be that of a sect apart from the central political policies of our nation, the churches must re-
learn their ancient teaching about war and trumpet them
in high places.   "Before the sun and the light, and the
moon, and the stars are darkened and the clouds return
after the rain; in the day when the keepers of the house
tremble, and the strong men are bent . . . and the doors on
the street are shut . . . and terrors are in the way" (Eccl. 12:
2-5), the churches must do what they can to restore the
ancient landmarks.   Whether Christianity is a sect in a
world gone mad and gone apolitical, or whether its teachings may still be regarded as a relevant context for high

policy-making, the churches need to know *where* are the principles by which the nations may be guided in this critical hour. To insure that *somewhere* these principles *are* in the allegiances of men is our most essential task.

In any case, military planners who (like Kahn) believe in "graduated deterrence" should admit, nay, even proclaim, the fact that this deterrence will work for a graduated range of weapons only up to the point where weapons become politically and militarily of no benefit for a fight-the-war policy, and not beyond this point. The church's doctrine of just war surely declares that a nation's military policy should be to maintain war-making capability by all manner of necessary means up to this point. To try to deter war by mounting force that exceeds this merely *seems* to succeed only because of the actually operative effect on the enemy's mind of the graduated range of force below this; and because of the moral and political resolve of a nation not to be deterred by its own massive deterrence, or by an enemy's possession of the same and his threats to use such weapons. In our final chapter we shall suggest an answer to the question where the line should be drawn between counter-forces and counter-people warfare, or between just war and murder, in view of the fire power of modern weapons.

Chapter Twelve

RATIONAL, POLITICALLY BENEFICIAL ARMAMENT

We have seen that the only weapons system that the Christian or any just man can possibly endorse is rationally beneficent, not irrationally malevolent, armament. The moralist, with his findings as to the moral law, and the military planner, with his findings of fact, need together to determine the nature of such a weapons system.

In order for us to consider soberly the question How *can* modern war be conducted justly? I propose, in conclusion, to examine the views of Mr. Thomas E. Murray (some of whose articles we have already treated) in his recent book *Nuclear Policy for War and Peace.*[1] This remarkable man, a distinguished public servant and a member of the Atomic Energy Commission from 1950 to 1957, is an outstanding example of the fact that the just-war theory may serve as the context for policy-making. He is also an example of the fact that in the midst of concrete policy-making itself a sensitive mind can come to greater clarity about the meaning of the moral principles of civilized warfare as regulative of policy. Theory and practice, the right and the feasible, are not alien to one another unless and until external norms are somehow imposed upon the political actualities. Instead, these things belong together. Since political policy and action is by nature a kind of moral ac

---

[1] Cleveland and New York: The World Publishing Co., 1960.

tion, men cannot otherwise obtain the goals they seek in politics.

"No scientific development has ever brought man face to face with the problem of good and evil more starkly than the achievement whereby he summoned atomic energy forth from the deep recesses of the universe," Murray declares at the outset; "I do not see how it is possible to write a meaningful book on the subject of atomic energy except from a moral standpoint."[2]   He is profoundly disturbed, as everyone should be, at "the appalling indifference of many persons in responsible positions to the moral aspects of public policy questions."[3]   He then rejects at once the "easy identification" of the "military face" of atomic power with evil and its "peaceful face with good."[4]   His volume, therefore, is about the morality *of* war and weapons, not war as the chief moral problem.[5]   He rightly assumes that a nation has "need for a force to repel unjust force"; and even that "an atomic war waged within the limits of military necessity may be not only something we are morally permitted to do; it may be something we are *morally obliged to do.*"[6]

Murray reiterates the appeal he has made for several years for a "restoration of the tradition of civilized warfare," which is "the Christian tradition of warfare."[7]   What, we may ask, does he understand this to mean? This means "the

---

[2] *Ibid.*, p. 15.

[3] *Ibid.*, p. 16.

[4] *Ibid.*, p. 22. Murray describes as "a perfect example of extreme American idealism," of potentially the "gravest consequence for our national security," the proposal of one of Harold Stassen's position papers in 1955 that the nations should agree that after a certain date "all future production of nuclear material anywhere in the world should be devoted exclusively to peaceful purposes."

[5] Murray's illuminating discussion of national policy for the peaceful use of atomic energy I shall omit from this review, except to cite in this connection Murray's belief that "we could have emphasized peaceful applications more without detracting from our defense capabilities" (*ibid.*, p. 122).

[6] *Op. cit.*, p. 23 (italics added).

[7] *Ibid.*, p. 27.

regulated use of force."[8]   Regulated in what manner and in what specific details? Among the limitations upon the use of force, and "one of the noblest features of the Western military tradition was the protective wall which was erected around civilian populations and peaceful activities—a wall which military men observed for several centuries with re- markable fidelity."[9]   Military action should be "limited to military components and not be directed against noncom- batants, *except accidentally*."[10]   Thus Murray clearly has in mind the moral immunity of noncombatants from *direct* attack in the meaning we have explained this to have, and not necessarily their (impossible) immunity from indirect attack.   Instead, today, "the great historic and moral right of the civilian population to immunity from violence has been attenuated."   Moreover, the objective of the action that is planned cannot be excused by any subterfuge about our subjective intentions.   "If," Murray writes, "we were as a matter of carefully premeditated strategic policy to drop multimegaton bombs on a large city, we can hardly escape the conclusion that our objective is to obliterate the city."[11]   Nor can this be excused by any *end* we may have in view. There is a morality of means and a morality or immorality in the conduct of war which Murray states as "the rule of minimal means," which it is the task of strategists and tac- ticians to determine how to apply.[12]   In summary, if we are compelled to fight a war,

we should make every effort to wage it according to the rule of minimal means, instead of operating from the very first hour according to the dialectic of wild excess. We should attempt to hold the use of force down to the minimum necessary for ac-

[8] *Ibid.,* p. 28.
[9] *Ibid.,* p. 29.
[10] *Ibid.,* p. 43 (italics added).
[11] *Ibid.,* p. 43-44.
[12] *Ibid.,* p. 43.

complishing the multiple ideas inherent in the moral idea of war—the military end of terminating the effective operations of the enemy's *armed forces;* the political end of achieving the proper order of power relationships for a stable and just international framework; and the moral end of peace itself.[13]

This clearly rules out counter-society warfare, and rules in counter-forces warfare, as the only conduct that can be justified in armed conflict between nations. This leads Murray to condemn the former type of warfare not only with our present weapons, but by any means:

In World War I a major strategic instrument was the naval blockade by which it was hoped to starve out both population and industry; in World War II a combination of blockade and strategic bombing was used; in World War III the strategy will call for striking industry and population directly, without the slow intermediate step of starvation. I submit that the strategy is immoral. It was immoral in previous decades, and it is immorality gone berserk today. The proper objective of military force must remain military force; the nation which takes as its objective the military force of its enemy will win the war. It will win the war if it can protect its own military force and if it has mobility and precision-type nuclear weapons, whether or not its cities are destroyed.[14]

Even in the Nuclear Age, it is possible to "draw the line between military action and sheer massacre of civilian populations, between the legitimate defense of human order and the destruction of all order in human life."[15] To complete the picture, we may even say that, in the final place and as a subordinate theme to his judgments about intrinsically immoral means, Murray also employs a calculus of proportionality in the consequences of action: "justice," he writes, "imperatively demands that we reject the concept of total

[13] *Ibid.,* p. 42 (italics added).
[14] *Ibid.,* p. 68.
[15] *Ibid.,* p. 40.

nuclear warfare, since it cannot be proportionated to any rational set of political objectives."[16]

This is the just-war theory completely intact. The various ingredients of this outlook (analyzed above) are compressed into Murray's "essential distinction between force and violence," the former justifiable, the latter never:

This is a political distinction, based on a moral premise. By violence I mean the use of military power in such an extensive, undiscriminating, or even unlimited, measure and manner that it becomes useless for the rational purposes of politics, which are always limited. By force I mean the use of power in such a proportionate measure and in such a discriminating manner as to constitute an apt means for the achievement of legitimate political goals.

Given the nature of man, the art of international politics cannot dispense with the use, or at least the threat, of force, any more than human society can dispense with law, which requires force to back it up. On the other hand, international politics perishes as an art if power is allowed to suffer moral debasement and become mere violence, which is destructive of the very idea of force and of law, too.

. . . .

For the last decades, we Americans have subscribed to a strategy not of force but of violence—excessive, incredible, and politically irrelevant.[17]

It is a failure of political intelligence not to see "the absurdity of violence" and also not to see "the rational necessity of force" for the purposes of politics.[18] "Politics needs force, but morals condemn violence."[19] The "spell" can be broken only by reasserting "the primacy of politics," beginning "an orderly surrender of weapons that are politically

[16] *Ibid.,* p. 45.
[17] *Ibid.,* pp. 223, 224.
[18] *Ibid.,* p. 235.
[19] *Ibid.,* p. 236.

useless," and replacing an "emphasis on inept violence" by an "emphasis on apt force."[20]

The fact is that it was no human judgment, no primarily political decision, by which our policy came to be controlled by the concept of violence. This came to pass because technology is now in the saddle and rides mankind. "A technological runaway, and technology itself rather than strategic and moral reason has determined the shape of our weapons program and our defense policy." Facts and the possibility of greater facts have made war more and more total. It has not been successfully argued by political reason that this should or must be so. In the manufacture of the first A-bomb, Murray points out, our political and military leaders did *not* tell the scientists and engineers that "so much fire power was needed to accomplish such and such an objective." Only "one limiting item of information" was furnished them: the size of the bomb bay into which the device had to fit. Thus "a purely mechanistic factor," not a policy, was put in operation; and the scientific determination of how much fire power *could* be released fixed the amount that would and *should* be used. "No one had thought out explicit reasons why we needed a weapon of this magnitude or even one of this nature." Since 1945 a carrier's ability to deliver bombs on a target alone has circumscribed the size of nuclear weapons to be manufactured.[21]

We are in need of a military policy and a weapons program geared not only to "deterrence" but also to "combat"—rational, justifiable combat. "For the last decade or more our weapons program has been dictated by what we *can* do, scientifically

---

[20] *Ibid.*, p. 234. The fact that the Communists may have few moral scruples does not mean that they are politically committed to a policy of "violence." Instead, their policies that "dictate the use of apt force, if force is necessary to insure success, also set limits to the force to be used and forbid the extremes of violence.... Limited force is an apt means to this success. Unlimited violence is an inept means, a useless means, a far too dangerous means" (*ibid.*, p. 238).

[21] *Ibid.*, pp. 33-34.

and technologically, rather than by what we *ought* to do, militarily, politically, and morally. Our military policy has been built backward. Beginning with the existence of multimegaton bombs, it then proceeded to a consideration of factors which rightly should have come first: military strategy and political objectives. The technological tail has been flying the policy kite.[22]

If there has been an "argument" in all this, it has been "the implicit argument that science and technology have advanced so far that man is now entitled to act like a barbarian."[23] But no one actually concluded that this was so. Instead, "the fatal error which we have made during the last decade and a half, and especially since 1953, is that of allowing weapons technology to determine the weapons program, and of allowing the weapons program to dictate national strategic policy."[24] Open-ended, unlimited physical power has been "the twentieth-century technician's dream—the counterpart of the fascinating idea of perpetual motion in the nineteenth century Steam Age." We *thoughtlessly* imagined that this gave us "a kind of abstract absolute strength" that could be used to hold at bay any external threat "by projecting the awful, unconquerable specter of utter ruin."[25] The stockpiles "have created their own strategy."[26] And we have continued to stockpile these weapons "in an almost complete vacuum of moral judgment," in an almost complete vacuum of political judgment.[27]

This determination of policy by technology seems likely to continue in the ICBM Age of the sixties. "Fascinated by

[22] *Ibid.*, p. 40. The opposite of civilization (in any but an unearthly conception of it) is not war but barbaric war; and Murray does not hesitate to use this expression for what must be refused by any just or charitable man: "I accept no sentence of doom to a regression into barbarism" (p. 47). "Technically, we could accumulate the megaton weapons in any numbers we wished, but we could never use them in quantity without crossing the line that separates civilized action from wanton barbarism." (p. 61).

[23] *Ibid.*, p. 40.

[24] *Ibid.*, p. 48.

[25] *Ibid.*, p. 50.

[26] *Ibid.*, p. 227.

[27] *Ibid.*, p. 35.

rocket weapons, we are already well on the way to abdicating our reason and falling down before the altar which bears the inscription: 'The strategic exigencies of the Rocket Age.' "[28]   This process must be reversed, and we should again assert the mastery of men over things, of politics over technics:

Here and now we should ask ourselves what kinds and sizes of war heads our missiles will carry and for what purposes. Are we going to look upon the missile as a discriminating weapon which can be used against military targets? Or do we intend to regard it as another instrument for the annihilation of metropolitan centers? It would seem that a missile by its very nature is less discriminating than a manned aircraft which can always be subjected to the control of human prudence. Because a ballistic missile is a purely mechanistic weapon which, once launched on its course, can be neither diverted nor recalled, we have a special obligation to think carefully about the war head which we attach to it. The moral problem . . . is not altered by the speed with which the delivery craft hurtles through space. It is impossible to justify the thermonuclear obliteration of cities and whole civilian populations, irrespective of whether it takes the carrier fifteen hours or fifteen minutes to reach its destination.[29]

Murray anticipates that years after the so-called missile gap has been closed, there will remain a "gap in our strategic-moral thinking."[30]   Here and now statesmen must begin to make policy, rather than have their minds determined by the strategist or the technologist. "The forthright making of this decision by government [namely, the decision to dismantle the stockpiles that have up to now fixed policy, or stockpiles of weapons too massive to be integrated within feasible policy] is the very condition for the restoration of

[28] *Ibid.*, p. 57.
[29] *Ibid.*, p. 58. Notice that in this volume Murray does not affirm, as he did in earlier articles, that missiles themselves are a "symbol" of the equation of immorality with insecurity. See above, chap. vii, in the text at n. 7.
[30] *Ibid.*, p. 59.

politics to its rightful place of primacy in the structure of American policy. *In no other way can the rupture between political purpose and military strategy be healed in its depths.*"[31]

Not only is it immoral, absurd, and infeasible to think of fighting a thermonuclear war, but also we can correctly assign to Mr. Murray the conviction that it is no less infeasible to attempt to construct a policy of deterrence by means of weapons which we cannot ever think of using. "Massive retaliation," "the destruction of the Soviet Union" are phrases that cannot possibly pretend to "enunciate a genuine military policy on which we intend to act."[32] Translated into megatonnage and its consequent radioactive fallout, "we shall find that the policy appears so nonsensical and irrational that it may be extremely risky for us to employ such resounding phrases." Anyway, in the actual world of international politics (as distinct from the abstract world of the strategist), by using ambiguous crises an enemy can "constantly probe our intentions" and readily maneuver us "into accepting our own deterrent policy as a *pro forma* bluff which we will pronounce with less conviction on each succeeding occasion."[33]   This consequence flows from the built-in contradiction within any policy that has to admit that "the very essence of such deterrent implements is that they should never be used," and has to admit that our reliance is solely on the hope that "we shall never have to demonstrate the complete failure of deterrence by using these weapons."[34]   A strategy of deterrence, when it completely monopolizes our policy thinking (because it is impossible to think through to the end the idea of purposefully choos-

[31] *Ibid.,* p. 227   (italics added).
[32] *Ibid.,* p. 36.
[33] *Ibid.,* p. 37.
[34] *Ibid.,* p. 39.

ing to fight a thermonuclear war) becomes "self-defeating."[35]
For war or for deterrence, "the weapons we manufacture
should be demonstrably useful for the purposes of actual
warfare." For this reason, there is "a kind of neurotic in-
stability and utter lack of realism in the school of thought
which advocates moving on to weapons of ever increasing
magnitude, while at the same time guiltily disclaiming the
intention to employ them."[36] Plainly, "force must be punitive precisely because it does not always deter; if it were
not at all punitive it would have little deterrent value."[37]
Even to begin to prevent a determined enemy from moving
into the *power* vacuum created by our reliance on deterrence by the threat of *violence,* a nation would have to act
more and more as if it were mad, all the while invoking perhaps the name of God in a vain attempt to render deterrence
credible and to make up for the vacuum of political principle in its strategic policy. This describes our times, and
shows why the conduct of international relations cannot be
carried out under the supposed umbrella of massive deterrence. No nation can raise the question of its own or mankind's survival every time an enemy manufactures a crisis.[38]
Policy-making is put in a strait jacket if an enemy, and many
of our own fellow citizens, can persuade us that limited action and limited war in answer to a probing, ambiguous
challenge is impossible without plunging the world into all
out H-war. We may also assume that the Communist power
does not want to achieve "a classless society of bone-cancer
patients."[39] The incredibility of his deterrent, too, requires
him to look more and more mad. The conclusion to which
we are forced by the incredibility of an infeasible deterrent

[35] *Ibid.,* p. 53.
[36] *Ibid.,* p. 69.
[37] *Ibid.,* p. 70.
[38] Cf. *ibid.,* pp. 179, 210.
[39] *Ibid.,* p. 45.

is that "it is absolutely necessary to remove from the cold war the issue of sheer physical survival. This issue has done nothing but darken counsel, paralyze purpose, and confuse policy. The issue is fundamentally false; survival should never be an issue in political struggles or even in war."[40] Only limited means can exert believable political pressures or prosecute a war, or provide the framework of power in which a nation's purposes can gain the form or incarnation they need in order to be actualized.

The foregoing states the principle of the thing; and it indicates as well how the mind is impelled, by an analysis of the asserted usefulness of modern weapons, to move *toward* the truth of the moral doctrine of just warfare as the only foundation for policy. Next, we need to examine the judgments Murray makes upon particular questions of application, and especially his views on multimegaton weapons as such, fractional kiloton weapons, and on nuclear testing. This will bring us decisively into the heart of the question, What is the nature of "rational, politically beneficial armament" today? Whether Murray's answer to this is correct or not, this is the chief question that should be debated today. Finally, we will consider Murray's signal proposal for "dismantling the era of terror," which can only mean *cutting back* our weapons system to rational armament (which may mean *building up* our weapons system, at greater cost in intellectual effort, moral resolve and money, to the level of rationally and beneficently requisite armament).

The multimegaton bomb, Murray writes, is "by its very nature a weapon of mass destruction. If we except a few appropriate targets, such as a naval fleet at sea, the H-bomb must be said to perform least efficiently against classical military objectives." It has a certain "terrible efficiency," of

---

[40] *Ibid.*, p. 233.

course, but this can "be linked to no reasonable military objective."[41]   When "some working set of figures is put into the concept of 'war of survival' to test its meaning realistically" (Murray estimates the unleashing of 3,500 megatons), the "inherent absurdity of 'all-out nuclear war' as an operational concept" is sufficiently demonstrated[42] (and at the same time the inherent absurdity of deterrence by means of multimegaton weapons which have usefulness only if we can fight such a war).   Therefore, Murray describes megaton weapons as "literally uncontrollable" and "by their nature . . . weapons of violence."[43]

Yet there is a certain hesitancy on Mr. Murray's part to make such a sweeping, unequivocal (though quite logical) condemnation of the H-bomb.   He says that "there is a definite limit to *the number* of large thermonuclear weapons we could employ under any conceivable circumstances with military and moral justification"; and, from this point of view, he seems only to oppose the movement toward bigger and bigger bombs and toward always accumulating more and more of those we now have.[44]   He describes the effect of a 20-megaton bomb exploded over New York (this would destroy immediately six million people, including one and one-half million children; and, if the wind were from the northeast, all persons as far south as Washington within forty-eight hours if they are not evacuated or in adequate shelters); and to this he appends the notation: "Such a weapon would do a satisfactory job on any legitimate target.   *There was no need to test anything larger than this.*"   Here again, his opposition seems only to be directed against "the unlimited stockpiling of large thermonuclears, and the effort to fashion even bigger ones."[45]   "We

[41] *Ibid.,* p. 52.
[42] *Ibid.,* p. 55.
[43] *Ibid.,* p. 226.
[44] *Ibid.,* p. 56 (italics added).
[45] *Ibid.,* p. 87 (italics added).

should cease the testing and the stockpiling of huge multi-megaton weapons which we can not justify in sizes or quantities greater than those already attained."[46]   Although the difference between thermonuclear megaton weapons and nuclear kiloton weapons is roughly 1000 to 1, and even though he speaks of "two orders of weapons," Murray says only that the former are "so excessive in their effects that they lend themselves to proper military uses against *very few targets*" and that it was "difficult to justify the continuation of tests of multimegaton weapons *larger* than we then had."[47]   In this age, perhaps one should be grateful for small policy proposals thrown across the path of increasingly irrational malevolence in our weapons.   In 1954, for example, Murray insisted that

the clean weapons argument should not be invoked as a pretext for testing larger thermonuclear weapons than we already had. Nor did I want the clean weapons to be looked upon as instruments which could be used to make our strategy of massive retaliation against civilian populations more palatable to the American people. I thought that we should set an upper limit to the size of all our weapons regardless of how clean they might be. But within the limits of a rational armaments program and a rational strategic policy, there is no doubt that weapons of reduced contamination should be part of any rational nuclear stockpile.[48]

One can be grateful that Murray was able to seize the heart of the issue, and not be lulled to sleep by sweet words about cleaning up the contamination that might incidentally result from an essentially immoral act.

Nevertheless, it should be pointed out that no arguments are advanced in this book, and no illustrations given of

[46] *Ibid.*, p. 112.
[47] *Ibid.*, pp. 80-81 (italics added). Cf. pp. 108 and 219: "two vastly different categories of weapons," and p. 175: "two substantially different categories of weapons, large and small."
[48] *Ibid.*, p. 85.

actual or hypothetical cases, and no strategic plans analyzed which go to the point of showing that there are *any* morally defensible and politically beneficial uses that can be made of multimegaton weapons. The only exception to this is the "exception" already cited, i.e., that an appropriate military target for an H-bomb might be a naval fleet at sea; and even in this instance it is not attempted to be shown that weapons of lesser firepower (whose existence would be less serious in their impact upon the conduct of international relations) would not be as or more efficient. Absent any reasoning or expert information to the contrary, the layman can only infer that Murray might, with greater consistency, have pressed his case for rational armament against the possession or use of any multimegaton bombs at all.

The explanation of this inconsistency or hesitation (if such it is) in applying the principles Murray has in mind may lie in the fact that, as he himself says, during his years as Atomic Energy Commisioner, "I was clarifying my thoughts and refining my position as I went along. . . ."[49] The explanation may lie in the fact that, earlier than the time to which that statement refers and while Murray's opinions were certainly not as clear and refined as they are today, he became more committed than he should have to the decision to develop the H-bomb. He apparently is proud, and from one point of view justifiably proud, of the leading part he played, during 1951, in the establishment of a Second Weapons Laboratory at Livermore, which led, only one year after it began to function under Dr. Edward Teller and some fifteen or twenty years earlier than had been predicted, on November 1, 1952, to the detonation of the first thermonuclear device (designed at Los Alamos under competitive stimulation, Murray believes, from the Second Lab-

[49] *Ibid.*, p. 79. This statement has reference to the test moratorium proposal of 1954.

oratory, which then immediately assumed leadership in designing deliverable thermonuclear weapons).[50] Is it not reasonable to suppose that Murray has not gone further in his condemnation of the moral and military inappropriateness of all thermonuclear weapons because of what he once did in their development (which, if he is now right in his more refined and clarified opinions upon this subject, would be equally as censurable as their use)? This would not be to deny him every credit for the clarity of his advice on many occasions to our political and military leaders.[51]

Murray's opinions on fractional kiloton weapons and on continued nuclear testing to develop them may be discussed together. For him, rational armament means rational *nuclear* armament. This nation needs a "nicely calculated measure of nuclear force—valid as a threat and valid in its use"; in this age of the vastly increased firepower of war, we need the capability "for waging in a civilized fashion every manner of warfare into which we might be forced."[52] This states, abstractly, both the upper and the lower limit of just war today. To mount less than the force that can possibly be used within the terms of the principles of counter-forces warfare we have discussed would be as wrong as to plan to use sheer violence against populations. The one would be to neglect to do what justly should be done; the other, to do injustice. This nation should immediately "embark upon a program of rational nuclear armament and rational nuclear disarmament."[53]

[50] *Ibid.*, p. 110-111.

[51] To President Truman on April 11, 1951, that nuclear weapons not be used in the Korean War unless and until we were prepared to become involved in war with Russia, and even then "only against targets which were military and not civilian in nature"; and his proposal in 1952 that, if the custody of weapons were transferred from the AEC to the military, "the Commission should formally recommend to the President that they never be used against primarily civilian targets" (*ibid.*, pp. 190-191).

[52] *Op. cit.*, pp. 60-61.

[53] *Ibid.*, p. 219.

The public generally knows what has happened to our conventional forces, or our capacity to fight and to deter limited wars (in the usual sense of this expression); Murray affirms outright that we also do not have any large number of small atomic weapons stockpiled.[54] These are needed to neutralize an enemy's superiority in conventional troops and to force him to avoid concentrating them in mass formation.[55] They are needed to fight justifiable war, and to deter war. Murray insists that what he calls the "third generation" nuclear devices would be "primarily antipersonnel in character,"[56] and therefore morally permissible if they are politically and militarily necessary.

In the past, it is Murray's belief, the American people have tended to "swing from pacifism to unlimited violence." We have believed, during peace, that war is "a horrible sin without justification"; and during war, that it is "a strategic game without rules," in which "the sky is the limit—and there is no more sky." Therefore "we feel guilty about using armed force when it might be used seasonably" and in due measure, "or else in the course of applying it we incur the guilt of using it excessively."[57] This same vacillation from one extreme to the other has confused our counsels in attempting to decide what we should mean by "rational armament," and especially the question whether this should include any nuclear weapons and the question of nuclear tests.

There is an "essential difference between the fallout from a kiloton bomb and that from a megaton bomb,"[58] in testing or in use. The fallout from small nuclear tests can be localized; the danger from testing them even in the

[54] *Ibid.*, p. 61.
[55] *Ibid.*, p. 65.
[56] *Ibid.*, p. 106.
[57] *Ibid.*, p. 26-27.
[58] *Ibid.*, p. 66.

atmosphere can readily be controlled.[59] But our high decision makers seemed to Murray not to base their proposals
on these or his foregoing distinctions in weapons policy. His
response to the Geneva Summit Meeting in mid-1955 was
this:

I had criticized [our] policy in 1955 because it admitted of no
cessation of tests, not even in the high megaton range. I was
now appalled to see that we had completely reversed our course
and were on the verge of a policy that apparently would admit
of no testing whatsoever, not even in the low kiloton range.
What an 'all or nothing' people we Americans are![60]

Nevertheless, by the fall of 1958, he was willing to support
the discontinuation of all atmospheric tests, in the belief
that a reasonable and still necessary program of testing for
fractional kiloton weapons could and should be conducted
either underground or far out in space.[61] He now acknowledges that ever since the first thermonuclear explosions in
1952-1953 (with which he had decisively to do, as we have
seen) "a ban on atmospheric tests has made a great deal of
sense"; but he does not believe that, then or now, the ban
should "go far beyond present-day technical feasibility, political necessity, and the irreducible requirements of national
security."[62] This is no all or nothing, no "either-or" proposition.[63] Some tests are imperative, others are not. Instead
of discriminating these in public debate,

we have badly fumbled the disarmament problem. We have
fumbled it because we previously fumbled the armament problem. We have failed miserably in the clash with the Soviets over
disarmament and testing because of our prior *failure to argue
out with ourselves, by ourselves, and for ourselves the entire
question of nuclear weapons*—military, political, and moral. So

[59] *Ibid.,* p. 80.
[60] *Ibid.,* p. 92 (italics added).
[61] *Ibid.,* p. 97.
[62] *Ibid.,* p. 105.
[63] *Ibid.,* p. 112.

long as *we remain internally confused about our purposes in accumulating arms,* we shall hardly be clear-minded about our
aims in negotiating for the control of them.[64]

The threat weighing down upon mankind is not nuclear
testing (nor is it to be resolved by banning the tests). It de-
rives rather "from the escape of nuclear technology from the
control of military doctrine and political purpose."[65] The
"primary issue is the stockpiled capacity for unlimited violence,"[66] and how we are to deal with this, while simultaneously arguing out with ourselves, and for ourselves and the
world, the meaning of rational armament today, and how
we are to obtain this. We should not have allowed anybody
to define something else, such as blanket cessation of tests
or total disarmament or the abolition of war, as more primary.

The issue as Murray sees it, an issue which he has been
trying for at least five years to have thoroughly debated in
the public forum, was concentrated yet still confused in that
single moment after we dropped the first A-bomb on Hiroshima when the American people themselves might possibly
have reversed the policies of their government. In a major
address during the presidential campaign of 1956, Adlai
Stevenson said, "I believe we should give prompt and earnest consideration to stopping further tests of the hydrogen
bomb, as Commissioner Murray of the Atomic Energy Commission recently proposed." Stevenson's proposal for unilateral suspension of H-bomb tests that are easily detectable
was classified by the Republicans as "catastrophic nonsense."
President Eisenhower called it a "theatrical national ges-
ture," and his view was that "weapons policy is manifestly
not a subject for detailed public discussion." The press
analyzed the difference between Stevenson's and Murray's

[64] *Ibid.,* p. 118 (italics added).
[65] *Ibid.,* p. 226.
[66] *Ibid.,* p. 232.

proposals; and as the campaign progressed Stevenson made
it clearer that he did not mean the suspension of *all* tests.
Looking back upon these events, Murray comments upon
"from what different premises our arguments—his and mine
—proceeded. His proposal flowed mainly from a fear of the
effects of radioactive fallout and of adverse world opinion.
My position was based on my analysis of national defense
needs." In other words, Stevenson had abstracted from
Murray's campaign (whom he cited more than once) for
"rational nuclear armament," and from his insistence that
our *war* and *weapons* policies be debated. Eisenhower
would have none of it. Thus, in Murray's sad commentary,
the presidential campaign of 1956 "made it evident that we
had not yet developed . . . the proper set of mature political
attitudes which would permit us to preserve this distinction
in practice"—the distinction between the morality of the
tests and the morality of weapons systems and of strategic
plans—and as a people we may not have had the political
maturity to keep in mind (had this been unambiguously
called to our attention) the enormously greater importance
of our coming to a sound conclusion upon the latter subject. Thus, the American people were not given the lead to
argue out with themselves, by themselves, and for themselves
the entire question of nuclear policy.[67]

I do not know whether Murray is correct in his belief
that rational, politically beneficial armament means rational
nuclear armament. Moreover, I do not see how the moralist, alone, can know this. However, as we have already
pointed out we should demand that Murray and others
more versed in the weapons field give proof that megaton

[67] *Ibid.*, pp. 214-218. That this situation is likely to continue is shown
by the fact that Nixon and Rockefeller, in their "fourteen point" agreement before the Republican Convention, made some discriminating statements about tests, but none about weapons policy or the kind of additional
military strength they agreed this nation should have.

weapons can have any usefulness in counter-forces warfare. At least, some reasonable argument should be advanced to show that megaton weapons as such are not exclusively instruments of barbaric violence against peoples and that this is not our only plan in manufacturing and possessing them. At the same time, the same has to be shown for kiloton weapons, at least in their upper ranges. Kiloton and fractional kiloton weapons, range from the dream of a nuclear bullet that can be fired with extreme accuracy at a target, all the way up to explosions of as great and greater power than the A-bombs dropped on Hiroshima and Nagasaki.[68] I tend to think that rational nuclear armament would need to be confined more to the lower range in such firepower, i.e., closer to the conventional weapons they will replace. Moreover, while Herman Kahn seems to agree with Thomas E. Murray on this point (when he says that "the difference between megaton and kiloton is very large, in some ways larger than the difference between kiloton and ton"), he also writes that "one of the advantages of limiting small wars to HE [high explosive capability] is that a violation of the rule is so clear-cut, so unambiguous. There is a genuine distinction between nuclear and chemical explosions. The fact that very low-yield nuclear weapons could be developed which would render this distinction fuzzy and vague does not change this. . . . The breaking of the precedent would seem to me to be much more significant than the advantages to be gained."[69]

[68] On July 30, 1960, the AEC announced the intensity of ninety-eight atomic and nuclear tests that have been conducted. (Seventy-one other tests remain secret.) These explosions ranged from, at the lowest, *fifteen one-hundredths* of a ton of TNT to, at the highest, 15,000,000 tons of TNT. (*New York Times*, July 31, 1960). "A megaton contains the energy equivalent to a million tons of TNT, or enough TNT to fill some 16,000 railroad coal cars. The TNT equivalent of a 20-megaton bomb would require a train of coal cars stretching from New York to Los Angeles" (Murray, *op. cit.*, p. 21 n.). The Hiroshima bomb was 20 kilotons.

[69] *Op. cit.*, Lect. III, chaps. vii and xi, pp. 313 and 540-541.

The precedent is, of course, of signal importance. In their distraught political and military affairs, the nations cannot afford to let go of even irrational limits upon the conduct of war, even if they are conventional limits founded only upon the vague feelings of countless people that if these are broken doom more swiftly approaches. It is notable that such analysts as Kissinger who formerly believed in the possibility of designing a limited nuclear war are now surrounding the use of such fractional nuclear weapons with more and more severe precautions. Perhaps even a majority of weapons analysts are now moving away from the position of Murray and Teller, more in the direction of conventional weapons as alone appropriate for a war planned to be fought, without escalation. We may wish that the asserted ground for this was not, in the views of some of these men, only precedent or the limits of custom alone; and it may be safely (or unsafely) predicted that, unless some more objective political and moral limit is discovered, any such limit will go the way of all flesh. There has to be more reason for submitting to a limit than simply the fact that it is *there*. For example, many a skillful designer of weapons systems can be found who agrees quite definitely that chemical and bacteriological weapons ought never to be used (or used first) and that the "conscience" against their use ought to be preserved. They value this limit upon the conduct of war for its stabilizing effect upon the context in which this nation's defense has to be planned. But often they can be heard saying that the reason for this is that they fear gas or germs may prove to be "the poor nation's atomic bomb" (only for the more powerful nations is it true that, in cost efficiency, nuclear weapons are a better means of producing mass destruction than RBC warfare). Thus, an existing standard becomes a mere weapon for this nation's security. Not just the existing standards or more or less accepted rules of war but *sound* conscience (if, indeed, this) will finally afford us firm limits. And sound conscience means the restriction of warfare to forces directly attacking or counter-attacking.

Broader political implications, of course, cannot be ignored. But, directing attention for the moment to weapons as such, I see no reason *a priori* for a radical distinction between nuclear and chemical bombs. As natural states or processes, nuclear and chemical explosions would seem to be morally and politically indistinguishable. It is only in their use, or in their integration into a nation's military plans, that they become significantly distinguishable. The question to be debated and resolved is whether the distinction between just use in counter-forces warfare and clearly unjust use in counter-people warfare follows exactly the distinction between chemical and nuclear explosions. However this question is answered, there is every reason to believe that the firepower of a justifiable war has today greatly increased; and there are no grounds in the morality of war for insisting that the nations, today and in the future, must unman themselves and *not* mount against a force that justly should be repelled *all* the force they can be justified in using in the conduct of a war. Indeed, the cause of justice requires that they do this; and even while they make every effort to avoid war and to settle disputes by diplomacy—and even in a period when peace may seem to have supervened—military establishments have to be charged with the responsibility for preparing a just, limited, and purposeful defense. Placing under analysis only weapons and war policy itself, the following case may be supposed. Suppose that the first A-bomb had been dropped, not on Hiroshima, but on a military target for the purpose of totally demolishing a harbor or some military installation, adjacent to a city, that had not been put out of the war by other less powerful means. Would this not have been more in accord with the reasonable meaning of an act of war than the use of the bomb directly against a Japanese city? Would this not even have been more justifiable than dropping it in some "uninhabited" place (let us also suppose at least one peasant woman and her child *known* to be living in the "experimental" target area), with the threat that we meant to use the next one against 165,000 noncombatants? Was there no militarily efficient use that could have been devised for a weapon of such power, and a needed use, that would not have made the United States guilty for all time to come of inaugurating this era of terrorized civilians and fear-stricken societies (or guilty of signally ratifying what was begun in the obliteration bombing of World War II)? Only if the layman and the moralist can answer these questions negatively can he say for sure that kiloton weapons in the quite powerful range can never be classed as rational armament or used in just war. Even so, it would have to be shown that weapons of lesser power, and less damaging to civilian life indirectly, would not have *equal* or greater military effectiveness against the target.

In any case, Murray is correct: the nature and meaning of rational armament is the chief question that should be argued today; and for this reason his views upon this subject should gain greater currency. With his full bodied analysis of the ethico-political principles regulative of policy making, Murray cannot be dismissed as only one of the "official scientists"; nor can his views on the requirements of a reasonable defense be charged to extreme anti-Communism or to the fact that he is, for example, an emigré Hungarian scientist.

In the shaping of the public mind by or against a program of rational *nuclear* armament, it may be well to reflect that hitherto judgments upon this subject have been somewhat deflected and confused by the fear that any use of nuclear weapons, or the use of any "miniaturized" nuclear weapons, might escalate into all-out use of thermonuclear violence on the part of this nation. Those who think it is sound policy for a nation to have and to hold and perhaps to use the most massive modern weapons may be right in thinking in this way. But this may only mean that they are deterred from sound analysis and decision setting a justifiably high upper limit to the power of the weapons that should actually be planned for use, because of the unjust conduct built into the massive weapons they still want to retain in the contradictory and self-defeating hope of never using them. This may only illustrate the fact that under the umbrella of massive deterrence, policy at every level lower than that is confused. Because of the fear that inept force may be used we are deterred from the use of apt force, and from vigorous thought about what apt force may be in this age.

This only shows that rational armament (or rational nuclear armament) simultaneously requires rational disarmament (or rational nuclear disarmament). It is Mr. Murray's opinion that because of a decade and a half of propaganda, and exceedingly confused thinking on the part of the American public, we have become "prone to assume, rather fatalistically, that once we make a certain policy decision, all the *possible* consequences of that decision will be realised automatically and immediately, as though neither we nor the other party will be able to exercise the slightest control over our actions any longer."[70] Why need we suppose that we will outwit ourselves and be unable to hold our position along a rational line of defense? To this confusion in the public mind, secular idealists and doubtless many churchmen have contributed by their ridicule of the just-war theory,

[70] *Op. cit.,* p. 67.

and by their repeated statements that there is no morality of war but that war itself is the only problem. Nevertheless, the *possibility* of escalation would always be present—from a firm stance in international relations to limited conventional war, from conventional war to limited nuclear war with fractional weapons, and from this to politically purposeless violence—*so long as* we deliberately or in a dreamless sleep retain the latter capability. This may be a decisive reason for proceeding at once to rational nuclear disarmament, in order that rational armament may be possible to plan rightly and feasible to exert as military force.

Here Murray makes his signal proposal for "dismantling" this era of senseless terror.

I suggest that an international agency be constituted on neutral territory and empowered to supervise the systematic destruction of the megaton weapons in the American and Soviet stockpiles. The destruction would be carried out on a matching basis, weapon for equal weapon. To begin with, the United States would hand over to the international agency one megaton weapon in the highest range. The Soviet Union would be expected simultaneously to hand over one weapon in the same category. Experts within the agency would be able to estimate, within a small percentage of error, whether the weapons are of equal yield. The "hardware" components of the weapons would be destroyed. Their content of highly enriched fissionable material would be placed at the disposal of an appropriate international authority for peaceful atomic uses.[71]

This proposal has since been ridiculed as the height of naïveté by Linus Pauling in public addresses, on the assumption that it would entail the Russians' agreeing to a one-by-one destruction of megaton weapons until they had *none* left and we still had, say, half our present megatonnage (U.S. stockpiles now being far the larger). This seems to me a complete misunderstanding of Murray's proposal.

[71] *Ibid.*, pp. 227-228.

If we take seriously the fact (pointed out above) that Muray assumes (without demonstration, I have said) that there may be some sort of *tactical* usefulness in *some* megaton weapons and in having them in stock, then he must assume that after the proposed dismantling has been carried out, there will still be a few of these weapons around— enough for feasible use, but not the excessive number and size of weapons we went on to accumulate.   Moreover, even if Murray believed consistently that *no* megaton weapon has any intrinsic military purpose, the feasibility of his proposal would not depend on the stockpiles of the Soviets and the United States *now* being of exactly the same megatonnage, so that weapon by weapon, these could be cut down to nothing without producing a politically unacceptable imbalance of strength.   He who raises this objection must believe, as Murray does not, that there is usable strength in such weapons.

His proposal is simply that we begin dismantling *at the top of the tonnage,* and by this dramatic action attack the era of terror there where the strength of nations is most impoverished by the weapons they possess.   What he asks is "clear, clean, and simple, free of the kind of detail that might give rise to resistance or bickering," or call for inspection (which would be "absolutely contingent upon the conversion of the U.S.S.R. from a totalitarian, closed society to a sophisticated liberal society like our own"[72]).   The work should be done "under the eyes, as it were, of all the world."[73]   In the first stage "enough megatonnage should be destroyed to affirm emphatically and at the outset a mutually serious intent to end the Era of Terror.   What would constitute such a quantity of megatonnage?" This last question he answers by asking another: "How many megatons

[72] *Ibid.,* p. 232.
[73] *Ibid.,* p. 228.

would be sufficient to create, if exploded, a serious threat
to civilization on a scale intolerable both to ourselves, the
legatees of Western civilization, and also to the artisans of
the Communist World Revolution?" Murray's figure is
3,500 megatons. The initial dismantling stage should destroy this much of the world's politically useless violence, in
approximately three years.[74] If there is enough megatonnage in existence, presumably this first stage might be
followed by another that would dismantle the same amount.
This proposal, Murray believes, is based on "hard and cold
self-interest, the common and coincident self-interest of both
parties," since "no national interest, American or Russian,
is served by maintaining and increasing a stockpile of weapons of violence that are utterly useless for any political purpose, Russian or American."[75] In other words, Murray
wants to reverse the decision to make the H-bomb; or, in
the event he would not go that far, he wants to reverse the
decision made soon thereafter to stockpile more and more
of such bombs.

Now, it seems very clear, indeed, that this proposal, and
the arguments for it, amount to the same as *unilateral*
megatonnage disarmament. It is unilateral rational disarmament, except that Murray wants to get the most mileage out
of the event politically. "Since this stockpile is now a mili-

---

[74] *Ibid.*, p. 229.

[75] *Ibid.*, p. 231. To invoke, as part of the above argument, the connection between force and purpose in Russian policy is a quite different thing
than invoking, as any part of the argument, a supposed "moral revulsion"
in the Russians to using these weapons. I believe what W. E. Hocking
stated as a fact, but do *not* suggest that this can be what we rely on in
public policy: "Whatever the mystery of Soviet motivation, however alien
the Slavonic temperament and capability and capacity for wile may be felt
to be, there can be no shadow of doubt that they who share with us an
official willingness to prepare weapons for the collective extinction of populations entertain not alone a fear of retaliation but an inward revulsion to
their use" (*The Strength of Men and Nations*, New York: Harper and Bros.,
1959, p. 188). Moreover, the contention is not that the Russians surely
know that they need only purposeful weapons (force, not violence), but
that in any case *we do*, and that any attempt to integrate into our policies
an irrationally malevolent weapon would not be possible, even if moral.

tary liability, we ought to make some political use of it."
Murray wants the nations to *celebrate* their return to sanity
(which would be a good thing to return to, with or without
the celebration, and with or without colleagues). This
means, if I may so express it, that the two leading nuclear
powers would perform each its own act of *unilateral* megatonnage disarmament in each other's presence, in co-ordination with the other, and before the eyes of the world; but
without insisting bilaterally on inspecting the tonnage the
other party may have remaining. Thus, "we would *give
witness in action* that we do not abdicate the right uses of
force, but that we do abjure the senseless uses of violence."[76]
This means, therefore and simultaneously, unilateral rational armament. Two coincident acts of unilateral rational
disarmament, however staged, may perhaps be described as
to be done mutually; but they need not be a single mutual
action, requiring inspection and all that, to justify it or to
guarantee the good of the outcome.

Something like this was, in fact, attempted, certainly
less dramatically and in fact rather heavy-handedly, in Henry
Cabot Lodge's address to the United Nations on August
16, 1960. Restating the United States government's current proposal in the test-ban negotiations at Geneva, but
adding "something to it which we think is very significant,"
Ambassador Lodge suggested a step in the direction of
"ending the production of fissionable material for weapons
purposes" that would reduce "directly the number of nuclear weapons now in national arsenals," without insisting on inspection of these arsenals as such. He indicated
the willingness of the United States government, "on a
reciprocal basis, to set aside 30,000 kilograms of weapons
grade U-235, as the amount which the United States and
the Soviet Union would each initially transfer." (That is

[76] *Ibid.*, p. 235 (italics added).

enough to generate an explosive force 1000 times greater than all the bombs dropped in World War II.) Asserting that this would mean "an immediate and sizeable reduction in nuclear threat," Lodge did not explain until the next day that the United States could not obtain that much U-235 without unpacking an unspecified number of bombs now in our arsenal. Moreover, the emphasis was on the virtue to be bestowed by the peaceful purposes to which this material would be devoted, and not resolutely upon *together* dismantling *unilaterally* the era of terror. Also, it was clearly possible for the United States to replenish its arsenal from new supplies of fissionable material; and, as to this, Lodge's second proposal linked international inspection with our willingness to shut down, one by one, our major plants producing enriched uranium and plutonium. This meant, in Russian eyes, that we still wanted inspection without disarmament, while we continue to accuse Russia of wanting disarmament without inspection. In any case, a proposed step in the direction of rational disarmament was trammeled by our widespread but erroneous opinion that these weapons are not so much a terror confusing policy as they are somehow necessary to a nation's strength, which can never be lessened without a guarantee of reciprocity.

Plainly, therefore, any argument in behalf of Murray's proposal would, in substance, be an argument for unilateral action in this direction (if that is the only way to accomplish it). In the opinion of the present writer, the case for unilateral rational armament and disarmament (or for Murray's version of this) is sufficiently demonstrated, politically, militarily, and morally. (To see and say this clearly is far more important today than for any one person to know where exactly the line is to be drawn.) Any case to the contrary rests on "a false concept of strength." As Murray says:

I do not consider it strength on our part to consent to the current deterioration of force into violence. This deterioration is, on the contrary, weakness. Surely, it is moral weakness; it amounts to a failure of the moral intelligence to understand what is going on, or a want of moral courage to stop this corrupting process. It is also political weakness; it is a failure of the political intelligence to see the absurdity of violence, and to see also the rational necessity of force, for the purposes of politics. Moreover, unless this process of moral degradation is checked by the courage of political decision, the result will be to continue or increase our military weakness: the weakness of a nuclear establishment whose political uselessness grows more and more apparent, and the weakness of a technology whose resources of power are exploited without purpose, because they lack due military and political direction.[77]

Any nation in the world today should indicate—whether dramatically or not, whether together with other nations or not—that it knows not to poison wells. If this seems daft, it is because it is deep—that other "deep truth" about modern weapons, which a just and reasonable man must believe on Tuesday, Thursday, and Saturday, and which the Christian must believe on these and every other day of the week because of what he believes, celebrates, and re-enacts on Sunday.

There will, of course, remain a lingering suspicion that this is somehow not quite true, and that we must prepare for the day on which an enemy brings forth in the form of a threat his clandestine cache of weapons of total violence. He who believes this is still in the power of the aggressor-defender war (which justifies *especially* the most absurd, purposeless, pushbutton retaliation). He is under the sway of the military concepts of the short, recent period of human history—concepts which did not prevail for most of the cen-

[77] *Ibid.*, p. 235.

turies of the past history of the West and which can afford
no foundation for the new age into which men must now
urgently press forward. He still believes in the feasibility
of fighting an unlimited war; or, if not this, he performs
an even more incredible act of faith and still believes in
the feasibility (for the first time in the entire history of warfare) of deterring such a war by means that are not intended
ever to be used. He has not yet plumbed to the bottom
the deep truth about modern weapons which commends itself to the mind on Monday, Tuesday, and Wednesday.

In the face of brandished missiles with megaton warheads, there is in no case any other recourse than to stand
firm in the right as God gives us to see the right and to
stand firm with arms that are the arms of a national purpose.
"I cherish the confident hope," Murray writes, "if that such
a threat of violence were ever to be made, the United States
would be secure enough in other forms of valid nuclear
strength [substitute: rational armament, if nuclear weapons
are no part of this] to have the courage simply to defy it."[78]
The courage to defy blackmail is the main ingredient
needed. This must in fact be exercised beneath the so-called
umbrella of nuclear deterrence.   At the moment, United
States policy toward Cuba, if this can be soundly determined
in its own right, has simply to ignore or disbelieve Soviet
threats, and this not because we have a believable massive
counter-threat or one we actually intend to use. Anyone
can see through the deterrent; in fact, everyone, in order
to conduct political affairs, *must insist* that he sees through
it. Who imagines that swift United Nations action in the
Congo did not simply have to go forward courageously
underneath rather irrelevant speculation about whether
Soviet threats were credible or only façade? (These were
more credible because they were counter-forces threats; and

[78] *Ibid.*, pp. 239-240.

as such had not to be ignored.) Nothing actually operative in these situations to strengthen or weaken our nation would be changed if we simply fold up the umbrella, and open another, namely a resolve to conduct international affairs in terms of policies that are backed up by only the purposeful use of just force. Disaster may come; so may earthquakes the like of which men have never seen, but we do not need to try vainly against the natural laws of warfare and of politics to make any such things the instruments of national policy.

The writer is proud to use, as the penultimate word of this book, Murray's words in conclusion of his:

Nor need we fear that the guidance of Divine Providence will be lacking to us as we thus work to dismantle the Era of Terror, which has grown increasing offensive to the moral conscience. The redemption of mankind from the dominion of terror is not alien to the purposes of God.[79]

The ultimate word has been constantly in mind in our entire account of the meaning and necessary *derivation* of the just-war theory: all that is required of men or of nations is that they do justice and love mercy—the mercy that strengthens, *definitely shapes,* enlightens and enlarges their justice— and to walk humbly with their God (*Micah* 6:8).

[79] *Ibid.,* p. 241.

Afterword

The definite fashioning of justice (in the concepts of the just war) by divine charity we have traced in detail. Love and mercy are the fulfilling of the law, or of the meaning expressed in the commandment, "Thou shalt not kill." The Christians who formulated the just-war theory were driven to make in this regard one, single, clearly defined and limited *exception*. That was what it was, an exception—nothing more. Those persons "formally" directing or participating in the military forces, or "materially" yet closely co-operating in the force that should be repelled are—this theory states—legitimate objects of direct violent repression. What was the reason for this conclusion? What was the motivation for this exception? We have seen that Christian conscience took the form of allowing any killing at all of men for whom Christ died only because military personnel were judged to stand at the point where there converged many multilateral relations of a Christian to his neighbors. Out of neighbor-regarding love for all one's fellow men, *preferential* decision among one's neighbors may and can and must be made. For love's sake (the very principle of the prohibition of killing) Christian thought and action were driven to posit this single exception: that forces should be repelled and the bearers or close co-operators in force directly repressed, by violent means if necessary, lest many more of God's little ones should be irresponsibly forsaken and suffer more harm than need be. This, then, was not really an "exception" but a determinate expression of justice and mercy.

We asked the question for us men today: Can there be any reason given for now allowing further "exception" to be made, or for now concluding that a wider circle of direct violence can be regarded as possibly compatible with the dictates of love, or mercy, or a love-informed justice, or even with simple justice? This question has to be answered in the negative as often as it is raised and clarified in the consciences of just or Christian men. Counter-forces warfare— the modern term for the just conduct of war—is the only kind of warfare in which just or merciful men can ever engage without a direct violation of those moral norms in terms of which they know they are ultimately judged, of which they know they often fall short, and whose reality surrounds and sustains them, and their "enemies," at all times in their participation in earthly kingdoms.

This book has been not about many things. It has not been about the solution of outstanding political problems anywhere in the world, or the goals of diplomacy, or military and political alliances and the need for regional confederations, or the possibility of conciliating an enemy, or how national sovereignty can or should be limited, or strengthening the United Nations, or a world someday ruled by law, or how much better just peace is than just war or a just endurable peace than a just endurable war; nor about arms control (except to say that this is the word for it). Our single theme has been weapons systems and weapons strategy and the just conduct of war. This is a problem of prime significance for Christian ethics, unless we are to say that Christianity is a sect to any military establishment and withdrawn from a main concern of political and military leadership today; and unless we are to say that war plans (no matter what they are) are altogether

beyond the pale and outside the concern of men of justice and mercy. Moreover, this is a problem that will be
with us, as Christians and as citizens, for a long while. Even
if one believes it is only for the time being, a considered
opinion on this subject is imperative—while also other approaches to the almost incorrigible problems of international relations are being taken.

If the argument of this book is correct, then, our present weapons of unlimited power should never be deposited
with the United Nations for any other purpose than getting
rid of them. Now is no time in the world's history to
weaken the United Nations. Now is no time to saddle the
United Nations with having to ask, in every international
crisis, whether it is worth it to defy blackmail or to venture
to initiate war against a people in order to get at some re-
calcitrant government. Better to remain in the present situation, in which the nations have to rely on a fragile, tacit
agreement never to use these weapons than to confuse the
councils and inhibit the decisions of the United nations,
by forcing that amorphous body—on which so much of the
hope of the people of the world depends—always to ask,
before it takes action (as the nuclear powers have now to ask
themselves) whether it is prepared to overwhelm with unlimited, unusable force a cache of the same sort of weapons
it would be child's play for any nation to conceal, or in the
future to obtain.

In short, no foreseeable international organization—not
even "world government"—can avoid decision in substance
upon this question: What is rational armament? And now
that nuclear power is an irrevocable possession of mankind,
no nation and no parliament of the world, can avoid the
moral-political decision to limit *its own* use of force to far
less than the force that is available to it. No nation, and
no parliament of mankind that had an executive and a war-

making or "police" arm, can avoid, today or in the future, the *moral-political decision* to limit the force in *its* possession to usable kinds and quantity; and, for the sake of its conduct of political affairs, resolve to be sensible in planning the use of armament, in actuality or as a deterrent. The nations, or the United Nations, would have to proceed to the business of nuclear disarmament, on sound principles as to what is apt force and what is not. Since we now must live with the permanent possibility of the threat, from some quarter, to use unlimited force, government as such (wherever it may be found, national or international) cannot avoid an essentially *unilateral* resolution to use only just and purposive means for legitimate and limited ends. This is inherent in an agreement of wills to be a nation, to be a power in the world, to be a force to any end, to be a government with effective policies.

What it would be immoral and inept for a nation to do in the field of force, it would also be immoral and inept for the representatives of the whole of mankind to do, or be prepared to do. The distinction between force and violence, or between counter-forces and counter-society warfare, has always been and will remain with us in principle. Only now that technology has released the power to destroy people from all physical limitation, this is a distinction that has to be made and preserved by moral will and political decision. And there is not, nor has ever been or shall be, a moral, volitional decision that does not entail a willingness firmly to do the right unilaterally (even if the more bilaterally, and in multilateral agreement with other wills, the better).

In actual policy decisions, this calls for *graduated unilateral steps* (but, one hopes, reciprocated steps) in the direction of rational or just disarmament and of rational and just armament. A program of gradual unilateral disarmament and rearmament would be based on two factors which are undeniable. The first is that explicit international agreements have to be based on prior tacit agreements, and these in turn on the actual policies and actions of governments. Actions speak louder than words in the matter of the return of armament and weapons systems to the control and limits of purposive policy. Other nations hear and may respond to what we do more than to what we say we might be willing to do. The second is the *moral* factor, the regulative guidance of military policy by the distinction between war and mass murder, between weapons aimed at forces and weapons aimed at people.

I have said that the just-war theory provides the moral *context* for policy decision and for the actual steps to be taken. There remains a gap between the just-war theory, even if this is a normative theory of and for practice, and the actual practice of statesmanship, if only because ethics is a practical *scientia* while political practice, like an art, requires *doing*. Only by venturing to put forth political actions can word and deed be brought together in the actual life and affairs of the nations. The statesman responsible for policy decisions lives in a realm where "the science of the possible" is definitive for all actions and in a realm of "deferrable repentance" so long as he remains convinced that politics is his vocation. This means that, under the guidance of moral *scientia,* just conduct must often first be made possible by prior acts, and by the patient play of moral reflection upon actual political conditions.

But this is to say that there is no essential difference between private morality and public morality. The judgmental criteria of the theory we have reviewed apply to both. Murder, or the intentional, direct killing of persons not immediately involved in force that should justly be repelled, means the same whether this is done by individuals against other individuals or by states against other nationals. It is equally wrong deliberately to enlarge the target and with direct intention and action to kill bystanders as a means of killing a dangerous criminal who resists other ways attempted to stop him, or to enlarge the target to retaliate against people as a means of stopping their forces. Moreover, readiness and preparation to kill the "innocent" partakes of the crime of actually doing so. Therefore, the statesman cannot escape from his evil necessities by asserting that his nation's power to retaliate against whole peoples is for the purpose of deterrence. No ethics—least of all Christian ethics—gives him leave, either in his private or his public capacity, to kill another man's children directly as a means of weakening that man's murderous intent or act. Preparation to do so—if that is the true and the only object of our weapons—is also intrinsically a grave moral evil and politically wrong.

Nevertheless, there is a difference between the actions of individuals and state acts. "Although persons and states are subjected to the same fundamental code of justice and the same norms of natural law, they are not subjected to them in exactly the same mode."[1] This means that politics and military planning are a realm of deferred repentance. Whatever is immoral the *individual in his private* capacity should cease doing at once. But it takes time for statesmanship to nurse and "persuade" necessity and to bring the pre-existent substance of international relations somewhat nearer even to the historically realizable criteria of a very earthy politics and into conformity to principles themselves oriented toward practice. There should be statesmen who themselves are quite clear as to the immorality of obliteration warfare (as well as the wrong of supposing to deter

[1] James E. Dougherty, "The Political Context," in *Morality and Warfare,* ed. William J. Nagle (Baltimore, Md.: Helicon Press, 1960), p. 30.

that great evil by readiness to do it) who are still willing to engage in negotiation directed to the end of limiting war to justifiable means and ends through a period of time in which they may have to defer their nation's repentance. But it is required of statesmanship to fashion policy in the right direction and to step without delay toward more purposive and feasible weapons systems.

This may be better than keeping personal conscience clean by getting out of office. Thus, it is likely that a "just war" Christian will on occasion find himself supporting his nation's preparations for unjust warfare—as there have been pacifist Christians in public office who have been willing to vote for military appropriations. The important thing is to make clear and keep clear in the public conscience the moral *context* that should surround every specific policy decision and should be the aim of political practice and of negotiation between nations. Just war must be made possible, and only just war should be allowed to be a possibility. Meantime, repentance may have to be deferred, if only to gain the time necessary to persuade public opinion to support that action which a statesman may wish to take. This is the main difference between public and private morality, between the different modes in which the same ethical requirements impinge upon them, and no case can be made for the view that what is wrong for a man may be right for a government. Nevertheless, even if the statesman is convinced that it is not by negotiation but by unilateral national resolve that the right can be done and a just-war weapons policy devised by the military, this would still be a policy decision which belongs to the art of politics. This takes time and requires the art of statesmanship to find the suitable occasion or mold that occasion. Therefore, as a policy decision even unilateral right action would not be immediately forthcoming even from the most practically oriented ethical principles, which are whatever they are for every occasion.

Nevertheless, there are certain realistic considerations which will come to the mind of a statesman, when he makes concrete policy decisions, which should incline him to judge that military plans and forces ought to be enclosed again within the possible political purposes of his nation— as quickly as possible, and if need be by unilateral resolve. In the remainder of this "afterword" I shall try to suggest that there are some policy considerations clearly oriented in the direction of this nation's resolve to maintain only just, rational, and politically purposive armament. This will be, at the same time, to summarize many of the themes of this book, and to bring them to focus on the task of policy making. To do this, it is *not* necessary for us first to answer the question where exactly the line is to be drawn, between conventional weapons and all nuclear weapons or between fractional atomic and multimegaton weapons. The moralist in any case cannot alone give the answer to this question. On the supposition of any given answer to it, we shall ask whether there are grounds for concluding that only usable weapons should be built and integrated into a nation's military preparedness whatever other powers may do, and to ask what steps can be devised to do this.

Our statesman ought not to be impressed by the argu-ment that, throughout the history of warfare and the ad-vance of military technology, any "improved" weapon or increase in the capacity to deliver violence has always at last been used. It is true that in the past new weapons have always been used, and no sentiment or horror in the face of increased power to kill and to maim has prevented this. But in the past the available weapons of war have not always or even usually been used *unlimitedly*. For all its bloodshed, history shows comparatively few Genghis

Khans. With whatever weapons, it shows few conquerers whose policy was to devastate without political purpose and without control by their hope of permanently gaining by conquest something worth possessing after victory. Of course, there have been Carthaginian policies carried out, and most wicked deeds against populations. But were this the rule rather than exception, warfare would long ago have ceased to serve any useful purpose (as threatens to be the case today); and if every weapon that became available was bound also to come into unlimited use, then no nation could ever have believed any weapon to be a possible instrument of its purpose as an organization of human power.

The situation today is that there are some weapons in the possession of the great powers whose use on a single occasion would be the equivalent of a decision, in any of the past ages of warfare, to use the weapons then available unlimitedly, irrationally and wantonly, and to no politically choiceworthy end. These weapons themselves transform policy into a policy of devastation without significant limit; they make every ruler willy-nilly a Genghis Khan in planning and making war. To say that these weapons, because they exist, are bound to be used is the same as saying that past weapons were bound to be used unlimitedly. By the same token, a political decision never to use an intrinsically unlimited weapon can be compared only with decisions in the past not to use available weapons unlimitedly. The renunciation of such weapons simply means the renunciation of political purposelessness. In the tortuous course of human civilization, the history of warfare has more often than not been the history of just warfare, in the sense that weapons have been used—all of them, so far—more often than not within limits and controllably to serve some cause. Now we have weapons which to use once can be for no cause. Their lack of limit or minimal purpose is in *any* use of them. It requires no extraordinary morality on the part of the present generation of men to recognize that no good or reasonable purpose can be secured by means of megaton bombs. By political resolve and by placing a limit on action, past weapons were not used, as at any time they might have been used, unlimitedly. By a similar political resolve, if at all, can the use of present weapons of the highest power be avoided.

Our policy maker ought not to be impressed by the argument that such weapons have at least this usefulness: that they deter war. We need not question the fact that in the past weapons that could be used to fight a war have also served the purpose of preventing war. But granting this, it has now to be said that some present-day weapons have escaped both purposes, and to the same degree and for the same reason. You cannot long deter with instruments you are unwilling to fight with. If the war itself is incredible because infeasible as a minimally purposive act of a nation, so also is the deterrent threat.

Of course, this is a world in which the incredible sometimes happens, and the infeasible is attempted. So we mount an incredible deterrent against an infeasible war. And we seem to be willing to guarantee *to ourselves* and to other nations that this will be done by building retaliation into computers and systems as automatic as possible in their reaction. Nevertheless, our statesman may well reflect upon what actually is operative in encounters of power between nations under the umbrella of massive deterrence. The actual use of those weapons has in any case simply to be disbelieved—whether out of complacency, or stupor, or hardened habit in the conduct of political affairs, or simply out of derring-do if not, as proposed here, by gradual stages and from resolute political decision—as nations go about effecting their policies by proper applications of power or credible threats of such applications. Blackmail has in any case simply to be resisted by the force of a nation's will when it has arms suitable to the purposes to be realized. Apart from the supposed deterrent effect on a potential enemy, the main domestic effect of preparing massive retaliation is that our own people will *think* they are protected, and that as a consequence they will irrationally have the courage to support their leaders in giving effect to limited policies in encounters of power. That sort of national determination, and not anything the massive weapons can actually accomplish, provides strength to the nation.

The transmilitary evil of maximum nuclear destruction can scarcely be faced by means of the concept of deterrence which derived its meaning from mankind's experience with weapons with which wars could be fought to a finish toward a choiceworthy peace beyond the cessation of hostilities. Meantime, by refusing to abandon this outmoded concept of deterrence and by continuing to act as if we believe we can deter with weapons that cannot be used for any national purpose, world politics suffers fundamental confusion in two respects: (1) we maintain the danger that any use of military force will quickly escalate into all-out nuclear war, and consequently (2) we try vainly to conduct international relations as if a nation's purpose could be achieved without its being possible and proper for this purpose to necessitate the use of armed force. In the vacuum of applicable power created in world politics by this so-called deterrent, communist politicians become more and more shrill and Western politicians more and more pious in the effort to convince themselves and others that these weapons will and should be used and that this is so certain that they will never have to be used. Thus the umbrella of massive deterrence has itself to be protected from degradation by incredible self-assertions and increasingly declaratory policies as a substitute for statesmanship and real power. It is difficult to imagine that the political life of mankind could be more disturbed than it now is by the abandonment of the so-called deterrent, and by the pursuit of political and military goals by means of rational, feasible armaments and credible threats, sheltered only by a national resolve never to yield to blackmail and never to attempt the impossible task of enforcing the nation's purposes by means that contradict them and repudiate the intrinsic laws of warfare subservient to the purpose of politics.

After emancipating himself from the notion that the history of warfare is the history of the unlimited use of available weapons and from the notion that the deterrence theory is any longer applicable, our statesman will scrutinize the emphasis currently placed on devising a system of inspection as a precondition to rational and justifiable disarmament. Nothing is more idealistic and vain than our present obsession with inspection. Currently the United States is proposing twenty-one inspection stations on Russian soil, and twenty on-the-spot inspections a year; while Russia wants three. If agreement were reached on our terms, it would take four years to construct the system. So the United States proposes that inspection go into operation as each station is built; while the Russians want to wait until the whole system is complete. This is an extension of the uninspected moratorium on weapons development (now already in its third year), which might be dangerous *if inspection* alone can guarantee the security of the West. Moreover, such a system when installed and operative will not be able to detect a great many powerful underground explosions. Therefore we are proposing joint research to improve the system, which will take still more time before we obtain the safety we seek through inspection. In the present stalemate between the Russian accusation that the

West wants "control without disarmament" and the United
States' charge that Russia wants "disarmament without controls" the difficulty is not only that we have been too rigid
about inspection. Our statesman might well reflect that
the emphasis on inspection, and the choice between weak
or strong guarantees, has been the thing in error. Certainly,
he should see that total and general disarmament as a goal
contains equally grave dangers; and he might conclude that
we have been beguiled into seeming to hold this forth as
a reasonable political goal in the world today because we
have not faced up to the fact that the real option before
any nation is the choice between rational and irrational
armaments. This choice will not go away simply by our
insistence on inspecting one another's irrational and purposeless armaments. Then statesmanship might conclude
that the attainment of politically purposive arms need not
wait on improbable guarantees, but may be the fruit of
graduated unilateral action and of tacit agreements.

It should be obvious that a system of inspection stations
and an agreed number of on-the-spot inspections to guarantee the West against surprise attack would require far more
openness in Soviet and in Chinese society than any communist dictatorship is likely to grant—particularly since we
have removed any incentive or reciprocal need on the part
of the USSR or Red China to have guarantees against surprise massive attack from the West by making it obvious
that we will never shoot first, in accord with that almost
worthless substitute for the just-war theory to which we
adhere, the aggressor-defender concept of war. For a while
President Eisenhower's "open skies" proposal, first advanced
at the Geneva Summit Conference in 1955 and subsequently
developed, seemed to provide the necessary guarantees without requiring the opening up of Soviet society. Even that
proposal, however, was an idealism designed for some other

world than this. Moreover, it may not provide the guarantees it was once believed to contain. Photographic reconnaissance might report that everything is quiet, or be unable to detect the degree of readiness of a missile, and an attack be launched fifteen minutes later.

For this reason, according to the New York *Times,* September 23, 1960 (and even while officially we were still justifying the U-2 flights as necessary to guard ourselves in the absence of an "open skies" agreement) the President did not renew the "open skies" proposal in his speech before the meeting of the General Assembly of the United Nations in the fall of 1960. Instead he proposed a most astonishing solution: "Today the danger of war by miscalculation could be reduced, in times of crisis, by the intervention, *when requested by any nation seeking to prove its own peaceful intention,* of an appropriate United Nations surveillance body. The question of methods could be left to the experts" (italics added). But it requires no expert to tell that no nation planning a surprise attack will be very much concerned to prove formally that it is not doing so, or willing to open its society momentarily and display its weapons to a host of United Nations inspectors. Moreover, it cannot be said that this would be a way to guarantee *the West* against surprise attack, but only to guarantee the nation *which may be suspected by the West of planning such attack* against a pre-emptive *strike against itself* by the West because of miscalculation! Since the enemy already has such weighty assurance of this by our granting him the first strike in our doctrines of defense and deterrence, he would have little reason to request United Nations intervention to allay our suspicions even at times he is not planning to attack, and none at all when he is. This alone he might cunningly suppose: that there might be some advantage to be gained by crying "no wolf" too often!

In any case, it seems very clear indeed that ordinary espionage and intelligence will yield more reliable information than any system of inspection the Chinese, if not the Russians, are going to agree to in this century. After an inspection system is adopted, only informal sanctions will be available to use against a violator of it. This means that it will have ultimately to be self-enforcing. It will rest upon the advantages to be gained, and the accord of the interests of nations. That in turn means we are back (or *down*) to unilateral action to preserve rational disarmament, and tacit agreements to this effect; or else we are back in an unlimited arms race. Our statesman may well reflect that the only limitation is, after all, self-limitation. Why the reiteration of inspection as a precondition should be regarded as anything but an idealogy from another world—like world government or the kingdom of God—is difficult to imagine. Yet it goes by the name of realism. The alternative to it, however, is not an agreement based on "trust" which the 1960 presidential candidates declared so eloquently they would never sign. The alternative is rather an agreement, or action taken by any state, based on the nature of just or counter-forces warfare. A state's action in line with this concept of warfare and directing its own weapons policy in this way must surely go ahead of and give rise to any of those tacit agreements among nations for the control of weapons and the moderation of the use of violence to within some barely human political purpose (all of which must precede formal agreements). Our statesman has reason to suppose that responsible action to bring national policy in line with the just conduct of war will serve to introduce new impulses into international politics at least as much as will repeated demands for inspection.

Moreover, our policy maker should reflect soberly upon the fact that he cannot avoid facing this nation's decision simply to moderate and limit the weapons we are planning to use (for war or deterrence), nor can he long postpone taking the steps such a decision requires. If he thinks about it for a while, he will know that total war cannot be made automatically impossible, that deterrent systems based on counter-people weapons cannot be permanently stabilized, that there is no hope of perfecting such systems, that war cannot be made technically self-limiting or just simply by mobile launching pads deep in the ocean, and that to attempt to make invulnerable the weapons whose ugly face is still turned toward populations is a vain hope. Grant that it might be possible to count on the Polaris submarine system to draw the firepower of nuclear weapons away from people—automatically abolishing total counter-people warfare and transforming it into counter-forces action. Still this may only divert military preparations to *other means* of warring against whole populations, such as bacteriological, radiological, and gaseous weapons. No purely technical means have yet been proposed for insuring that war by these means must necessarily be germ-counter-germ warfare. There may be no way to force an enemy and compel ourselves to concentrate on finding a way to get at his germs before destroying his people by bacteriological warfare, preemptively or in counter-retaliation. There may not be technical ways of automatically changing RBC warfare, while still threatening populations, into counter-germ or counter-forces warfare. It is clear that today there are many weapons of potential mass obliteration which have escaped the limits of counter-forces warfare, to which they can be returned only by a decision that this should be done, and by actions that speak louder than wishing with spoken words that this were so. What is mankind to do with these weapons? We can no longer avoid a decision by fleeing in thought into another world where there is world government with international forces or such peace that nations no longer need to mount every justifiable form of force or open societies with inspection agreements or technical ways of limiting war without appealing to political morality and to a nation's resolve.

Here a political decision is unavoidable, by gradual stages, at least, returning war to the limits of legitimate military and political policy. For a time, of course, the implicit agreement not to use these weapons may be expected to stand and to continue to exercise some limitation upon the means used for war or for deterrence. And any limit upon the conduct of nations is worth preserving if possible, even if the objection to these weapons of mass destruction may be based only on such irrational factors as horror and their inefficiency in producing enough destruction per "buck" in comparison to nuclear weapons in the hands of great powers. The achievement of the control of nuclear weapons, or the technical stabilization of nuclear deterrence, would remove one reason total RBC warfare may not now be an important part of the arsenal of the West. The remaining "rationality of irrationality" of maintaining a tacit agreement not to use these means, because of horror over their possible use, cannot be expected to endure for long. Only rational, political limits such as those expressed in the distinction between just and unjust war can be expected to endure, if indeed these. Here plainly our statesman cannot relieve himself of responsibility for unilateral steps to control war as an instrument of national policy. And he will find no reason to believe it is possible to limit the *objectives* for which wars are fought while *means* cannot be modified. It is not at all self-evident that nations can be exhorted to limit the goals, which if limitless are productive of the fury of total war, while they have no other recourse than to go in the direction of making retaliatory obliteration certain and automatic as the only way of limiting the military means they are preparing.

Our statesman, therefore, should reflect upon how senseless it is to count on perfect invulnerability of retaliatory forces as the only way to limit their use; and he must know that agreements to limit them must be preceded not only by tacit agreements to do so but by action going already in that direction. He might then be driven to demand that our military planners put greater intellectual effort into the development of defense against obliteration warfare, surveillance, anti-missile and anti-sumbarine forces, etc., and into *a persistent effort to make counter-forces warfare effective.* Moreover, if this seems perilous (even though up to the present time the sound political direction of our weapons policy has been so lacking as to leave this an open and largely unexplored question), he will nevertheless have to conclude that no more could be lost by a resolve to perfect and to fight only counter-forces warfare than by preparing in earnest to fight war in its present shape (even so as to be able to deter it)—by placing a sector of the population and a living part of the economy underground, and by actually *choosing* to fight a thermonuclear war, hopefully in some sanitary fashion, to a meaningful victory or meaningful survival beyond. RBC weapons and technological development yet to come, and not only megaton bombs, face the statesman with the unavoidable decision for or against just warfare. He cannot refer to "strengthening the United Nations" or to "one final effort" to get an arms control agreement, or to technically automatic counter-germ or counter-radiological warfare or to an outmoded concept of deterrence in order to avoid facing, and leading his nation to face, the decision which alone has any hope of returning weapons to politically purposive control. This will involve the decision, somewhere along the line, that a situation in which one people is destroyed is to be chosen over a situation in which two peoples are destroyed in retaliatory and counter-retaliatory warfare in any of its forms.

Finally, in a cool hour our statesman will be driven to reflect that if the foregoing considerations are insufficient to restore to influence just-war theory and practice, if our only defense is to be always on the offensive in the preparation of weapons too horrible ever to use for any of the finite ends of policy, then that pale shadow of the just-war doctrine—the "aggressor-defender" concept of war—should be seriously re-examined. If it is truly impossible to shape weapons policy for defense in accord with the use of just and limited means alone, if defense can no longer be justly conducted, in short, if it is impossible for nations to mount a just defense (on one side of the hyphen in the "aggressor-defender" situation), then it may be questioned whether we should much longer be bound by our only remaining notion of the justification of war in this simplicist moral distinction between aggression and defense. For very little is at stake in who strikes first. Bound by Western political morality in this absurdly attenuated form, we yield the first strike on every imaginable occasion in the armed encounter of nations. This reduces deterrence completely to our power to reply after suffering the first strike, deprives an enemy of any incentive to make an arms control agreement to guard himself against surprise attack, and abdicates political initiative to nations prepared to threaten, at least, the first strike, and to threaten this in the loudest voice and in the most irrational manner. If we are to go on believing in the rationality of irrational behavior in the second instance, then there may be some rationality in more irrational behavior in the first instance. If we are not going to make a resolute effort to initiate the control of weapons and subdue them to policy, in the presence of other nations and to the end of tempering the relations between us, then there is much to be said in behalf of freeing our policy from this one remaining extrinsic limit. There would then be some apparent justification for an application of power *whether for defense or offense* altogether in terms of military or diplomatic necessity, preserving a measure of ambiguity about what we shall do, limited only by the determination that we shall not be wantonly cruel but will inflict only a barely intolerable damage upon an enemy people in order to bend or defeat their government's will. If it is right to do this in order to *defend*, it is right to do this in order to *effect* our national purpose. Moreover, this might be less costly and less dangerous for us than to continue to be victimized by modern weapons technology and at the same time by that surrogate moral justification of an act of war: the aggressor-defender doctrine. Since our statesman may not have the stomach for preventive war plans or even for pre-emptive war (which Einstein called "anticipatory retaliation"), he should take decisive, if graduated, unilateral action to fashion his nation's military and weapons system in accord with the only doctrine of war that is morally or politically justifiable.

Index

Moralist, function distinguished from weapons expert, 162, 166
Morality: public and private, 11-12, 146 n., 308, 309; and security, 274, 280 n., 302
Morgenstern, Oskar: on limited objectives, 7 n.; on stabilizing the deterrent, 218-221; on defense of economy, 221-223; on survival, 223-224
Morrison, C. C., 26 n.
Murray, John Courtney, xxii n., 61; on papal proscription of aggression even if just, 84-88; on just war theory, 102-103; on limited war, 137; on need for military doctrine, 140; on failure of moral theologians, 142; on planned surrender, 152 n.
Murray, Thomas E.: on morality and security, 138-140, 274, 280 n., 302; on just war theory, 275-277; on force and violence, 277-278, 282; on determination of policy by technology, 278-281, 290; on civilization and barbarism, 279 n.; on incredibility of deterrence, 281-283; on nuclear testing, 283-290; on fractional kiloton weapons, 283-295; on decision to make H-bomb, 286-287; and Adlai Stevenson, 290-291; on escalation, 296-297; proposal for dismantling the era of terror, 297-304
Muste, A. J., 155, 184

Nagasaki, 142, 161, 292
National Planning Association, 232
Natural law, 4, 32, 33, 34, 35; and love in genesis of just war, xviii-xxii; absolute and relative, 18-19; right of self-defense, 55; of war, 167-168; means, 176, 183; and Protestant ethics, 177. See also Justice, natural
Nazism, 187-188
Nelson, J. O., 225
Nicolson, Nigel, 204, 205
Niebuhr, H. Richard, 112
Niebuhr, Reinhold, 5, 26 n., 111; on justice and order, 88-89; on public and private morality, 146 n.
Nixon, Richard, 291 n.
Nonaggression treaty, 240
Noncombatant immunity, xix-xx, 275-276; genesis of, 34-59; today,

66-73; basic definition, 67-68, 135-137, 143-145; burden of proof, 69; from destruction of property, 73-74; derived from proportionality, 94; in John Bennett, 148; applied to future victims of nuclear tests, 215-216; and tradition of civilized warfare, 275-276
Nuclear pacifism, 88, 154, 155, 226
Nuclear testing, 139, 210-217, 283-290

Obligation, objective and subjective, 79, 175-176, 187
Obliteration bombing, xix-xx, 60-74, 187, 276, 280
O'Brien, William V., 160 n.
Oceanic system, 220-221
Official declaration of war, 114-124
Open skies, 317, 318
Osgood, Robert, 29, 139
Over-kill, 262
Oxford Conference, 88

Pacifism: early Christian, xv-xvi, 305-306; recent history of, 3; nuclear, 88, 155, 154, 226; and degenerate Calvinism, 93; vocational, 129, 156, 158 n.; prudential, 155; and just war, 226
Patijn, C. L., 91 n., 107 n., 108
Pauling, Linus, 138, 297
Pax-ordo, 120, 122, 124, 205
Peace churches, 88, 129
Peaceful uses of atomic energy, 217, 274
Penance for fighting, 115, 133
"Permitted effect," 202-203. See also Double effect, rule of
Pius XII, 83-87
Poison gas. See RBC warfare
Polaris submarine missile system, 220-221, 232, 233, 241, 320
Policy decision: in context of just war theory, 219, 230, 273, 309-312; determined by technology, 278-281, 290. See also Decision making
Political theory. See Commonwealth
Politics as deferred repentance, 11-13, 163
Pollard, William G.: on natural hydrogen bombs, 196-197; on actions that make the earth less habitable, 206-207
Population problem, 207